PRAISE FOR THE

ALMANAC *of* ARCHITECTURE & DESIGN

"No comparable resource exists."
LIBRARY JOURNAL

....

"The definitive fact book on architecture and design."
THE AMERICAN INSTITUTE OF ARCHITECTS

....

"This is the book that informs decision makers like no other."
SOCIETY FOR MARKETING PROFESSIONAL SERVICES

....

*"This Almanac, filled with resources, can help all those involved in
the building arts to better fulfill this unusual moment's potential."*
ARCHITECTURAL RECORD

....

*"A core reference title for personal, professional,
and academic reference collections."*
MIDWEST BOOK REVIEW

....

*"A comprehensive media guide to architecture
and design's defining moments."*
THE DESIGN FUTURES COUNCIL

DesignIntelligence®

ALMANAC *of* ARCHITECTURE & DESIGN 2013

14TH EDITION

DesignIntelligence®

ALMANAC of ARCHITECTURE & DESIGN 2013
14TH EDITION

FOUNDING EDITOR AND PUBLISHER
JAMES P. CRAMER

EDITOR
JANE PARADISE WOLFORD, PH.D.

östberg

Library of Design Management

Greenway Communications

Almanac of Architecture & Design

Publisher and Founding Editor:	James P. Cramer, Hon. AIA, Hon. IIDA, CAE
Almanac Editor:	Jane Paradise Wolford, Ph.D., LEED AP
Associate Publisher	Mary Pereboom
Art Director:	Austin M. Cramer
Graphic Design and Layout:	Karen Berube
Editorial Advisor:	Jennifer Evans Yankopolus
Web Development Advisor:	Ryan James Cramer
Market Data Advisor:	Arol Wolford, Hon. AIA
Research Editors:	Dawn Hunt, Margot Montouchet, Connor O'Neill, Doug Parker, AIA, Ian McClain Shelton, Alexa Smith, Tonya Smith, Dave Zimmerman and Greenway Group Research

Greenway Communications, LLC

President/CEO:	James P. Cramer
Principal for Research and Administration:	Mary Pereboom
Principal for Management Consulting:	Doug Parker
Membership Director, Design Futures Council:	Tonya Smith
Art Director and Managing Editor:	Austin M. Cramer
Manager, Östberg Library of Design Management:	Dawn Hunt

SEE 17 '13

Greenway Communications,
a division of The Greenway Group
25 Technology Parkway South, Suite 101
Atlanta, GA 30092
(800) 726-8603
www.greenway.us
www.di.net

Publisher's Cataloging-in-Publication

Almanac of architecture & design / James P. Cramer
and Jane Paradise Wolford, editors

    2013 ed.

    p. cm.

    Almanac of architecture and design

    Includes bibliographical references and index

    ISBN-13 978-0-9852743-7-5

    ISBN-10 0-9852743-7-9

    1. Architecture—Directories. 2. Architectural design. 3.
Architecture—United States. I. Title: Almanac of architecture
and design

NA9.A27 2011   720

Contents

Note: Please visit us online at www.di.net/almanac/ for enhanced searchability throughout the entire expanded online version of the *Almanac*.

Introduction: Rankings, Ratings, and the Conditions of Success

Welcome to the *Almanac of Architecture & Design 2013*. We're happy you are here.

There is a supposition, even among the most talented architects and designers, that there is something arbitrary about success. We don't agree, of course. Nevertheless, we hear about good buildings going unrecognized or clients who don't understand the value of design or the financial failings of Louis Kahn in architecture or Ian McHarg in landscape architecture. Genius dying broke. In the halls of academia we hear professors saying to their students, "If you want to make money or achieve great acclaim for your work, don't go into architecture." In 1962 the late Robert McLaughlin—then chairman of the School of Architecture at Princeton University—put a similar sounding twist on the mythology. In his book *Architect: Creating Man's Environment*, he wrote that "the profession is far from the best field in which to earn the most money for the least work."

Some things change. Today, talent and design leadership is more likely to foster both monetary success and recognition. Top architects and designers are increasingly being paid a premium for the value they bring. Designers may be self-employed or they may share ownership in professional practices that are well run and give adequate attention to their marketing and operations as well as professional responsibilities. And great design is being recognized, too. Front covers of popular magazines feature new forms and solutions in design and architecture. The Internet is full of sites educating visitors about global design feats and models. No longer do we see coverage of architecture and design topics relegated only to trade journals. Design has gone mainstream. Architects are more often celebrated in their communities and as they travel worldwide. Some are celebrities.

Thus, it can be argued that the conditions of success are increasingly being met at higher levels, going beyond regional peer recognition and critical acclaim. Indeed, there are raving clients who are not only fans of good design but who also provide patronage to their preferred architects and designers. Design today is not only an aesthetic quality of preference but also an investment in brand and business success. Design is powerful.

In this *Almanac* we make lists and we rank firms. In Chapter 1, we rank the 333 largest architectural design firms and provide statistics relative to their current condition. In Chapter 2, America's Leading Architecture & Design Firms, we feature alphabetical listings of the approximately 1,000 top design firms in North America, providing data about the type of services they offer, their size and geography, and the market segments they work in. The DI Index is a system formulated by Greenway Group to provide categorical recognitions that measure peer repute, critical recognition, business recognition, and public acclaim. It's an imperfect science. We search the media, read press releases, constantly scan the Internet, and observe first-hand many of the projects that are making the news.

Our system has five tiers. In our work advising competitions and designer selection processes this system has proven to work well over the last fifteen years. *Tier one* is at the top and is earned by firms we consider to be world class and who have categorical leader recognition. Sometimes this is in one or more building sectors; other times it is for a signature: a form-giving unique value proposition to a variety of projects. *Tier two* is assigned to firms who excel at the national level and are also categorical leaders; these are firms who are winning awards, are featured in the media and have a strong brand position. A *tier three* rating is given to strong regional firms who sometimes also work nationally. Many of these are up-and-coming firms that are winning awards at local and state levels. They are currently more likely to be recognized in their respective cities and regions than in national publications.

In this *Almanac* we are only able to show the top three tiers. However, in tiers four and five there are also notable and growing firms with emerging categorical recognition. These firms may be newer or may be sole practitioners. They can be highly competitive organizations with considerable talent but are not yet operating with a strong national or global brand voice. There are good firms who are not listed, of course. We discover new firms each week. And some firms don't participate in our surveys, making it difficult for us to ascertain their current condition of service value.

Every day our staff gathers information about records, rankings, and achievements. Accolades in architecture and design are not absolute or final; they are sustained each year by talent and commitment, and must be earned.

Each month our Web site is updated so that the freshest information is available about new awards and new individual noteworthy achievements or changes. Visit us online at www.di.net/almanac/.

We are pleased to have you with us as we navigate the future of the architecture and design professions. As progress unfolds, we'll be keeping score.

Jane Paradise Wolford, Ph.D. LEED AP
James P. Cramer, Hon AIA, Hon IIDA, CAE

DesignIntelligence 333 |

This chapter features a ranking of America's top 333 architecture firms, along with useful contact information and pertinent data.

DesignIntelligence 333

The *DesignIntelligence* 333 ranks the top 333 architecture and design firms in North America. To compile the most accurate and up-to-date information, firms throughout the United States and Canada were surveyed during the spring and summer of 2012. Under the direction of the editors, extensive research was conducted by the *Almanac* staff and the research staff of *DesignIntelligence* to compile a comprehensive geographically and demographically diverse group of firms that would qualify for inclusion. Professional associations, media lists, client organizations, and conference registrations of the Design Futures Council were also studied to determine the most active leading firms. The Greenway Group also researched additional media sources, such as leading professional and business publications read by clients in each of the areas of specialty.

The firms were mailed a letter inviting them to participate in the survey, along with a copy of the survey. The survey asked for information regarding their areas of specialty, employment counts, number of offices, fields of professional practice, 2011 gross professional fee revenues, leading officers of the firms, and other relevant information. The data collected was also used for the *Almanac*'s Directory of America's Leading Architecture and Design Firms.

Telephone calls and emails followed mailed surveys if additional information was needed. Each firm included in this *Almanac* was contacted a minimum of three times by mail, email, or telephone. When firms did not respond, estimates were made based on previous surveys completed by the firms for *DesignIntelligence*, listings in business media, Greenway's private research databases, reliable information on the Internet regarding employee counts, and other credible sources. At least three independent sources were used to estimate gross revenues when the firms did not supply these figures. Blank fields in the ranking section or missing profile information were due to the firm not returning its survey. The number of reported firm locations and actual locations may differ. Totals may not equal 100 percent due to rounding.

To fill out a survey for next year's *Almanac*, visit www.di.net/almanac/, call *DesignIntelligence* at (678) 879-0929, or contact the editor at jwolford@di.net.

Note: n/p = not provided

Gensler

Shanghai Tower, Shanghai, China | Gensler

1 | Gensler

2 Harrison Street
San Francisco, CA 94105
(415) 433-3700
www.gensler.com
Andy Cohen, Executive Director
David Gensler, Executive Director
Diane Hoskins, Executive Director

WORLDWIDE REVENUE	$764,081,273
US REVENUE	$563,209,298
WORLDWIDE STAFF	3,500
HEADQUARTERS	San Francisco, CA
YEAR ESTABLISHED	1965
RECENT REPRESENTATIVE PROJECT	
	L.A. Live, Los Angeles, CA

GEOGRAPHIC ANALYSIS OF WORK IN THE US

GEOGRAPHIC ANALYSIS OF WORK OUTSIDE THE US

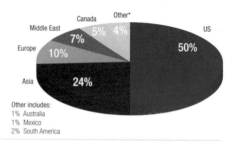

Other includes:
1% Australia
1% Mexico
2% South America

PRIMARY SERVICES OFFERED

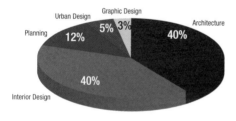

MARKET SEGMENTS

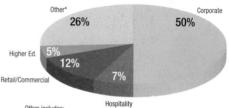

Other includes:
1% Healthcare   3% Government
2% Sports   18% Transportation; Mixed Use/
2% Museum/Cultural   Entertainment; Data Center

LOCATIONS

Atlanta, GA	Las Vegas, NV	San Francisco, CA	Hong Kong, China
Austin, TX	Los Angeles, CA	San Jose, CA	London, UK
Baltimore, MD	Miami, FL	San Ramon, CA	San Jose, Costa Rica
Boston, MA	Minneapolis, MN	Seattle, WA	Sao Paulo, Brazil
Charlotte, NC	Morristown, NJ	Tampa, FL	Seoul, South Korea
Chicago, IL	New York, NY	Washington, DC	Shanghai, China
Dallas, TX	Newport Beach, CA	Abu Dhabi, UAE	Singapore
Denver, CO	Phoenix, AZ	Bangalore, India	Tokyo, Japan
Detroit, MI	Pittsburgh, PA	Bangkok, Thailand	Toronto, ON, Canada
Houston, TX	Raleigh, NC	Beijing, China	
La Crosse, WI	San Diego, CA	Dubai, UAE	**Gensler**

American Hospital Dubai Expansion, Dubai, UAE | AECOM

Velti Headquarters, San Francisco, CA | AECOM

2 | AECOM (Architecture)

555 South Flower Street
Los Angeles, CA 90071
(213) 593-8000
www.aecom.com
Jason Prior, CEO
Rick Lincicome, Executive VP
Jacinta McCann, Executive VP

WORLDWIDE REVENUE	$687,520,000
US REVENUE	$384,822,000
WORLDWIDE STAFF	3,900
HEADQUARTERS	Los Angeles, CA
YEAR ESTABLISHED	1990

RECENT REPRESENTATIVE PROJECT

Envision Energy Headquarters,
Jiangyin, China

GEOGRAPHIC ANALYSIS OF WORK IN THE US

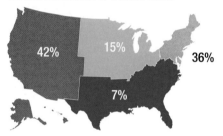

GEOGRAPHIC ANALYSIS OF WORK OUTSIDE THE US

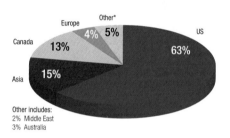

Other includes:
2% Middle East
3% Australia

PRIMARY SERVICES OFFERED

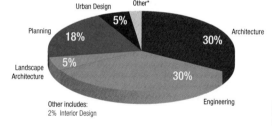

Other includes:
2% Interior Design

MARKET SEGMENTS

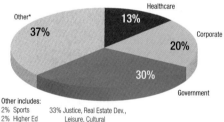

Other includes:
2% Sports   33% Justice, Real Estate Dev.,
2% Higher Ed   Leisure, Cultural

LOCATIONS

Albuquerque, NM	Minneapolis, MN	Seattle, WA	Hong Kong, China
Arlington, VA	New York, NY	Virginia Beach, VA	London, UK
Atlanta, GA	Orange, CA	Washington, DC	Shanghai, China
Baltimore, MD	Orlando, FL	Abu Dhabi, UAE	Shenzhen, China
Birmingham, AL	Philadelphia, PA	Auckland, New Zealand	Singapore
Boston, MA	Phoenix, AZ	Bangalore, India	Sydney, Australia
Charlotte, NC	Portland, OR	Beijing, China	Taipei, Taiwan
Chicago, IL	Providence, RI	Calgary, AB, Canada	Tokyo, Japan
Dallas, TX	Raleigh, NC	Doha, Qatar	Vancouver, BC, Canada
Kansas City, MO	Roanoke, VA	Dubai, UAE	
Los Angeles, CA	San Francisco, CA	Hamilton, New Zealand	

AECOM

Joonhwan Yoon

New Songdo City Central Park I & II, Incheon, South Korea | HOK

3 | HOK

211 North Broadway, Suite 700
St. Louis, MO 63102
(314) 421-2000
www.hok.com
Patrick MacLeamy, Chairman & CEO
William Hellmuth, President
Clark Davis, Vice Chairman

WORLDWIDE REVENUE	$447,472,000
US REVENUE	$246,786,000
WORLDWIDE STAFF	1,695
HEADQUARTERS	St. Louis, MO
YEAR ESTABLISHED	1955

RECENT REPRESENTATIVE PROJECT

Indira Gandhi International Airport, Terminal 3, Dehli, India

GEOGRAPHIC ANALYSIS OF WORK IN THE US

GEOGRAPHIC ANALYSIS OF WORK OUTSIDE THE US

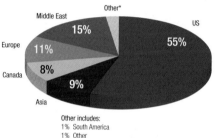

Other includes:
1% South America
1% Other

PRIMARY SERVICES OFFERED   MARKET SEGMENTS

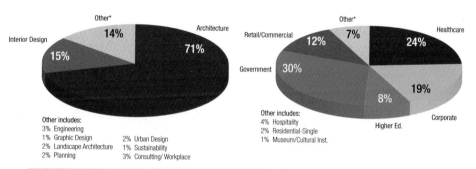

Other includes:
3% Engineering
1% Graphic Design   2% Urban Design
2% Landscape Architecture   1% Sustainability
2% Planning   3% Consulting/ Workplace

Other includes:
4% Hospitality
2% Residential-Single
1% Museum/Cultural Inst.

LOCATIONS

Atlanta, GA	San Francisco, CA	Ho Chi Minh City,	Singapore
Chicago, IL	Seattle, WA	Vietnam	Toronto, ON,
Dallas, TX	St. Louis, MO	Hong Kong, China	Canada
Denver, CO	Tampa, FL	London, UK	Vancouver, BC,
Houston, TX	Washington, DC	Mumbai, India	Canada
Los Angeles, CA	Beijing, China	Ottawa, ON,	
Miami, FL	Calgary, AB, Canada	Canada	
New York, NY	Dubai, UAE	Shanghai, China	

© James Steinkamp, Steinkamp Photography

Rush University Medical Center, Chicago, IL | Perkins+Will

4 | Perkins+Will

330 North Wabash Avenue, Suite 3600
Chicago, IL 60611
(312) 755-0770
www.perkinswill.com

WORLDWIDE REVENUE	$372,000,000
US REVENUE	$306,000,000
WORLDWIDE STAFF	1,517
HEADQUARTERS	23 Global Offices
YEAR ESTABLISHED	1935

RECENT REPRESENTATIVE PROJECT

Texas Children's Hospital Duncan
Neurological Institute, Houston, TX

GEOGRAPHIC ANALYSIS OF WORK IN THE US

GEOGRAPHIC ANALYSIS OF WORK OUTSIDE THE US

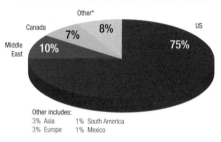

Other includes:
3% Asia   1% South America
3% Europe   1% Mexico

PRIMARY SERVICES OFFERED

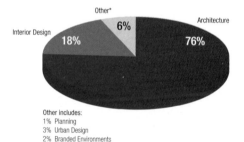

Other includes:
1% Planning
3% Urban Design
2% Branded Environments

MARKET SEGMENTS

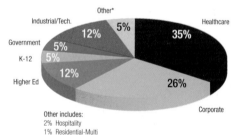

Other includes:
2% Hospitality
1% Residential-Multi
2% Museum/Cultural Inst.

LOCATIONS

Atlanta, GA	Miami, FL	San Francisco, CA	Canada
Boston, MA	Minneapolis, MN	Seattle, WA	London, UK
Charlotte, NC	New York, NY	Washington, DC	Shangai, China
Chicago, IL	Orlando, FL	Dubai, UAE	Toronto, ON,
Dallas, TX	Philadelphia, PA	Dundas, ON,	Canada
Houston, TX	Research Triangle	Canada	Vancouver, BC,
Los Angeles, CA	Park, NC	Ottawa, ON,	Canada

PERKINS
+WILL

© 2012 Thomas McConnell

University of Texas at Arlington College Park Mixed-Use Development, Arlington, TX | Jacobs (Architecture)

5 | Jacobs (Architecture)

1111 South Arroyo Parkway

Pasadena, CA 91105

(626) 578-6988

www.jacobs.com

H. Thomas McDuffie Jr., Group Vice President

Brad Simmons, VP/National Design Operations

Richard Keating, Managing Principal/Design

WORLDWIDE REVENUE	$353,710,000
US REVENUE	$220,020,000
WORLDWIDE STAFF	2,800
HEADQUARTERS	Pasadena, CA
YEAR ESTABLISHED	1947
RECENT REPRESENTATIVE PROJECT	

3161 Michelson, Irvine, CA

GEOGRAPHIC ANALYSIS OF WORK IN THE US

GEOGRAPHIC ANALYSIS OF WORK OUTSIDE THE US

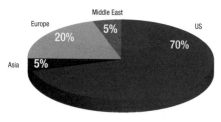

PRIMARY SERVICES OFFERED

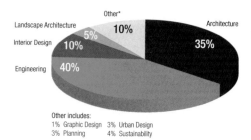

Other includes:
1% Graphic Design   3% Urban Design
3% Planning   4% Sustainability

MARKET SEGMENTS

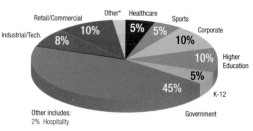

Other includes:
2% Hospitality

LOCATIONS

Arlington, VA	Louisville, KY	San Antonio, TX	Calgary, Canada
Atlanta, GA	Madison, WI	San Diego, CA	Hong Kong, China
Austin, TX	Miami, FL	San Francisco, CA	Leeds, UK
Baltimore, MD	Minneapolis, MN	Seattle, WA	London, UK
Boston, MA	Nashville, TN	St. Louis, MO	Madrid, Spain
Charleston, SC	New York, NY	Tampa, FL	Melbourne, Australia
Chicago, IL	Oklahoma City, OK	Tucson, AZ	Milan, Italy
Cincinnati, OH	Orlando, FL	Tulsa, OK	Moscow, Russia
Dallas, TX	Philadelphia, PA	Washington, DC	Mumbai, India
Denver, CO	Phoenix, AZ	Abu Dhabi, UAE	New Delhi, India
Honolulu, HI	Pittsburgh, PA	Al-Khobar, Saudi Arabia	Paris, France
Houston, TX	Portland, OR	Antwerp, Belgium	Shanghai, China
Indianapolis, IN	Providence, RI	Athens, Greece	Singapore
Irvine, CA	Raleigh, NC	Aylesbury, UK	Toronto, ON, Canada
Las Vegas, NV	Sacramento, CA	Beijing, China	Vancouver, BC, Canada
Los Angeles, CA	Salt Lake City, UT	Birmingham, UK	

9400 Dodge, Omaha, NE | HDR Architecture, Inc.

6 | HDR Architecture, Inc.

8404 Indian Hills Drive
Omaha, NE 68114
(402) 399-1000
www.hdrarchitecture.com
Merle S. Bachman, President
Michael Doiel, Senior VP
Doug Wignall, Senior VP

WORLDWIDE REVENUE	$310,000,000
US REVENUE	$232,480,000
WORLDWIDE STAFF	1,612
HEADQUARTERS	Omaha, NE
YEAR ESTABLISHED	1917
RECENT REPRESENTATIVE PROJECT	

Georgia State University Parker H. Petit
Science Center, Atlanta, GA

GEOGRAPHIC ANALYSIS OF WORK IN THE US

GEOGRAPHIC ANALYSIS OF WORK OUTSIDE THE US

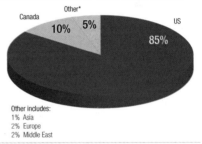

Other includes:
1% Asia
2% Europe
2% Middle East

PRIMARY SERVICES OFFERED

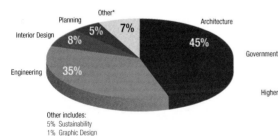

Other includes:
5% Sustainability
1% Graphic Design
1% Landscape Architecture

MARKET SEGMENTS

Other includes:
1% Sports
1% Museum/Cultural Inst.
18% Justice, Labs

LOCATIONS

Alexandria, VA	Lexington, KY	Rochester, MN	Beijing, China
Atlanta, GA	Lincoln, NE	Sacramento, CA	Dubai, UAE
Bethesda, MD	Los Angeles, CA	San Antonio, TX	Kingston, ON, Canada
Boise, ID	Madison, WI	San Diego, CA	London, ON, Canada
Boston, MA	New York, NY	San Francisco, CA	London, UK
Charleston, SC	Oklahoma City, OK	Seattle, WA	Ottawa, ON, Canada
Charlotte, NC	Omaha, NE	St. Paul, MN	Shanghai, China
Chicago, IL	Orlando, FL	Tacoma, WA	Sydney, Australia
Dallas, TX	Phoenix, AZ	Tampa, FL	Toronto, ON, Canada
Denver, CO	Portland, OR	Tucson, AZ	
Houston, TX	Princeton, NJ	Abu Dhabi, UAE	

© SOM | MIR

Suzhou Center, Wujiang, China | Skidmore, Owings & Merrill

7 | Skidmore, Owings & Merrill

224 South Michigan Avenue, Suite 1000
Chicago, IL 60604
(312) 554-9090
www.som.com
Gary Haney, Partner
Jeffrey J. McCarthy, Partner
Gene Schnair, Partner

WORLDWIDE REVENUE	$252,500,000
US REVENUE	$113,200,000
WORLDWIDE STAFF	788
HEADQUARTERS	Chicago, IL
YEAR ESTABLISHED	1936
RECENT REPRESENTATIVE PROJECT	

UCSF Neurosciences Lab & Clinical
Research Bldg 19A, San Francisco, CA

GEOGRAPHIC ANALYSIS OF WORK IN THE US

GEOGRAPHIC ANALYSIS OF WORK OUTSIDE THE US

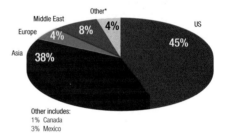

Other includes:
1% Canada
3% Mexico

PRIMARY SERVICES OFFERED

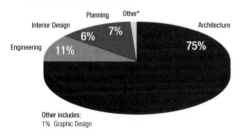

Other includes:
1% Graphic Design

MARKET SEGMENTS

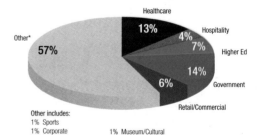

Other includes:
1% Sports
1% Corporate   1% Museum/Cultural
1% Residential-Multifamily   53% Not specified

LOCATIONS

Chicago, IL	Abu Dhabi, UAE
Los Angeles, CA	Hong Kong, China
New York, NY	London, UK
San Francisco, CA	Mumbai, India
Washington, DC	Shanghai, China

Blake Marvin/HKS, Inc.

Capital Health Medical Center, Hopewell-Pennington, NJ | HKS, Inc.

8 | HKS, Inc.

1919 McKinney Avenue
Dallas, TX 75201
(214) 969-5599
www.hksinc.com
H. Ralph Hawkins, Chairman/CEO
Nunzio M. DeSantis, Executive VP
Craig Beale, Executive VP
Dan Noble, Executive VP

WORLDWIDE REVENUE	$225,000,000
US REVENUE	$206,000,000
WORLDWIDE STAFF	940
HEADQUARTERS	Dallas, TX
YEAR ESTABLISHED	1939

RECENT REPRESENTATIVE PROJECT

Salt River Fields at Talking Stick, Phoenix, AZ

GEOGRAPHIC ANALYSIS OF WORK IN THE US

GEOGRAPHIC ANALYSIS OF WORK OUTSIDE THE US

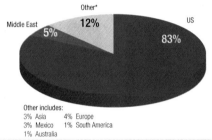

Other includes:
3% Asia   4% Europe
3% Mexico   1% South America
1% Australia

PRIMARY SERVICES OFFERED

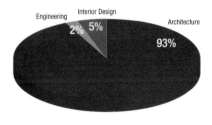

MARKET SEGMENTS

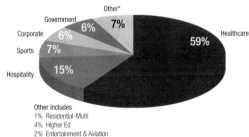

Other includes
1% Residential-Multi
4% Higher Ed
2% Entertainment & Aviation

LOCATIONS

Atlanta, GA	Los Angeles, CA	Richmond, VA	London, UK
Chicago, IL	Miami, FL	Salt Lake City, UT	Mexico City, Mexico
Dallas, TX	Nashville, TN	San Diego, CA	New Dehli, India
Denver, CO	New York, NY	San Francisco, CA	Sao Paulo, Brazil
Detroit, MI	Orange County, CA	Tampa, FL	Shanghai, China
Fort Worth, TX	Orlando, FL	Washington, DC	
Indianapolis, IN	Palo Alto, CA	Abu Dhabi, UAE	
Las Vegas, NV	Phoenix, AZ	Chennai, India	

Björg Magnea Architectural & Interior Photography

Kaleida Health, Clinical and Medical Research Building, Gates Vascular Institute and UB Clinical Translational Research Center/Incubator, Buffalo, NY ㅣ Cannon Design

9 | Cannon Design

2170 Whitehaven Road
Grand Island, NY 14072
(716) 773-6800
www.cannondesign.com
Mark Mendell, Co-Chairman/President
Gary R. Miller, Co-Chairman/CEO
M. Kent Turner, President/ Cannon Design North America

WORLDWIDE REVENUE	$218,808,718
US REVENUE	$116,064,000
WORLDWIDE STAFF	1,053
HEADQUARTERS	17 Global Offices
YEAR ESTABLISHED	1945

RECENT REPRESENTATIVE PROJECT
Cannon Design Regional Office,
St. Louis, MO

GEOGRAPHIC ANALYSIS OF WORK IN THE US

GEOGRAPHIC ANALYSIS OF WORK OUTSIDE THE US

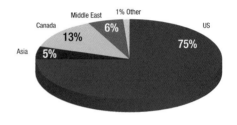

PRIMARY SERVICES OFFERED

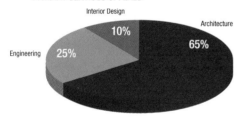

MARKET SEGMENTS

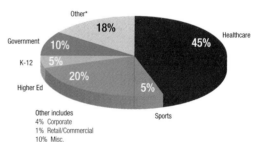

Other includes
4% Corporate
1% Retail/Commercial
10% Misc.

LOCATIONS

Baltimore, MD
Boston, MA
Buffalo, NY
Chicago, IL
Los Angeles, CA
New York, NY
Phoenix, AZ

San Francisco, CA
St. Louis, MO
Washington, DC
Mumbai, India
Shanghai, China
Toronto, ON,
    Canada

Vancouver, BC,
    Canada
Victoria, BC, Canada

CANNONDESIGN

RTKL Associates Inc./Charles Davis, AIA

San Antonio Military Medical Center, San Antonio, TX | RTKL Associates Inc.

10 | RTKL Associates Inc.

901 South Bond Street

Baltimore, MD 21231

(410) 537-6000

www.rtkl.com

Lance K. Josal, President/CEO

Randall S. Pace, CFO

Allan M. Pinchoff, General Counsel

WORLDWIDE REVENUE $201,933,000

US REVENUE $102,745,000

WORLDWIDE STAFF 925+

HEADQUARTERS Baltimore, MD

YEAR ESTABLISHED 1946

RECENT REPRESENTATIVE PROJECT

National Geospatial-Intelligence Agency, New Campus East, Fort Belvoir, VA

GEOGRAPHIC ANALYSIS OF WORK IN THE US

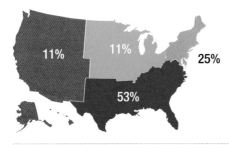

11% 11% 25%

53%

GEOGRAPHIC ANALYSIS OF WORK OUTSIDE THE US

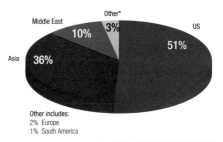

Other* 3%
Middle East 10%
US 51%
Asia 36%

Other includes:
2% Europe
1% South America

PRIMARY SERVICES OFFERED

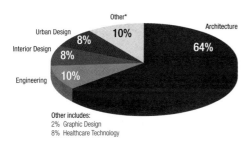

Other* 10%
Urban Design 8%
Interior Design 8%
Engineering 10%
Architecture 64%

Other includes:
2% Graphic Design
8% Healthcare Technology

MARKET SEGMENTS

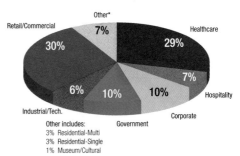

Other* 7%
Retail/Commercial 30%
Healthcare 29%
Hospitality 7%
Corporate 10%
Government 10%
Industrial/Tech. 6%

Other includes:
3% Residential-Multi
3% Residential-Single
1% Museum/Cultural

LOCATIONS

Baltimore, MD
Chicago, IL
Dallas, TX
Los Angeles, CA
Miami, FL
Washington, DC
Abu Dhabi, UAE

Beijing, China
Dubai, UAE
Jeddah, Saudi
  Arabia
London, UK
Shanghai, China

Tim Griffith, courtesy NBBJ

City of Capitals Tower, Moscow, Russia | NBBJ

11 | NBBJ

223 Yale Avenue North
Seattle, WA 98109
(206) 223-5555
www.nbbj.com
Steven McConnell, Managing Partner
Scott Wyatt, Managing Partner
Joann Lohkamp, Managing Partner

WORLDWIDE REVENUE	$182,000,000
US REVENUE	$145,000,000
WORLDWIDE STAFF	675
HEADQUARTERS	Seattle, WA
YEAR ESTABLISHED	1943
RECENT REPRESENTATIVE PROJECT	

Massachusetts General Hospital Lunder
Building, Boston, MA

GEOGRAPHIC ANALYSIS OF WORK IN THE US

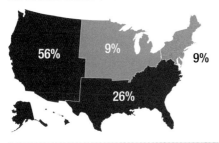

GEOGRAPHIC ANALYSIS OF WORK OUTSIDE THE US

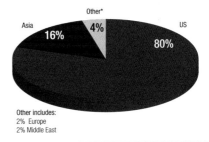

Other includes:
2% Europe
2% Middle East

PRIMARY SERVICES OFFERED

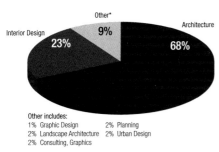

Other includes:
1% Graphic Design   2% Planning
2% Landscape Architecture   2% Urban Design
2% Consulting, Graphics

MARKET SEGMENTS

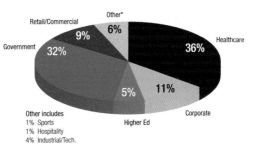

Other includes
1% Sports
1% Hospitality
4% Industrial/Tech.

LOCATIONS

Boston, MA	Seattle, WA
Columbus, OH	Beijing, China
Los Angeles, CA	London, UK
New York, NY	Pune, India
San Francisco, CA	Shanghai, China

12 | Stantec Architecture (US)

901 Market Street
San Francisco, CA 94105
(415) 882- 9500
www.stantec.com
Pete Moriarty, VP
Roger Swanson, VP
Stanis Smith, Senior VP

WORLDWIDE REVENUE	$172,425,000
US REVENUE	$53,295,000
WORLDWIDE STAFF	1,244
HEADQUARTERS	Edmonton, AB, Canada
YEAR ESTABLISHED	1954
RECENT REPRESENTATIVE PROJECT	

Laguna Honda, San Francisco, CA

GEOGRAPHIC ANALYSIS OF WORK IN THE US

GEOGRAPHIC ANALYSIS OF WORK OUTSIDE THE US

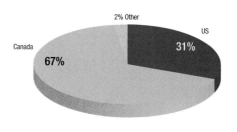

PRIMARY SERVICES OFFERED

MARKET SEGMENTS

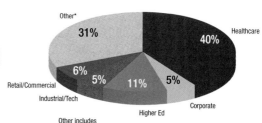

Other includes
3% Hospitality
28% Unspecified

LOCATIONS

Boston, MA
Boulder, CO
Butler, PA
Cleveland, OH
Columbus, OH
Petaluma, CA
Philadelphia, PA -
  Market Street

Philadelphia, PA -
  Spring Garden
Pittsburgh, PA
Redlands, CA
Sacramento, CA
San Francisco, CA
State College, PA
Washington, DC
Abu Dhabi, UAE

Ahmedabad, India
Calgary, AB, Canada
Doha, Qatar
Dubai, UAE
Edmonton, AB, Canada
Hamilton, ON, Canada
Kamloops, BC, Canada
London, UK
Ottawa, ON, Canada

Regina, SK, Canada
Saskatoon, SK,
  Canada
Toronto, ON, Canada
Vancouver, BC, Canada
Victoria, BC, Canada
Winnipeg, MB, Canada
Yellowknife, NT,
  Canada

13 | SmithGroupJJR

500 Griswold Street, Suite 1700
Detroit, MI 48226
(313) 983-3600
www.smithgroupjjr.com
David R.H. King, Chairman/Design Director
Carl Roehling, President/CEO
Randal Swiech, COO

WORLDWIDE REVENUE	$160,000,000
US REVENUE	$158,040,000
WORLDWIDE STAFF	747
HEADQUARTERS	11 Global Offices
YEAR ESTABLISHED	1853
RECENT REPRESENTATIVE PROJECT	

Chandler City Hall, Chandler, AZ

GEOGRAPHIC ANALYSIS OF WORK IN THE US

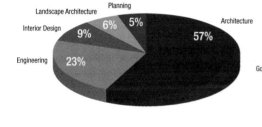

GEOGRAPHIC ANALYSIS OF WORK OUTSIDE THE US

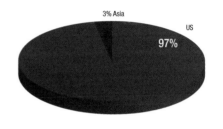

3% Asia
US
97%

PRIMARY SERVICES OFFERED

Planning
Landscape Architecture
Interior Design
Engineering
Architecture
6% 5%
9%
23%
57%

MARKET SEGMENTS

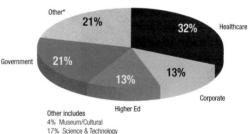

Other*
Government
Healthcare
Corporate
Higher Ed
21%
21%
13%
13%
32%

Other includes
4% Museum/Cultural
17% Science & Technology

LOCATIONS

Ann Arbor, MI
Chicago, IL
Dallas, TX
Detroit, MI
Durham, NC
Los Angeles, CA
Madison, WI

Phoenix, AZ
San Francisco, CA
Washington, DC

Virtua Voorhees Hospital, Voorhees, NJ | HGA Architects and Engineers

14 | HGA Architects and Engineers

701 Washington Avenue North
Minneapolis, MN 55401
(612) 758-4000
www.hga.com
Daniel Avchen, CEO
Stephen Fiskum, COO
Loren Ahles, VP

WORLDWIDE REVENUE	$134,200,000
US REVENUE	$131,900,000
WORLDWIDE STAFF	610
HEADQUARTERS	Minneapolis, MN
YEAR ESTABLISHED	1953
RECENT REPRESENTATIVE PROJECT	

Calif. State University Valley Performing Arts Center, Northridge, CA

GEOGRAPHIC ANALYSIS OF WORK IN THE US

GEOGRAPHIC ANALYSIS OF WORK OUTSIDE THE US

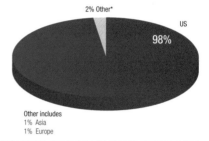

Other includes
1% Asia
1% Europe

PRIMARY SERVICES OFFERED

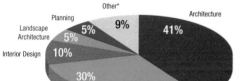

Other includes
2% Graphic Design
2% Urban Design
5% Sustainability

MARKET SEGMENTS

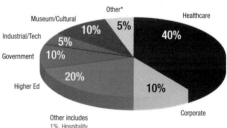

Other includes
1% Hospitality
2% Retail/Commercial
2% Religious

LOCATIONS

Los Angeles, CA
Milwaukee, WI
Minneapolis, MN
Rochester, MN

Sacramento, CA
San Francisco, CA
Washington, DC

China Mobile Beijing IT Park, Beijing, China | LEO A DALY

Georgia Gwinnett College Library, Lawrenceville, GA | LEO A DALY

15 | LEO A DALY

8600 Indian Hills Drive
Omaha, NE 68114
(402) 391-8111
www.leodaly.com
Leo A. Daly III, Chairman/CEO
Charles D. Dalluge, Executive VP
Robert L. Luhrs, VP/CFO

WORLDWIDE REVENUE	$132,000,000
US REVENUE	$118,000,000
WORLDWIDE STAFF	810
HEADQUARTERS	Omaha, NE
YEAR ESTABLISHED	1915
RECENT REPRESENTATIVE PROJECT	

Lockheed Martin Ctr for Leadership
Excellence, Washington, DC

GEOGRAPHIC ANALYSIS OF WORK IN THE US

GEOGRAPHIC ANALYSIS OF WORK OUTSIDE THE US

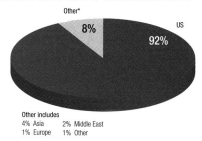

Other includes
4% Asia   2% Middle East
1% Europe   1% Other

PRIMARY SERVICES OFFERED

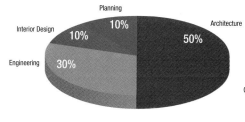

MARKET SEGMENTS

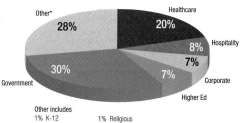

Other includes
1% K-12   1% Religious
1% Industrial/Tech   25% Aviation, Transportation, Water

LOCATIONS

Atlanta, GA	Omaha, NE	Dallas, TX	Beijing, China
Dallas, TX	Phoenix, AZ	Fort Worth, TX	Hong Kong, China
Denver, CO	Tampa, FL	Houston, TX	Istanbul, Turkey
Honolulu, HI	Washington, DC	Miami, FL	Moscow, Russia
Houston, TX	West Palm Beach,	Phoenix, AZ	Riyadh, Saudi Arabia
Las Vegas, NV	FL	Sacramento, CA	
Los Angeles, CA	(LAN offices)	San Antonio, TX	
Miami, FL	Austin, TX	San Marcos, TX	
Millburn, NJ	Chicago, IL	Waco, TX	
Minneapolis, MN	College Station, TX	Abu Dhabi, UAE	

Park Wan Soon

Kumkang Peneterium IT Tower, Seoul, South Korea | Perkins Eastman

16 | Perkins Eastman

115 Fifth Avenue
New York, NY 10003
(212) 353-7200
www.perkinseastman.com
Bradford Perkins, Chairman/CEO
J. David Hoglund, President/COO
Mary-Jean Eastman, Principal/Executive Director

WORLDWIDE REVENUE	$130,000,000
US REVENUE	$97,500,000
WORLDWIDE STAFF	675
HEADQUARTERS	New York, NY
YEAR ESTABLISHED	1981
RECENT REPRESENTATIVE PROJECT	

Elizabeth Seton Pediatric Center, Yonkers, NY

GEOGRAPHIC ANALYSIS OF WORK IN THE US

GEOGRAPHIC ANALYSIS OF WORK OUTSIDE THE US

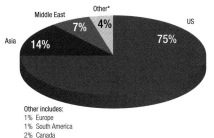

Other includes:
1% Europe
1% South America
2% Canada

PRIMARY SERVICES OFFERED

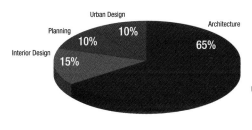

MARKET SEGMENTS

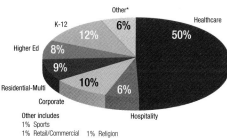

Other includes
1% Sports
1% Retail/Commercial   1% Religion
1% Museum/Cultural   2% Government

LOCATIONS

Boston, MA
Charlotte, NC
Chicago, IL
New York, NY
Pittsburgh, PA

San Francisco, CA
Stamford, CT
Washington, DC
Dubai, UAE
Guayaquil, Ecuador

Mumbai, India
Shanghai, China
Toronto, ON,
    Canada

Perkins Eastman

17 | SSOE Group

1001 Madison Avenue
Toledo, OH 43604
(419) 255-3830
www.ssoe.com
Tony Damon, CEO
David Verner, Senior VP
Lee Warnick, VP

WORLDWIDE REVENUE	$126,535,500
US REVENUE	$113,495,400
WORLDWIDE STAFF	858
HEADQUARTERS	Toledo, OH
YEAR ESTABLISHED	1948
RECENT REPRESENTATIVE PROJECT	

Volkswagen Assembly Plant,
Chattanooga, TN

GEOGRAPHIC ANALYSIS OF WORK IN THE US

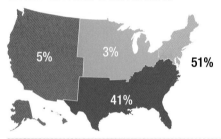

GEOGRAPHIC ANALYSIS OF WORK OUTSIDE THE US

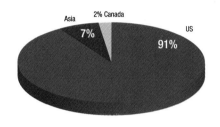

PRIMARY SERVICES OFFERED

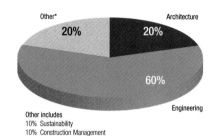

Other includes
10% Sustainability
10% Construction Management

MARKET SEGMENTS

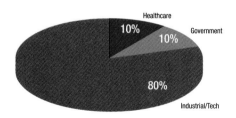

LOCATIONS

Alliance, OH	Kalamazoo, MI	Seattle, WA	Shanghai, China
Birmingham, AL	Lima, OH	St. Paul, MN	Tianjin, China
Cedar Rapids, IA	Midland, MI	Toledo, OH	Toronto, ON,
Chicago, IL	Nashville, TN	Troy, MI	Canada
Cincinnati, OH	Omaha, NE	Washington, DC	
Columbus, OH	Phoenix, AZ	Beijing, China	
Huntsville, AL	Pittsburgh, PA	Mumbai, India	
Irvine, CA	Raleigh, NC	Sao Paulo, Brazil	

18 | RMJM

275 Seventh Avenue, 24th Floor
New York, NY 10001
(212) 629-4100
www.rmjm.com
Peter Schubert, Design Principal
Roger Klein, Design Principal
Sean Roche, Principal

WORLDWIDE REVENUE	$125,660,000
US REVENUE	$14,280,000
WORLDWIDE STAFF	712
HEADQUARTERS	New York, NY
YEAR ESTABLISHED	1956
RECENT REPRESENTATIVE PROJECT	

Duke University Graduate Medical School, Singapore

GEOGRAPHIC ANALYSIS OF WORK IN THE US   GEOGRAPHIC ANALYSIS OF WORK OUTSIDE THE US

PRIMARY SERVICES OFFERED   MARKET SEGMENTS

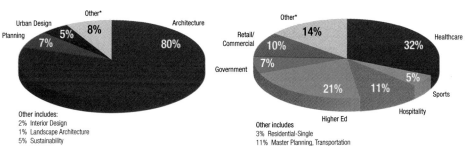

Other includes:
2% Interior Design
1% Landscape Architecture
5% Sustainability

Other includes
3% Residential-Single
11% Master Planning, Transportation

LOCATIONS

New York, NY
Washington, DC
Abu Dhabi, UAE
Dubai, UAE
Edinburgh, UK
Glasgow, UK

Hong Kong, China
Istanbul, Turkey
London, UK
Manama, Bahrain
Moscow, Russia
Shanghai, China

Singapore
St. Petersburg,
   Russia
Vladivostok, Russia

19 | Kohn Pedersen Fox

11 West 42nd Street
New York, NY 10036
(212) 977-6500
www.kpf.com
A. Eugene Kohn, Chairman
Paul Katz, Managing Principal
James von Klemperer, Design Principal

WORLDWIDE REVENUE	$123,600,000
US REVENUE	N/A
WORLDWIDE STAFF	500
HEADQUARTERS	New York, NY
YEAR ESTABLISHED	1976
RECENT REPRESENTATIVE PROJECT	

University of Michigan Ross School of
Business, Ann Arbor, MI

GEOGRAPHIC ANALYSIS OF WORK IN THE US

GEOGRAPHIC ANALYSIS OF WORK OUTSIDE THE US

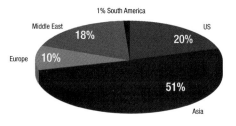

PRIMARY SERVICES OFFERED

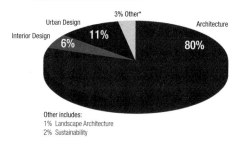

Other includes:
1% Landscape Architecture
2% Sustainability

MARKET SEGMENTS

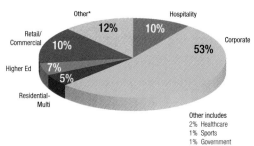

Other includes
2% Healthcare
1% Sports
1% Government
8% Transportation

LOCATIONS

New York, NY
Abu Dhabi, UAE
Hong Kong, China
London, UK
Seoul, Korea
Shanghai, China

20 | ZGF Architects

1223 S.W. Washington Street, Suite 200
Portland, OR 97205
(503) 224-3860
www.zgf.com
Robert Packard, Managing Partner
Robert Frasca, Partner in Charge of Design

WORLDWIDE REVENUE	$120,248,889
US REVENUE	$113,109,262
WORLDWIDE STAFF	426
HEADQUARTERS	Portland, OR
YEAR ESTABLISHED	1959
RECENT REPRESENTATIVE PROJECT	

Randall Children's Hospital at Legacy
Emanuel, Portland, OR

GEOGRAPHIC ANALYSIS OF WORK IN THE US

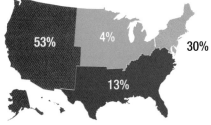

53%
4%
30%
13%

GEOGRAPHIC ANALYSIS OF WORK OUTSIDE THE US

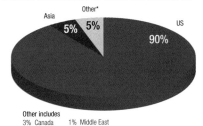

Other*
Asia
5% 5%
US
90%

Other includes
3% Canada   1% Middle East
1% Europe

PRIMARY SERVICES OFFERED

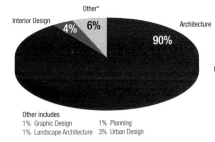

Other*
Interior Design
4% 6%
Architecture
90%

Other includes
1% Graphic Design   1% Planning
1% Landscape Architecture   3% Urban Design

MARKET SEGMENTS

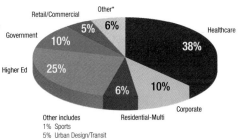

Other*
Retail/Commercial
5% 6%
Healthcare
Government
10%
38%
Higher Ed
25%
6% 10%
Corporate
Residential-Multi

Other includes
1% Sports
5% Urban Design/Transit

LOCATIONS

Los Angeles, CA
New York, NY
Portland, OR
Seattle, WA
Washington, DC

MetLife Stadium Solar Ring, East Rutherford, NJ I DLR Group

Santa Monica College Performing Arts Center Expansion, Santa Monica, CA I DLR Group

21 | DLR Group

400 Essex Court
Omaha, NE 68114
(877) DLR Group
www.dlrgroup.com
Griff Davenport, Managing Principal
Jon Pettit, Managing Principal
Steven McKay, Sr. Principal/Design Leader

WORLDWIDE REVENUE	$110,000,000
US REVENUE	$108,500,000
WORLDWIDE STAFF	502
HEADQUARTERS	21 Global Offices
YEAR ESTABLISHED	1966
RECENT REPRESENTATIVE PROJECT	

Marysville Getchell High School,
Marysville, WA

GEOGRAPHIC ANALYSIS OF WORK IN THE US

55%   40%   0%
5%

GEOGRAPHIC ANALYSIS OF WORK OUTSIDE THE US

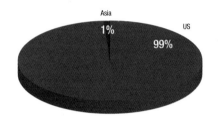

Asia
1%   US
99%

PRIMARY SERVICES OFFERED

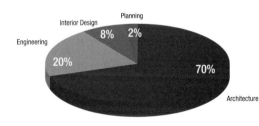

Interior Design   Planning
Engineering   8%   2%
20%   70%
Architecture

MARKET SEGMENTS

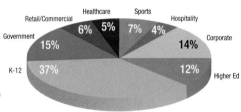

Retail/Commercial   Healthcare   Sports
Government   6%   5%   7%   4%   Hospitality
15%   Corporate
14%
K-12   37%   12%
Higher Ed

LOCATIONS

Chicago, IL
Colorado Springs,
CO
Denver, CO
Des Moines, IA
Honolulu, HI

Las Vegas, NV
Lincoln, NE
Minneapolis, MN
Omaha, NE
Orlando, FL
Overland Park, KS

Palm Springs, CA
Pasadena, CA
Phoenix, AZ
Portland, OR
Riverside, CA
Sacramento, CA

Santa Monica, CA
Seattle, WA
Tucson, AZ
Shanghai, China

 DLR Group

33
Understanding Change
& the Change in Understanding

By Richard Saul Wurman

$22.00   ISBN: 978-0-9818989-8-8

You might describe Richard Saul Wurman as a provocateur, a pioneer, a creative genius. Inspirational, innovative, larger-than-life ... legendary, even. Others have. But the most apt description of this singular individual — this architect, designer, creator of the celebrated TED Conference, and prolific author — is storyteller.

Springing to life from the mind of the world's original information architect is *33: Understanding Change & the Change in Understanding*. A book that breaks out of any traditional (dare we say even rational) story-telling framework, 33 invites readers to journey through its pages as they will.

A fable re-imagined three decades after its original telling as a conference keynote address, 33 chronicles the adventures and musings of an eccentric (yet oddly familiar) character: the Commissioner of Curiosity and Imagination. This bemused, amused, and roundish imp waddles through the city of What-If in the land of Could-Be, trying to make sense of the myriad changes that have transpired in the past 33 years.

The story is presented in an ingenious, multi-layered format – "information upon information," as the Commissioner himself might say – with the original fable at its core. Surrounding this is an updated tale as presented through 33 episodes and accompanying graphics.

Order online at www.di.net/store

800.726.8603
www.greenway.us

Greenway Communications
25 Technology Parkway South, Suite 101
Norcross, GA 30092

22 | Dewberry (Architecture)

8401 Arlington Boulevard
Fairfax, VA 22031
(703) 849-0100
www.dewberry.com
Sidney O. Dewberry, Chairman
Donald E. Stone Jr., CEO
Randall E. Gibson, Architects, Practice Manager

WORLDWIDE REVENUE	$106,284,000
US REVENUE	$106,284,000
WORLDWIDE STAFF	1,800
HEADQUARTERS	Fairfax, VA
YEAR ESTABLISHED	1956
RECENT REPRESENTATIVE PROJECT	New Youth Detention Center, Baltimore, MD

GEOGRAPHIC ANALYSIS OF WORK IN THE US

GEOGRAPHIC ANALYSIS OF WORK OUTSIDE THE US

US
100%

PRIMARY SERVICES OFFERED

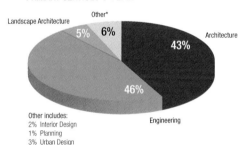

Landscape Architecture — Other* 6% — 5%
Architecture 43%
Engineering 46%

Other includes:
2% Interior Design
1% Planning
3% Urban Design

MARKET SEGMENTS

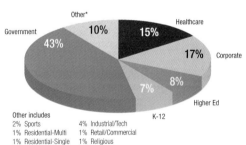

Government 43% — Other* 10% — Healthcare 15%
Corporate 17%
Higher Ed 8%
K-12 7%

Other includes
2% Sports   4% Industrial/Tech
1% Residential-Multi   1% Retail/Commercial
1% Residential-Single   1% Religious

LOCATIONS

Arlington, VA	Danville, VA	Leesburg, VA	Philadelphia, PA
Atlanta, GA	Denton, TX	Los Angeles, CA	Phoenix, AZ
Baltimore, MD	Denver, CO	Mount Laurel, NJ	Raleigh, NC
Bloomfield, NJ	Elgin, IL	New Haven, CT	Richmond, VA
Boston, MA	Fairfax, VA	New Orleans, LA	Sacramento, CA
Carlisle, PA	Frederick MD	New York, NY	Tampa, FL
Chapel Hill, NC	Gainesville, VA	Orlando, FL	Tulsa, OK
Charlotte, NC	Gaithersburg, MD	Parsippany, NJ	Virginia Beach, VA
Dallas, TX	Lanham, MD	Peoria, IL	

San Francisco State University, J. Paul Leonard and Sutro Library, San Francisco, CA | HMC Architects

23 | HMC Architects

633 West 5th Street, 3rd Floor
Los Angeles, CA 90071
(800) 350-9979
www.hmcarchitects.com
Brian Staton, President/CEO
Ric Mangum, Regional Managing Principal

WORLDWIDE REVENUE	$87,973,699
US REVENUE	$87,791,874
WORLDWIDE STAFF	411
HEADQUARTERS	Ontario, CA
YEAR ESTABLISHED	1940

RECENT REPRESENTATIVE PROJECT

Orchard School Library, San Jose, CA

GEOGRAPHIC ANALYSIS OF WORK IN THE US

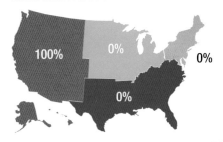

GEOGRAPHIC ANALYSIS OF WORK OUTSIDE THE US

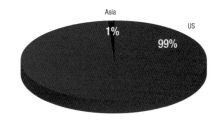

PRIMARY SERVICES OFFERED

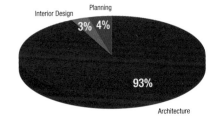

MARKET SEGMENTS

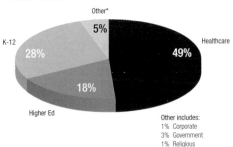

Other includes:
1% Corporate
3% Government
1% Religious

LOCATIONS

Fresno, CA	Phoenix, AZ	San Francisco, CA
Las Vegas, NV	Reno, NV	San Jose, CA
Los Angeles, CA	Sacramento, CA	Santiago, Chile
Ontario, CA	San Diego, CA	

24 | Populous

300 Wyandotte Street
Kansas City, MO 64105
(816) 221-1500
www.populous.com

WORLDWIDE REVENUE	$86,000,000
US REVENUE	$46,000,000
WORLDWIDE STAFF	333
HEADQUARTERS	Kansas City, MO
YEAR ESTABLISHED	1983

RECENT REPRESENTATIVE PROJECT

Marlins Park, Miami, FL

GEOGRAPHIC ANALYSIS OF WORK IN THE US   GEOGRAPHIC ANALYSIS OF WORK OUTSIDE THE US

PRIMARY SERVICES OFFERED   MARKET SEGMENTS

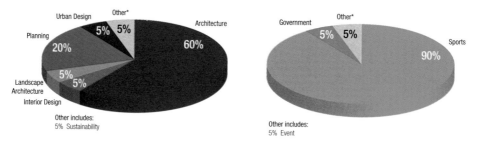

Other includes:
5% Sustainability

Other includes:
5% Event

LOCATIONS

Denver, CO	Auckland, New Zealand	London, UK	Taipei, Taiwan
Kansas City, MO	Brisbane, Australia	Melbourne, Australia	
Knoxville, TN	Hong Kong, China	New Delhi, India	
Norman, OK		Singapore	

25 | Gresham, Smith and Partners

511 Union Street, Suite 1400
Nashville, TN 37219
(615) 770-8100
www.gspnet.com
Brackney J. Reed, Chairman/COO
James W. Bearden, CEO

WORLDWIDE REVENUE	$85,953,500
US REVENUE	$84,150,000
WORLDWIDE STAFF	625
HEADQUARTERS	Nashville, TN
YEAR ESTABLISHED	1967
RECENT REPRESENTATIVE PROJECT	

Nissan Americas Corporate Facility, Franklin, TN

GEOGRAPHIC ANALYSIS OF WORK IN THE US

GEOGRAPHIC ANALYSIS OF WORK OUTSIDE THE US

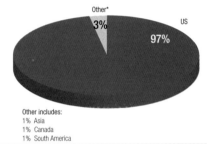

Other includes:
1% Asia
1% Canada
1% South America

PRIMARY SERVICES OFFERED

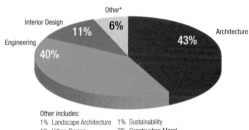

Other includes:
1% Landscape Architecture   1% Sustainability
1% Urban Design   3% Construction Mgmt.

MARKET SEGMENTS

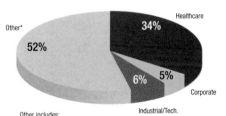

Other includes:
52% Transportation, Water Services, Aviation

LOCATIONS

Atlanta, GA	Dallas, TX	Louisville, KY	Shanghai, China
Birmingham, AL	Ft. Lauderdale, FL	Memphis, TN	
Chipley, FL	Jackson, MS	Nashville, TN	
Cincinnati, OH	Jacksonville, FL	Richmond, VA	
Columbus, OH	Knoxville, TN	Tampa, FL	

DesignIntelligence®

Where Business Meets the Future of Design

www.DI.net

26 | Rafael Viñoly Architects

50 Vandam Street
New York, NY 10013
(212) 924-5060
www.rvapc.com
Rafael Vinoly, President

WORLDWIDE REVENUE	$84,966,000
WORLDWIDE STAFF	510
HEADQUARTERS	New York, NY
YEAR ESTABLISHED	1983

27 | PageSoutherlandPage

400 West Cesar Chavez, Suite 500
Austin, TX 78701
(512) 472-6721
www.pspaec.com

WORLDWIDE REVENUE	$84,429,100
WORLDWIDE STAFF	415
HEADQUARTERS	Dallas, TX
YEAR ESTABLISHED	1898
RECENT REPRESENTATIVE PROJECT	

Architecture of Discovery Green,
Houston, TX

28 | HNTB (Architecture)

715 Kirk Drive
Kansas City, MO 64105
(816) 472-1201
www.hntb.com
Terry Miller, CEO

WORLDWIDE REVENUE	$83,334,000
WORLDWIDE STAFF	101-450
HEADQUARTERS	Kansas City, MO
YEAR ESTABLISHED	1914

29 | Corgan Associates

401 North Houston Street
Dallas, TX 75202
(214) 748-2000
www.corgan.com
David Lind, Chairman/Managing Principal
Bob Morris, CEO/Managing Principal
Jon Holzheimer, COO/Managing Principal

WORLDWIDE REVENUE	$81,782,000
WORLDWIDE STAFF	301
HEADQUARTERS	Dallas, TX
YEAR ESTABLISHED	1938
RECENT REPRESENTATIVE PROJECT	

Blue Cross Blue Shield of Texas,
Richardson, TX

Great Hall, Tom Bradley International Terminal Expansion, Los Angeles International Airport | Fentress Architects

University of California, Irvine, Humanities Gateway-West Facade, Irvine, CA | Fentress Architects

30 | EYP Architecture & Engineering

257 Fuller Road, NanoFab East
Albany, NY 12203
(518) 795-3800
www.eypaedesign.com
Tom Birdsey, President/CEO
John Pocorobba, VP/Operations
Leila Kamal, VP/Design Expertise

WORLDWIDE REVENUE	$72,681,105
WORLDWIDE STAFF	300
HEADQUARTERS	Albany, NY
YEAR ESTABLISHED	1972

RECENT REPRESENTATIVE PROJECT
University of Scranton Loyola Science
Center, Scranton, PA

31 | Fentress Architects

421 Broadway
Denver, CO 80203
(303) 722-5000
www.fentressarchitects.com
Curtis Fentress, President/Principal-in-Charge of Design
Agatha Kessler, CEO
Karen Gilbert, Principal, Marketing Director

WORLDWIDE REVENUE	$70,698,507
WORLDWIDE STAFF	137
HEADQUARTERS	Denver, CO
YEAR ESTABLISHED	1980

RECENT REPRESENTATIVE PROJECT
Mineta San Jose International Airport,
Terminal B, San Jose, CA

32 | Clark Nexsen

6160 Kempsville Circle
Norfolk, VA 23502
(757) 455-5800
www.clarknexsen.com
Tom Winborne, CEO
David A. Keith, Director of Architecture

WORLDWIDE REVENUE	$66,300,000
WORLDWIDE STAFF	505
HEADQUARTERS	Norfolk, VA
YEAR ESTABLISHED	1920

RECENT REPRESENTATIVE PROJECT
Walter Reed Medical Center, Warrior
Transition Unit, Bethesda, MD

33 | EwingCole

100 North 6th Street
Philadelphia, PA 19106
(215) 923-2020
www.ewingcole.com
John Gerbner, President
S. Mark Hebden, Executive VP
Donald Dissinger, Executive VP

WORLDWIDE REVENUE	$64,566,000
WORLDWIDE STAFF	330
HEADQUARTERS	Philadelphia, PA
YEAR ESTABLISHED	1961

RECENT REPRESENTATIVE PROJECT
New Meadowlands Stadium,
East Rutherford, NJ

David Whittaker, Kasian Architecture, Interior Design and Planning LTD

Esker Foundation Art Gallery, Calgary, AB, Canada | Kasian Architecture Interior Design and Planning

34 | SHW Group

5717 Legacy Drive
Plano, TX 75024
(888) SHW-1019
www.shwgroup.com
Marjorie Simmons, CEO
Kyle Bacon, COO
Matt Snider, CFO

WORLDWIDE REVENUE $59,796,231
WORLDWIDE STAFF 240
HEADQUARTERS Plano, TX
YEAR ESTABLISHED 1945
RECENT REPRESENTATIVE PROJECT
Carl Wunsche Senior High School,
Spring, TX

35 | NELSON

222-230 Walnut Street
Philadelphia, PA 19106
(215) 925-6562
www.nelsononline.com
John "Ozzie" Nelson, President/CEO

WORLDWIDE REVENUE $55,533,900
WORLDWIDE STAFF 450
HEADQUARTERS Philadelphia, PA
YEAR ESTABLISHED 1977
RECENT REPRESENTATIVE PROJECT
Bank of America Infomart, Dallas, TX

36 | Kasian Architecture Interior Design and Planning

1555 West Pender Street, Suite 350
Vancouver, BC V6G 2T1
(604) 683-4145
www.kasian.com
Don Kasian, President

WORLDWIDE REVENUE $55,000,000
WORLDWIDE STAFF 248
HEADQUARTERS Vancouver, Canada
YEAR ESTABLISHED 1985

37 | Ennead Architects

320 West 13th Street
New York, NY 10014
(212) 807-7171
www.ennead.com

WORLDWIDE REVENUE $52,200,000
WORLDWIDE STAFF 172
HEADQUARTERS New York, NY
YEAR ESTABLISHED 1963

City Target, Seattle, WA | MulvannyG2 Architecture

Wuxi Chong'an Temple, Wuxi, China | MulvannyG2 Architecture

38 | Callison

1420 5th Avenue, Suite 2400
Seattle, WA 98101
(206) 623-4646
www.callison.com
John Jastrem, Chairman/CEO

WORLDWIDE REVENUE	$52,015,000
WORLDWIDE STAFF	800
HEADQUARTERS	Seattle, WA
YEAR ESTABLISHED	1975
RECENT REPRESENTATIVE PROJECT	
	Bloomingdale's Dubai, Dubai, UAE

39 | Robert A.M. Stern Architects

460 West 34th Street
New York, NY 10001
(212) 967-5100
www.ramsa.com
Robert Stern, Senior Partner

WORLDWIDE REVENUE	$51,811,410
WORLDWIDE STAFF	220
HEADQUARTERS	New York, NY
YEAR ESTABLISHED	1969
RECENT REPRESENTATIVE PROJECT	
	Fifteen Central Park West, New York, NY

40 | Wimberly Allison Tong & Goo (WATG)

8001 Irvine Center Drive, Suite 500
Irvine, CA 92618
(949) 574-8500
www.watg.com
Michael R. Seyle, President/CEO
Peter Priebe, VP/CFO
Rajesh Chandnani, VP/Strategy Director

WORLDWIDE REVENUE	$51,000,000
WORLDWIDE STAFF	301
HEADQUARTERS	Irvine, CA
YEAR ESTABLISHED	1945
RECENT REPRESENTATIVE PROJECT	
	Viceroy Anguilla, Anguilla

41 | MulvannyG2 Architecture

MULVANNY|G2
ARCHITECTURE

1110 112th Avenue Northeast, Suite 500
Bellevue, WA 98004
(425) 463-2000
www.mulvannyg2.com
Mitch Smith, CEO
Ming Zhang, President

WORLDWIDE REVENUE	$50,000,000
WORLDWIDE STAFF	308
HEADQUARTERS	Bellevue, WA
YEAR ESTABLISHED	1971
RECENT REPRESENTATIVE PROJECT	
	Gashora Girls Academy, Gashora, Rwanda

Arriton Grass/ESTO

University of Wisconsin-Madison, School of Human Ecology, Madison, WI | Sasaki Associates, Inc.

Pease Photography

Lorain County Community College iLoft Building, Elyria, OH | Sasaki Associates, Inc.

42 | Sasaki Associates, Inc.

S A S A K I

64 Pleasant Street
Watertown, MA 02472
(617) 926-3300
www.sasaki.com
James Miner, Managing Partner
Mark O. Dawson, Managing Partner
Pablo Savid-Buteler, Managing Principal

WORLDWIDE REVENUE	$48,335,000
WORLDWIDE STAFF	222
HEADQUARTERS	Watertown, MA
YEAR ESTABLISHED	1953

RECENT REPRESENTATIVE PROJECT

Port of Los Angeles Wilmington
Waterfront Park, Los Angeles, CA

43 | LPA

5161 California Avenue
Irvine, CA 92617
(949) 769-6219
www.lpainc.com
Robert O. Kupper, CEO/Sr. Principal
Dan Heinfeld, President/Sr. Principal
Glenn Carels, Principal-of-Design

WORLDWIDE REVENUE	$48,194,126
WORLDWIDE STAFF	220
HEADQUARTERS	Irvine, CA
YEAR ESTABLISHED	1965

RECENT REPRESENTATIVE PROJECT

Orangewood Charter School,
Santa Ana, CA

44 | Flad Architects

644 Science Drive, PO Box 44977
Madison, WI 53711
(608) 238-2661
www.flad.com
William (Bill) Bula, President/CEO
Jeffrey C. Zutz, Managing Principal
Laura Stillman, Principal

WORLDWIDE REVENUE	$46,818,000
WORLDWIDE STAFF	101-450
HEADQUARTERS	Madison, WI
YEAR ESTABLISHED	1927

45 | LS3P Associates Ltd.

205 1/2 King Street
Charleston, SC 29407
(843) 577-4444
www.LS3P.com
Michael Tribble, Chairman
Frank Lucas, Chairman Emeritus
Thompson Penney, President/CEO

WORLDWIDE REVENUE	$46,470,000
WORLDWIDE STAFF	200
HEADQUARTERS	Charleston, SC
YEAR ESTABLISHED	1963

RECENT REPRESENTATIVE PROJECT

Clemson Univ. ICAR Center for Emerging
Technologies, Greenville, NC

Roosevelt University Academic, Student Life and Residence Center, Chicago, IL | VOA Associates

46 | Little

5815 Westpark Drive
Charlotte, NC 28217
(704) 525-6350
www.littleonline.com
Philip Kuttner, CEO
John Komisin, President/COO
Jim Williams, National Design Director

WORLDWIDE REVENUE $46,200,000
WORLDWIDE STAFF   210
HEADQUARTERS   Charlotte, NC
YEAR ESTABLISHED   1966
RECENT REPRESENTATIVE PROJECT
Adventist Health Systems Corporate
Headquarters, Orlando, FL

47 | BSA LifeStructures

9365 Counselors Row
Indianapolis, IN 46240
(317) 819-7878
www.bsals.com
Keith H. Smith, President
Michael D. Castor, Managing Director/Practice Groups
Shawn P. Mulholland, Managing Director/Client Acquisition

WORLDWIDE REVENUE $45,326,151
WORLDWIDE STAFF   247
HEADQUARTERS   Indianapolis, IN
YEAR ESTABLISHED   1975
RECENT REPRESENTATIVE PROJECT
Lakeland HealthCare Inpatient Pavilion,
St. Joseph, MI

48 | VOA Associates

222 South Michigan Avenue, Suite 1400
Chicago, IL 60604
(312) 554-1400
www.voa.com
Michael A. Toolis, Chairman/CEO
Percy "Rebel" Roberts III, President/COO
Theodore Fery, Secretary

WORLDWIDE REVENUE $45,300,000
WORLDWIDE STAFF   262
HEADQUARTERS   Chicago, IL
YEAR ESTABLISHED   1969
RECENT REPRESENTATIVE PROJECT
Roosevelt University Vertical Campus,
Chicago, IL

49 | Cuningham Group Architecture

201 Main Street Southeast, Suite 325
Minneapolis, MN 55414
(612) 379-3400
www.cuningham.com
John Cuningham, Founder
John Quiter, Chairman
Timothy Dufault, President/CEO

WORLDWIDE REVENUE $44,188,852
WORLDWIDE STAFF   229
HEADQUARTERS   Minneapolis, MN
YEAR ESTABLISHED   1968
RECENT REPRESENTATIVE PROJECT
Epic Systems Corporation Headquarters,
Verona, WI

50 | GHAFARI

17101 Michigan Avenue
Dearborn, MI 48126
(313) 441-3000
www.ghafari.com

WORLDWIDE REVENUE	$42,861,710
WORLDWIDE STAFF	101-450
HEADQUARTERS	Dearborn, MI
YEAR ESTABLISHED	1982

51 | FKP Architects

8 Greenway Plaza, Suite 300
Houston, TX 77046
(713) 621-2100
www.fkp.com

WORLDWIDE REVENUE	$42,424,000
WORLDWIDE STAFF	130
HEADQUARTERS	Houston, TX
YEAR ESTABLISHED	1937

52 | RSP Architects

RSP ARCHITECTS

1220 Marshall Street Northeast
Minneapolis, MN 55413
(612) 677-7100
www.rsparch.com

WORLDWIDE REVENUE	$42,228,000
WORLDWIDE STAFF	236
HEADQUARTERS	Minneapolis, MN
YEAR ESTABLISHED	1978

53 | STUDIOS Architecture

1625 M Street Northwest
Washington, DC 20036
(202) 736-5900
www.studiosarchitecture.com

WORLDWIDE REVENUE	$41,100,000
WORLDWIDE STAFF	212
HEADQUARTERS	Washington, DC
YEAR ESTABLISHED	1985

54 | CTA Architects Engineers

13 North 23rd Street
Billings, MT 59102
(406) 248-7455
www.ctagroup.com

WORLDWIDE REVENUE	$40,800,000
WORLDWIDE STAFF	344
HEADQUARTERS	Billings, MT
YEAR ESTABLISHED	1938

55 | Swanke Hayden Connell Architects

295 Lafayette Street
New York, NY 10012
(212) 226-9696
www.shca.com

WORLDWIDE REVENUE	$40,698,000
WORLDWIDE STAFF	250
HEADQUARTERS	New York, NY
YEAR ESTABLISHED	1906

56 | The SLAM Collaborative

80 Glastonbury Boulevard

Glastonbury, CT 06033

(860) 657-8077

www.slamcoll.com

WORLDWIDE REVENUE	$39,475,964
WORLDWIDE STAFF	155
HEADQUARTERS	Glastonbury, CT
YEAR ESTABLISHED	1976

57 | Perkowitz+Ruth Architects

111 West Ocean Boulevard, 21st Floor

Long Beach, CA 90802

(562) 628-8000

www.prarchitects.com

WORLDWIDE REVENUE	$39,000,000
WORLDWIDE STAFF	201
HEADQUARTERS	Long Beach, CA
YEAR ESTABLISHED	1979

58 | Cooper Carry

191 Peachtree Street Northeast, Suite 2400

Atlanta, GA 30303

(404) 237-2000

www.coopercarry.com

WORLDWIDE REVENUE	$38,005,433
WORLDWIDE STAFF	161
HEADQUARTERS	Atlanta, GA
YEAR ESTABLISHED	1960

59 | NTD Architecture

9655 Granite Ridge Drive, Suite 400

San Diego, CA 92123

(858) 565-4440

www.ntd.com

WORLDWIDE REVENUE	$36,822,000
WORLDWIDE STAFF	300
HEADQUARTERS	San Diego, CA
YEAR ESTABLISHED	1953

60 | tvsdesign

1230 Peachtree Street Northeast, Suite 2700

Atlanta, GA 30309

(404) 888-6600

www.tvs-design.com

WORLDWIDE REVENUE	$35,600,000
WORLDWIDE STAFF	167
HEADQUARTERS	Atlanta, GA
YEAR ESTABLISHED	1968

61 | Langdon Wilson International

1055 Wilshire Boulevard, Suite 1500

Los Angeles, CA 90017

(213) 250-1186

www.langdonwilson.com

WORLDWIDE REVENUE	$35,300,000
WORLDWIDE STAFF	280
HEADQUARTERS	Los Angeles, CA
YEAR ESTABLISHED	1951

Maconochie Photography

Wayne State University Paul A. Schaap Chemistry Building, Detroit, MI | Harley Ellis Devereaux

62 | KMD Architects

222 Vallejo Street	WORLDWIDE REVENUE	$35,143,453
San Francisco, CA 94111	WORLDWIDE STAFF	163
(415) 398-5191	HEADQUARTERS	San Francisco, CA
www.kmdarchitects.com	YEAR ESTABLISHED	1963

63 | Beyer Blinder Belle

41 East 11th Street	WORLDWIDE REVENUE	$34,986,423
New York, NY 10003	WORLDWIDE STAFF	175
(212) 777-7800	HEADQUARTERS	New York, NY
www.beyerblinderbelle.com	YEAR ESTABLISHED	1968

64 | Harley Ellis Devereaux

HARLEY ELLIS DEVEREAUX

26913 Northwestern Highway, Suite 200	WORLDWIDE REVENUE	$34,026,000
Southfield, MI 48033	WORLDWIDE STAFF	208
(248) 262-1500	HEADQUARTERS	Detroit, MI
www.harleyellisdevereaux.com	YEAR ESTABLISHED	1908

65 | Payette

290 Congress Street, Fifth Floor	WORLDWIDE REVENUE	$33,582,508
Boston, MA 02210	WORLDWIDE STAFF	115
(617) 895-1000	HEADQUARTERS	Boston, MA
www.payette.com	YEAR ESTABLISHED	1932

66 | EDSA

1512 East Broward Boulevard, Suite 110	WORLDWIDE REVENUE	$32,538,000
Fort Lauderdale, FL 33301	WORLDWIDE STAFF	175
(954) 524-3330	HEADQUARTERS	Fort Lauderdale, FL
www.edsaplan.com	YEAR ESTABLISHED	1960

67 | Ayers Saint Gross

1040 Hull Street, Suite 100	WORLDWIDE REVENUE	$32,040,000
Baltimore, MD 21230	WORLDWIDE STAFF	130
(410) 347-8500	HEADQUARTERS	Baltimore, MD
www.asg-architects.com	YEAR ESTABLISHED	1912

68 | Fanning/Howey Associates

1200 Irmscher Boulevard
Celina, OH 45822
(888) 499-2292
www.fhai.com

WORLDWIDE REVENUE	$31,447,134
WORLDWIDE STAFF	173
HEADQUARTERS	Celina,OH
YEAR ESTABLISHED	1961

69 | Roger Ferris + Partners

285 Riverside Avenue
Westport, CT 06880
(203) 222-4848
www.ferrisarch.com

WORLDWIDE REVENUE	$31,298,700
WORLDWIDE STAFF	40
HEADQUARTERS	Westport, CT
YEAR ESTABLISHED	1986

70 | Arquitectonica

2900 Oak Avenue
Miami, FL 33131
(305) 372-1812
www.arquitectonica.com

WORLDWIDE REVENUE	$30,039,000
WORLDWIDE STAFF	355
HEADQUARTERS	Miami, FL
YEAR ESTABLISHED	1977

71 | Shepley Bulfinch Richardson and Abbott

2 Seaport Lane
Boston, MA 02210
(617) 423-1700
www.shepleyfbulfinch.com

WORLDWIDE REVENUE	$29,800,000
WORLDWIDE STAFF	134
HEADQUARTERS	Boston, MA
YEAR ESTABLISHED	1874

72 | Lionakis

1919 Nineteenth Street
Sacramento, CA 95811
(916) 558-1900
www.lionakis.com

WORLDWIDE REVENUE	$29,376,000
WORLDWIDE STAFF	21-100
HEADQUARTERS	Sacramento, CA
YEAR ESTABLISHED	1909

73 | HLW International

115 Fifth Avenue, Suite 500
New York, NY 10003
(212) 353-4600
www.hlw.com

WORLDWIDE REVENUE	$29,355,000
WORLDWIDE STAFF	149
HEADQUARTERS	New York, NY
YEAR ESTABLISHED	1885

74 | Architects Hawaii

1001 Bishop Street, Suite 200	WORLDWIDE REVENUE $29,002,680
Honolulu, HI 96813	WORLDWIDE STAFF 87
(808) 523-9636	HEADQUARTERS Honolulu, HI
www.ahldesign.com	YEAR ESTABLISHED 1946

75 | Aedas

315 Hudson Street	WORLDWIDE REVENUE $28,779,300
New York, NY 10013	WORLDWIDE STAFF 151
(212) 633-4700	HEADQUARTERS New York, NY
www.aedas.com	YEAR ESTABLISHED 1952

76 | Adrian Smith + Gordon Gill Architecture

111 West Monroe, Suite 2300	WORLDWIDE REVENUE $28,500,000
Chicago, IL 60603	WORLDWIDE STAFF 110
(312) 920-1888	HEADQUARTERS Chicago, IL
www.smithgill.com	YEAR ESTABLISHED 2006

77 | Murphy/Jahn

35 East Wacker Drive, Suite 300	WORLDWIDE REVENUE $28,197,900
Chicago, IL 60601	WORLDWIDE STAFF 80
(312) 427-7300	HEADQUARTERS Chicago, IL
www.murphyjahn.com	YEAR ESTABLISHED 1937

78 | Lord, Aeck & Sargent

1201 Peachtree Street Northeast, Suite 300	WORLDWIDE REVENUE $28,152,000
Atlanta, GA 30361	WORLDWIDE STAFF 144
(877) 929-1400	HEADQUARTERS Atlanta, GA
www.lordaecksargent.com	YEAR ESTABLISHED 1942

79 | RDG Planning & Design

301 Grand Avenue	WORLDWIDE REVENUE $27,808,028
Des Moines, IA 50309	WORLDWIDE STAFF 175
(515) 288-3141	HEADQUARTERS Des Moines, IA
www.rdgusa.com	YEAR ESTABLISHED 1966

80 | FXFOWLE Architects

22 West 19th Street	WORLDWIDE REVENUE $27,250,000
New York, NY 10011	WORLDWIDE STAFF 108
(212) 627-1700	HEADQUARTERS New York, NY
www.fxfowle.com	YEAR ESTABLISHED 1978

81 | TRO Jung | Brannen

22 Boston Wharf Road	WORLDWIDE REVENUE $27,100,000
Boston, MA 02210	WORLDWIDE STAFF 170
(617) 502-3400	HEADQUARTERS Boston, MA
www.trojungbrannen.com	YEAR ESTABLISHED 1909

82 | JCJ Architecture

38 Prospect Street	WORLDWIDE REVENUE $27,050,000
Hartford, CT 06103	WORLDWIDE STAFF 107
(860) 247-9226	HEADQUARTERS Hartford, CT
www.jcj.com	YEAR ESTABLISHED 1936

83 | GreenbergFarrow

1430 West Peachtree Street	WORLDWIDE REVENUE $26,924,200
Atlanta, GA 30309	WORLDWIDE STAFF 140
(404) 601-4000	HEADQUARTERS Atlanta, GA
www.greenbergfarrow.com	YEAR ESTABLISHED 1974

84 | Lawrence Group

319 North 4th Street, Suite 1000	WORLDWIDE REVENUE $26,550,610
St. Louis, MO 63102	WORLDWIDE STAFF 145
(866) 680-5700	HEADQUARTERS St. Louis, MO
www.thelawrencegroup.com	YEAR ESTABLISHED 1983

85 | Ballinger

833 Chestnut Street, Suite 1400	WORLDWIDE REVENUE $26,356,800
Philadelphia, PA 19107	WORLDWIDE STAFF 125
(215) 446-0900	HEADQUARTERS Philadelphia, PA
www.ballinger-ae.com	YEAR ESTABLISHED 1878

86 | GBBN Architects

332 East Eighth Street	WORLDWIDE REVENUE $26,100,000
Cincinnati, OH 45202	WORLDWIDE STAFF 112
(513) 241-8700	HEADQUARTERS Cincinnati, OH
www.gbbn.com	YEAR ESTABLISHED 1948

87 | Elkus Manfredi Architects

300 A Street	WORLDWIDE REVENUE $26,099,930
Boston, MA 02210	WORLDWIDE STAFF 120
(617) 426-1300	HEADQUARTERS Boston, MA
www.elkus-manfredi.com	YEAR ESTABLISHED 1988

88 | Davis Partnership Architects

225 Main Street, Unit C101	WORLDWIDE REVENUE $26,076,759
Edwards, CO 81632	WORLDWIDE STAFF 21-100
(970) 926-8960	HEADQUARTERS Edwards, CO
www.davispartner.com	YEAR ESTABLISHED 1967

89 | SLCE Architects

841 Broadway, 7th Floor	WORLDWIDE REVENUE $25,097,100
New York, NY 10003	WORLDWIDE STAFF 5-20
(212) 979-8400	HEADQUARTERS New York, NY
www.slcearch.com	YEAR ESTABLISHED 1941

90 | BWBR Architects

380 Saint Peter Street	WORLDWIDE REVENUE $25,000,000
St. Paul, MN 55102	WORLDWIDE STAFF 104
(651) 222-3701	HEADQUARTERS St. Paul, MN
www.bwbr.com	YEAR ESTABLISHED 1922

91 | gkkworks

2355 Main Street, Suite 220	WORLDWIDE REVENUE $24,837,873
Irvine, CA 92614	WORLDWIDE STAFF 102
(949) 250-1500	HEADQUARTERS Irvine, CA
www.gkkworks.com	YEAR ESTABLISHED 1991

92 | FFKR Architects

730 Pacific Avenue

Salt Lake City, UT 84104

(801) 521-6186

www.ffkr.com

WORLDWIDE REVENUE	$24,806,400
WORLDWIDE STAFF	121
HEADQUARTERS	Salt Lake City, UT
YEAR ESTABLISHED	1976

93 | Solomon Cordwell Buenz

625 North Michigan Avenue, Suite 800

Chicago, IL 60611

(312) 896-1100

www.scb.com

WORLDWIDE REVENUE	$24,730,953
WORLDWIDE STAFF	120
HEADQUARTERS	Chicago, IL
YEAR ESTABLISHED	1931

94 | Arrowstreet

212 Elm Street

Somerville, MA 02144

(617) 623-5555

www.arrowstreet.com

WORLDWIDE REVENUE	$24,380,040
WORLDWIDE STAFF	95
HEADQUARTERS	Somerville, MA
YEAR ESTABLISHED	1961

95 | CO Architects

5055 Wilshire Boulevard, 9th Floor

Los Angeles, CA 90036

(323) 525-0500

www.coarchitects.com

WORLDWIDE REVENUE	$24,200,000
WORLDWIDE STAFF	75
HEADQUARTERS	Los Angeles, CA
YEAR ESTABLISHED	1996

96 | NAC|Architecture

1203 West Riverside Avenue

Spokane, WA 99201

(509) 838-8240

www.nacarchitecture.com

WORLDWIDE REVENUE	$24,199,811
WORLDWIDE STAFF	123
HEADQUARTERS	Spokane, WA
YEAR ESTABLISHED	1960

97 | H+L Architecture

1755 Blake Street, Suite 400

Denver, CO 80202

(303) 298-4700

www.hlarch.com

WORLDWIDE REVENUE	$23,628,590
WORLDWIDE STAFF	81
HEADQUARTERS	Denver, CO
YEAR ESTABLISHED	1963

Francis Cauffman

New Bed Tower, Hospital for Special Surgery, New York, NY | Francis Cauffman

98 | WHR Architects

1111 Louisiana Street, 26th Floor	WORLDWIDE REVENUE	$23,581,538
Houston, TX 77002	WORLDWIDE STAFF	114
(713) 665-5665	HEADQUARTERS	Houston, TX
www.whrarchitects.com	YEAR ESTABLISHED	1979

99 | Cambridge Seven Associates

1050 Massachusetts Avenue	WORLDWIDE REVENUE	$23,500,000
Cambridge, MA 02138	WORLDWIDE STAFF	67
(617) 492-7000	HEADQUARTERS	Cambridge, MA
www.c7a.com	YEAR ESTABLISHED	1962

100 | Francis Cauffman

Francis Cauffman

2000 Market Street, Suite 600	WORLDWIDE REVENUE	$23,476,000
Philadelphia, PA 19103	WORLDWIDE STAFF	105
(215) 568-8250	HEADQUARTERS	Philadelphia, PA
www.franciscauffman.com	YEAR ESTABLISHED	1954

101 | Mancini - Duffy

1350 Avenue of the Americas, Second Floor	WORLDWIDE REVENUE	$23,448,015
New York, NY 10019	WORLDWIDE STAFF	60
(212) 938-1260	HEADQUARTERS	New York, NY
www.manciniduffy.com	YEAR ESTABLISHED	1920

102 | Hord Coplan Macht

750 East Pratt Street, Suite 1100	WORLDWIDE REVENUE	$23,200,000
Baltimore, MD 21202	WORLDWIDE STAFF	107
(410) 837-7311	HEADQUARTERS	Baltimore, MD
www.hcm2.com	YEAR ESTABLISHED	1977

103 | OZ Architecture

3003 Larimer Street	WORLDWIDE REVENUE	$23,000,000
Denver, CO 80205	WORLDWIDE STAFF	100
(303) 861-5704	HEADQUARTERS	Denver, CO
www.ozarch.com	YEAR ESTABLISHED	1964

Goettsch Partners

Abu Dhabi Office Tower, Abu Dhabi, UAE | **Goettsch Partners**

104 | Goettsch Partners

GP GOETTSCH PARTNERS

224 South Michigan Avenue, 17th Floor	WORLDWIDE REVENUE	$22,748,000
Chicago, IL 60604	WORLDWIDE STAFF	90
(312) 356-0600	HEADQUARTERS	Chicago, IL
www.gpchicago.com	YEAR ESTABLISHED	1938

105 | Jerde

913 Ocean Front Walk	WORLDWIDE REVENUE	$22,500,000
Venice, CA 90291	WORLDWIDE STAFF	115
(310) 399-1987	HEADQUARTERS	Los Angeles, CA
www.jerde.com	YEAR ESTABLISHED	1977

106 | AC Martin

444 South Flower Street, Suite 1200	WORLDWIDE REVENUE	$22,485,645
Los Angeles, CA 90071	WORLDWIDE STAFF	101-150
(213) 683-1900	HEADQUARTERS	Los Angeles, CA
www.acmartin.com	YEAR ESTABLISHED	1906

107 | Cromwell Architects Engineers

101 South Spring Street	WORLDWIDE REVENUE	$22,440,000
Little Rock, AR 72201	WORLDWIDE STAFF	114
(501) 372-2900	HEADQUARTERS	Little Rock, AR
www.cromwell.com	YEAR ESTABLISHED	1885

108 | Helman Hurley Charvat Peacock/Architects

222 West Maitland Boulevard	WORLDWIDE REVENUE	$22,362,072
Maitland, FL 32751	WORLDWIDE STAFF	21-100
(407) 644-2656	HEADQUARTERS	Maitland, FL
www.hhcp.com	YEAR ESTABLISHED	1975

109 | McKissack & McKissack

1401 New York Avenue Northwest, Suite 900	WORLDWIDE REVENUE	$22,339,000
Washington, DC 20005	WORLDWIDE STAFF	150
(202) 347-1446	HEADQUARTERS	Washington, DC
www.mckissackdc.com	YEAR ESTABLISHED	1990

110 | Astorino

227 Fort Pitt Boulevard
Pittsburgh, PA 15222
(412) 765-1700
www.astorino.com

WORLDWIDE REVENUE	$22,100,000
WORLDWIDE STAFF	97
HEADQUARTERS	Pittsburgh, PA
YEAR ESTABLISHED	1972

111 | Richard Meier & Partners Architects

475 Tenth Avenue, 6th Floor
New York, NY 10018
(212) 967-6060
www.richardmeier.com

WORLDWIDE REVENUE	$22,050,000
WORLDWIDE STAFF	100
HEADQUARTERS	New York, NY
YEAR ESTABLISHED	1963

112 | Michael Graves & Associates

341 Nassau Street
Princeton, NJ 08540
(609) 924-6409
www.michaelgraves.com

WORLDWIDE REVENUE	$22,000,000
WORLDWIDE STAFF	100-120
HEADQUARTERS	Princeton, NJ
YEAR ESTABLISHED	1964

113 | Goody Clancy

420 Boylston Street
Boston, MA 02116
(617) 262-2760
www.goodyclancy.com

WORLDWIDE REVENUE	$21,968,490
WORLDWIDE STAFF	96
HEADQUARTERS	Boston, MA
YEAR ESTABLISHED	1955

114 | Smallwood, Reynolds, Stewart, Stewart & Associates

3565 Piedmont Road NE, One Piedmont Center, Suite 303
Atlanta, GA 30305
(404) 233-5453
www.srssa.com

WORLDWIDE REVENUE	$21,642,756
WORLDWIDE STAFF	137
HEADQUARTERS	Atlanta, GA
YEAR ESTABLISHED	1979

115 | Steelman Partners

3330 West Desert Inn Road
Las Vegas, NV 89012
(702) 873-0221
www.steelmanpartners.com

WORLDWIDE REVENUE	$21,500,000
WORLDWIDE STAFF	175
HEADQUARTERS	Las Vegas, NV
YEAR ESTABLISHED	1987

116 | Symmes Maini & McKee Associates

1000 Massachusetts Avenue
Cambridge, MA 02138
(617) 547-5400
www.smma.com

WORLDWIDE REVENUE	$21,318,000
WORLDWIDE STAFF	135
HEADQUARTERS	Cambridge, MA
YEAR ESTABLISHED	1955

117 | RNL

1050 17th Street, Suite A200
Denver, CO 80265
(303) 295-1717
www.rnldesign.com

WORLDWIDE REVENUE	$21,129,700
WORLDWIDE STAFF	126
HEADQUARTERS	Denver, CO
YEAR ESTABLISHED	1956

118 | Hart | Howerton

One Union Street
San Francisco, CA 94111
(415) 439-2200
www.harthowerton.com

WORLDWIDE REVENUE	$20,909,000
WORLDWIDE STAFF	80
HEADQUARTERS	New York, NY & San Francisco, CA
YEAR ESTABLISHED	1967

119 | L. R. Kimball (Architecture)

615 West Highland Avenue
Ebensburg, PA 15931
(814) 472-7700
www.lrkimball.com

WORLDWIDE REVENUE	$20,583,600
WORLDWIDE STAFF	465
HEADQUARTERS	Edensburg, PA
YEAR ESTABLISHED	1953

120 | Gould Evans

4041 Mill Street
Kansas City, MO 64111
(800) 297-6655
www.gouldevans.com

WORLDWIDE REVENUE	$20,443,990
WORLDWIDE STAFF	119
HEADQUARTERS	Kansas City, MO
YEAR ESTABLISHED	1974

121 | Moody - Nolan

300 Spruce Street, Suite 300
Columbus, OH 43215
(877) 530-4984
www.moodynolan.com

WORLDWIDE REVENUE	$20,414,280
WORLDWIDE STAFF	21-100
HEADQUARTERS	Columbus, OH
YEAR ESTABLISHED	1982

Courtesy of Armani Hotels& Resorts

Armani Hotel Dubai, Dubai, UAE | Wilson Associates

122 | Pei Cobb Freed & Partners Architects

88 Pine Street
New York, NY 10005
(212) 751-3122
www.pcf-p.com

WORLDWIDE REVENUE	$20,351,770
WORLDWIDE STAFF	73
HEADQUARTERS	New York, NY
YEAR ESTABLISHED	1955

123 | Handel Architects

150 Varick Street
New York, NY 10013
(212) 595-4112
www.handelarchitects.com

WORLDWIDE REVENUE	$20,236,350
WORLDWIDE STAFF	105
HEADQUARTERS	New York, NY
YEAR ESTABLISHED	1994

124 | Wilson Associates

WILSON /// ASSOCIATES

3811 Turtle Creek Boulevard, 16th Floor
Dallas, TX 75219
(214) 521-6753
www.wilsonassociates.com

WORLDWIDE REVENUE	$20,100,000
WORLDWIDE STAFF	375
HEADQUARTERS	Dallas, TX
YEAR ESTABLISHED	1978

125 | Niles Bolton Associates

3060 Peachtree Road Northwest, Suite 600
Atlanta, GA 30305
(404) 365-7600
www.nilesbolton.com

WORLDWIDE REVENUE	$20,050,000
WORLDWIDE STAFF	90
HEADQUARTERS	Atlanta, GA
YEAR ESTABLISHED	1975

126 | Hixson

659 Van Meter Avenue
Cincinnati, OH 45202
(513) 241-1230
www.hixson-inc.com

WORLDWIDE REVENUE	$20,000,000
WORLDWIDE STAFF	125
HEADQUARTERS	Cincinnati, OH
YEAR ESTABLISHED	1948

127 | Steffian Bradley Architects

100 Summer Street
Boston, MA 02110
(617) 305-7100
www.steffian.com

WORLDWIDE REVENUE	$19,700,000
WORLDWIDE STAFF	125
HEADQUARTERS	Boston, MA
YEAR ESTABLISHED	1932

PROVIDING FORESIGHT
AND INSIGHT

If you have ever witnessed a trend unfolding and said to yourself, I should have seen this coming, then you are beginning to understand the value of the services of the Greenway Group.

The Greenway Group is a management consulting and research firm serving as trusted advisors to the design, construction, and real estate sectors of the global economy.

Our singularity is the depth of understanding we bring to the task, an intensity of knowledge that is fueled by an intelligence network unparalleled in our industry.

- STRATEGIC PLANNING
- LEADERSHIP DEVELOPMENT AND COACHING
- OWNERSHIP TRANSFER
- VISION AND STRATEGIC RETREATS
- MANAGEMENT CONSULTING AND RESEARCH
- BUSINESS MODELS AND GROWTH STRATEGIES
- COMPENSATION AND EXECUTIVE EQUITY PLANS

Greenway Group
Foresight for the Business of Design

(678) 879-0929 or *www.greenway.us*

128 | ARC/Architectural Resources Cambridge

Five Cambridge Center
Cambridge, MA 02142
(617) 547-2200
www.arcusa.com

WORLDWIDE REVENUE	$19,573,800
WORLDWIDE STAFF	65
HEADQUARTERS	Cambridge, MA
YEAR ESTABLISHED	1969

129 | Wight & Company

2500 North Frontage Road
Darien, IL 60561
(630) 969-7000
www.wightco.com

WORLDWIDE REVENUE	$19,509,540
WORLDWIDE STAFF	105
HEADQUARTERS	Darien, IL
YEAR ESTABLISHED	1939

130 | Morris Architects

1001 Fannin Street, Suite 300
Houston, TX 77002
(713) 622-1180
www.morrisarchitects.com

WORLDWIDE REVENUE	$19,454,000
WORLDWIDE STAFF	105
HEADQUARTERS	Houston, TX
YEAR ESTABLISHED	1938

131 | CBT

110 Canal Street
Boston, MA 02114
(617) 262-4354
www.cbtarchitects.com

WORLDWIDE REVENUE	$19,380,000
WORLDWIDE STAFF	220
HEADQUARTERS	Boston, MA
YEAR ESTABLISHED	1967

132 | BHDP Architecture

302 West 3rd Street, Suite 500
Cincinnati, OH 45202
(513) 271-1634
www.bhdp.com

WORLDWIDE REVENUE	$19,000,000
WORLDWIDE STAFF	99
HEADQUARTERS	Cincinnati, OH
YEAR ESTABLISHED	1937

133 | BBG-BBGM

161 Sixth Avenue
New York, NY 10013
(212) 888-7667
www.bbg-bbgm.com

WORLDWIDE REVENUE	$18,768,000
WORLDWIDE STAFF	120
HEADQUARTERS	New York, NY
YEAR ESTABLISHED	1984

JH Photo

Butler High School, Vandalia, OH | SHP Leading Design

134 | Gehry Partners

12541 Beatrice Street
Los Angeles, CA 90066
(310) 482-3000
www.foga.com

WORLDWIDE REVENUE	$18,727,200
WORLDWIDE STAFF	125
HEADQUARTERS	Los Angeles, CA
YEAR ESTABLISHED	1962

135 | Kirksey

6909 Portwest Drive
Houston, TX 77024
(713) 850-9600
www.kirksey.com

WORLDWIDE REVENUE	$18,662,294
WORLDWIDE STAFF	106
HEADQUARTERS	Houston, TX
YEAR ESTABLISHED	1971

136 | WDG Architecture

1025 Connecticut Avenue NW, Suite 300
Washington, DC 20036
(202) 857-8300
www.wdgarch.com

WORLDWIDE REVENUE	$18,462,000
WORLDWIDE STAFF	21-100
HEADQUARTERS	Washington, DC
YEAR ESTABLISHED	1938

137 | Grimm + Parker Architects

11720 Beltsville Drive, Suite 600
Calverton, MD 20705
(301) 595-1000
www.grimmandparker.com

WORLDWIDE REVENUE	$18,360,000
WORLDWIDE STAFF	72
HEADQUARTERS	Calverton, MD
YEAR ESTABLISHED	1972

138 | ADD Inc

311 Summer Street
Boston, MA 02210
(617) 234-3100
www.addinc.com

WORLDWIDE REVENUE	$18,202,665
WORLDWIDE STAFF	125
HEADQUARTERS	Boston, MA
YEAR ESTABLISHED	1971

139 | SHP Leading Design

4805 Montgomery Road
Cincinnati, OH 45212
(513) 381-2112
www.shp.com

WORLDWIDE REVENUE	$18,000,000
WORLDWIDE STAFF	83
HEADQUARTERS	Cincinnati, OH
YEAR ESTABLISHED	1901

Charles Davis Smith, AIA

Hunt Oil Corporate Headquarters, Dallas, TX | The Beck Group (Architecture)

140 | FreemanWhite

8845 Red Oak Boulevard	WORLDWIDE REVENUE	$17,900,000
Charlotte, NC 28217	WORLDWIDE STAFF	106
(704) 523-2230	HEADQUARTERS	Charlotte, NC
www.freemanwhite.com	YEAR ESTABLISHED	1892

141 | Dekker/Perich/Sabatini

7601 Jefferson Northeast, Suite 100	WORLDWIDE REVENUE	$17,717,400
Albuquerque, NM 87109	WORLDWIDE STAFF	150
(505) 761-9700	HEADQUARTERS	Albuquerque, NM
www.dpsdesign.org	YEAR ESTABLISHED	1998

142 | The Beck Group (Architecture)   BECK 100

1807 Ross Avenue, Suite 500	WORLDWIDE REVENUE	$17,686,000
Dallas, TX 75201	WORLDWIDE STAFF	85
(214) 303-6200	HEADQUARTERS	Dallas, TX
www.beckgroup.com	YEAR ESTABLISHED	1912

143 | Highland Associates

102 Highland Avenue	WORLDWIDE REVENUE	$17,635,800
Clarks Summit, PA 18411	WORLDWIDE STAFF	21-100
(570) 586-4334	HEADQUARTERS	Clarks Summit, PA
www.highlandassociates.com	YEAR ESTABLISHED	1988

144 | Davis Carter Scott

1676 International Drive, Suite 500	WORLDWIDE REVENUE	$17,504,730
McLean, VA 22102	WORLDWIDE STAFF	21-100
(703) 556-9275	HEADQUARTERS	McLean, VA
www.dcsdesign.com	YEAR ESTABLISHED	1968

145 | William Rawn Associates, Architects, Inc.

10 Post Office Square, Suite 1010	WORLDWIDE REVENUE	$17,500,000
Boston, MA 02109	WORLDWIDE STAFF	41
(617) 423-3470	HEADQUARTERS	Boston, MA
www.rawnarch.com	YEAR ESTABLISHED	1983

146 | Epstein

600 West Fulton
Chicago, IL 60661
(312) 454-9100
www.epsteinglobal.com

WORLDWIDE REVENUE	$17,340,000
WORLDWIDE STAFF	300+
HEADQUARTERS	Chicago, IL
YEAR ESTABLISHED	1921

147 | FRCH Design Worldwide

311 Elm Street, Suite 600
Cincinnati, OH 45202
(513) 241-3000
www.frch.com

WORLDWIDE REVENUE	$17,151,300
WORLDWIDE STAFF	101- 450
HEADQUARTERS	Cincinnati, OH
YEAR ESTABLISHED	1968

148 | Shalom Baranes Associates

3299 K Street Northwest, Suite 400
Washington, DC 20007
(202) 342-2200
www.sbaranes.com

WORLDWIDE REVENUE	$17,136,000
WORLDWIDE STAFF	21-100
HEADQUARTERS	Washington, DC
YEAR ESTABLISHED	1981

149 | Kahler Slater

111 West Wisconsin Avenue
Milwaukee, WI 53203
(414) 272-2000
www.kahlerslater.com

WORLDWIDE REVENUE	$17,100,000
WORLDWIDE STAFF	95
HEADQUARTERS	Milwaukee, WI
YEAR ESTABLISHED	1908

150 | EDI International

2800 Post Oak Boulevard, Suite 3800
Houston, TX 77056
(877) 375-1401
www.ediarchitecture.com

WORLDWIDE REVENUE	$16,719,840
WORLDWIDE STAFF	101
HEADQUARTERS	Houston, TX
YEAR ESTABLISHED	1976

151 | Mahlum

71 Columbia, Floor 4
Seattle, WA 98104
(206) 441-4151
www.mahlum.com

WORLDWIDE REVENUE	$16,700,000
WORLDWIDE STAFF	90
HEADQUARTERS	Seattle, WA
YEAR ESTABLISHED	1938

152 | RBB Architects

10980 Wilshire Boulevard
Los Angeles, CA 90024
(310) 473-3555
www.rbbinc.com

WORLDWIDE REVENUE	$16,500,000
WORLDWIDE STAFF	75
HEADQUARTERS	Los Angeles, CA
YEAR ESTABLISHED	1952

153 | ASD

55 Ivan Allen Junior Boulevard, Suite 100
Atlanta, GA 30308
(404) 688-3318
www.asdnet.com

WORLDWIDE REVENUE	$16,400,000
WORLDWIDE STAFF	85
HEADQUARTERS	Atlanta, GA
YEAR ESTABLISHED	1963

154 | Hobbs+Black Architects

100 North State Street
Ann Arbor, MI 48104
(734) 663-4189
www.hobbs-black.com

WORLDWIDE REVENUE	$16,275,000
WORLDWIDE STAFF	98
HEADQUARTERS	Ann Arbor, MI
YEAR ESTABLISHED	1969

155 | BOORA Architects

720 Southwest Washington, Suite 800
Portland, OR 97205
(503) 226-1575
www.boora.com

WORLDWIDE REVENUE	$16,231,260
WORLDWIDE STAFF	65
HEADQUARTERS	Portland, OR
YEAR ESTABLISHED	1958

156 | Wallace Roberts & Todd

1700 Market Street, Suite 2800
Philadelphia, PA 19103
(215) 732-5215
www.wrtdesign.com

WORLDWIDE REVENUE	$16,109,713
WORLDWIDE STAFF	130
HEADQUARTERS	Philadelphia, PA
YEAR ESTABLISHED	1963

157 | RMW architecture & interiors

160 Pine Street
San Francisco, CA 94111
(415) 781-9800
www.rmw.com

WORLDWIDE REVENUE	$16,096,998
WORLDWIDE STAFF	63
HEADQUARTERS	San Francisco, CA
YEAR ESTABLISHED	1970

158 | Devenney Group Architects

201 West Indian School Road
Phoenix, AZ 85013
(602) 943-8950
www.devenneygroup.com

WORLDWIDE REVENUE	$16,000,000
WORLDWIDE STAFF	63
HEADQUARTERS	Phoenix, AZ
YEAR ESTABLISHED	1962

159 | DES Architects + Engineers

399 Bradford Street
Redwood City, CA 94063
(650) 364-6453
www.des-ae.com

WORLDWIDE REVENUE	$15,800,000
WORLDWIDE STAFF	94
HEADQUARTERS	Redwood City, CA
YEAR ESTABLISHED	1973

160 | Fletcher Thompson

Three Corporate Drive, Suite 500
Shelton, CT 06484
(203) 225-6500
www.fletcherthompson.com

WORLDWIDE REVENUE	$15,651,900
WORLDWIDE STAFF	101- 450
HEADQUARTERS	Shelton, CT
YEAR ESTABLISHED	1910

161 | Good Fulton & Farrell

2808 Fairmount Street, Suite 300
Dallas, TX 75201
(214) 303-1500
www.gff.com

WORLDWIDE REVENUE	$15,616,200
WORLDWIDE STAFF	60
HEADQUARTERS	Dallas, TX
YEAR ESTABLISHED	1982

162 | RATIO Architects

107 South Pennsylvania Street, Suite 100
Indianapolis, IN 46204
(317) 633-4040
www.ratioarchitects.com

WORLDWIDE REVENUE	$15,613,786
WORLDWIDE STAFF	81
HEADQUARTERS	Indianapolis, IN
YEAR ESTABLISHED	1982

163 | Carrier Johnson + CULTURE

1301 3rd Avenue
San Diego, CA 92101
(619) 239-2353
www.carrierjohnson.com

WORLDWIDE REVENUE	$15,558,060
WORLDWIDE STAFF	40
HEADQUARTERS	San Diego, CA
YEAR ESTABLISHED	1977

164 | Nadel

1990 South Bundy Drive, 4th Floor
Los Angeles, CA 90025
(310) 826-2100
www.nadelarc.com

WORLDWIDE REVENUE	$15,300,000
WORLDWIDE STAFF	90
HEADQUARTERS	Los Angeles, CA
YEAR ESTABLISHED	1973

165 | ka

1468 West 9th Street, Suite 600
Cleveland, OH 44113
(216) 781-9144
www.kainc.com

WORLDWIDE REVENUE	$14,908,320
WORLDWIDE STAFF	105
HEADQUARTERS	Cleveland, OH
YEAR ESTABLISHED	1960

166 | Lee, Burkhart, Liu

13335 Maxella Avenue
Marina del Rey, CA 90292
(310) 829-2249
www.lblarch.com

WORLDWIDE REVENUE	$14,825,700
WORLDWIDE STAFF	55
HEADQUARTERS	Marina Del Rey, CA
YEAR ESTABLISHED	1986

167 | Shremshock Architects

6130 South Sunbury Road
Westerville, OH 43081
(614) 545-4550
www.shremshock.com

WORLDWIDE REVENUE	$14,800,000
WORLDWIDE STAFF	101
HEADQUARTERS	Westerville, OH
YEAR ESTABLISHED	1976

168 | CMA

219 North Second Street
Minneapolis, MN 55401
(612) 338-6677
www.cmarch.com

WORLDWIDE REVENUE	$14,750,000
WORLDWIDE STAFF	106
HEADQUARTERS	Minneapolis, MN
YEAR ESTABLISHED	1977

169 | Ratcliff

RATCLIFF

5856 Doyle Street
Emeryville, CA 94608
(510) 899-6400
www.ratcliffarch.com

WORLDWIDE REVENUE	$14,600,000
WORLDWIDE STAFF	55
HEADQUARTERS	Emeryville, CA
YEAR ESTABLISHED	1906

170 | Hanbury Evans Wright Vlattas + Company

120 Atlantic Street
Norfolk, VA 23510
(757) 321-9600
www.hewv.com

WORLDWIDE REVENUE	$14,500,000
WORLDWIDE STAFF	75
HEADQUARTERS	Norfolk, VA
YEAR ESTABLISHED	1985

171 | Humphreys & Partners Architects

5339 Alpha Road
Dallas, TX 75240
(972) 701-9636
www.humphreys.com

WORLDWIDE REVENUE	$14,331,000
WORLDWIDE STAFF	127
HEADQUARTERS	Dallas, TX
YEAR ESTABLISHED	1991

172 | Dattner Architects

1385 Broadway
New York, NY 10018
(212) 247-2660
www.dattner.com

WORLDWIDE REVENUE	$14,000,000
WORLDWIDE STAFF	68
HEADQUARTERS	New York, NY
YEAR ESTABLISHED	1964

173 | Baskervill

101 South 15th Street, Suite 200
Richmond, VA 23219
(804) 343-1010
www.baskervill.com

WORLDWIDE REVENUE	$13,929,000
WORLDWIDE STAFF	104
HEADQUARTERS	Richmond, VA
YEAR ESTABLISHED	1897

174 | Arcturis

720 Olive Street, Suite 200
St. Louis, MO 63101
(314) 206-7100
www.arcturis.com

WORLDWIDE REVENUE	$13,899,132
WORLDWIDE STAFF	101
HEADQUARTERS	St. Louis, MO
YEAR ESTABLISHED	1977

175 | Hunton Brady Architects

800 North Magnolia Avenue, Suite 600
Orlando, FL 32803
(407) 839-0886
www.huntonbrady.com

WORLDWIDE REVENUE	$13,777,000
WORLDWIDE STAFF	71
HEADQUARTERS	Orlando, FL
YEAR ESTABLISHED	1947

176 | Johnson Fain

1201 North Broadway
Los Angeles, CA 90012
(323) 224-6000
www.johnsonfain.com

WORLDWIDE REVENUE	$13,590,480
WORLDWIDE STAFF	21-100
HEADQUARTERS	Los Angeles, CA
YEAR ESTABLISHED	1931

177 | Stevens & Wilkinson

100 Peachtree Street Northwest, Suite 2500
Atlanta, GA 30303
(404) 522-8888
www.stevenswilkinson.com

WORLDWIDE REVENUE	$13,500,000
WORLDWIDE STAFF	85
HEADQUARTERS	Atlanta, GA
YEAR ESTABLISHED	1919

178 | THW Design

2100 RiverEdge Parkway, Suite 900
Atlanta, GA 30328
(404) 252-8040
www.thw.com

WORLDWIDE REVENUE	$13,485,500
WORLDWIDE STAFF	40
HEADQUARTERS	Atlanta, GA
YEAR ESTABLISHED	1975

179 | Miller Hull Partnership

71 Columbia Street, Suite 600
Seattle, WA 98104
(206) 682-6837
www.millerhull.com

WORLDWIDE REVENUE	$13,276,668
WORLDWIDE STAFF	62
HEADQUARTERS	Seattle, WA
YEAR ESTABLISHED	1977

180 | Gruen Associates

6330 San Vicente Boulevard, Suite 200
Los Angeles, CA 90048
(323) 937-4270
www.gruenassociates.com

WORLDWIDE REVENUE	$13,172,320
WORLDWIDE STAFF	21-100
HEADQUARTERS	Los Angeles, CA
YEAR ESTABLISHED	1946

181 | Tsoi/Kobus & Associates

One Brattle Square, PO Box 9114
Cambridge, MA 02238
(617) 475-4000
www.tka-architects.com

WORLDWIDE REVENUE	$13,100,000
WORLDWIDE STAFF	58
HEADQUARTERS	Cambridge, MA
YEAR ESTABLISHED	1983

182 | Mithun

1201 Alaskan Way, Suite 200
Seattle, WA 98101
(206) 623-3344
www.mithun.com

WORLDWIDE REVENUE	$13,056,000
WORLDWIDE STAFF	143
HEADQUARTERS	Seattle, WA
YEAR ESTABLISHED	1949

183 | Pieper O'Brien Herr Architects

3000 Royal Boulevard South
Alpharetta, GA 30022
(770) 569-1706
www.poharchitects.com

WORLDWIDE REVENUE	$13,014,180
WORLDWIDE STAFF	38
HEADQUARTERS	Alpharetta, GA
YEAR ESTABLISHED	1971

184 | BNIM Architects

106 West 14th Street, Suite 200
Kansas City, MO 64105
(816) 783-1500
www.bnim.com

WORLDWIDE REVENUE	$13,000,000
WORLDWIDE STAFF	68
HEADQUARTERS	Kansas City, MO
YEAR ESTABLISHED	1970

185 | Ascension Group Architects

1250 East Copeland Road, Suite 500
Arlington, TX 76011
(817) 226-1917
www.ascensiongroup.biz

WORLDWIDE REVENUE	$12,852,000
WORLDWIDE STAFF	38
HEADQUARTERS	Arlington, TX
YEAR ESTABLISHED	2001

186 | TSP

1112 North West Avenue
Sioux Falls, SD 57104
(605) 336-1160
www.teamtsp.com

WORLDWIDE REVENUE	$12,760,200
WORLDWIDE STAFF	101-450
HEADQUARTERS	Sioux Falls, SD
YEAR ESTABLISHED	1930

187 | BOKA Powell

8070 Park Lane, Suite 300
Dallas, TX 75231
(972) 701-9000
www.bokapowell.com

WORLDWIDE REVENUE	$12,758,160
WORLDWIDE STAFF	75
HEADQUARTERS	Dallas, TX
YEAR ESTABLISHED	1975

188 | Architects Design Group

333 North Knowles Avenue
Winter Park, FL 32789
(407) 647-1706
www.adgusa.org

WORLDWIDE REVENUE	$12,683,700
WORLDWIDE STAFF	40
HEADQUARTERS	Winter Park, FL
YEAR ESTABLISHED	1971

189 | Goodwyn, Mills & Cawood

2660 EastChase Lane, Suite 200
Montgomery, AL 36117
(334) 271-3200
www.gmcnetwork.com

WORLDWIDE REVENUE	$12,452,160
WORLDWIDE STAFF	310
HEADQUARTERS	Montgomery, AL
YEAR ESTABLISHED	1975

190 | Gwathmey Siegel & Associates Architects

475 Tenth Avenue
New York, NY 10018
(212) 947-1240
www.gwathmey-siegel.com

WORLDWIDE REVENUE	$12,437,880
WORLDWIDE STAFF	45
HEADQUARTERS	New York, NY
YEAR ESTABLISHED	1968

191 | Legat Architects

651 West Washington Boulevard, Suite 1
Chicago, IL 60661
(312) 258-9595
www.legat.com

WORLDWIDE REVENUE	$12,396,060
WORLDWIDE STAFF	21-100
HEADQUARTERS	Chicago, IL
YEAR ESTABLISHED	1964

192 | Altoon + Porter Architects

444 South Flower Street, 48th Floor
Los Angeles, CA 90071
(213) 225-1900
www.altoonporter.com

WORLDWIDE REVENUE	$12,051,300
WORLDWIDE STAFF	45
HEADQUARTERS	Los Angeles, CA
YEAR ESTABLISHED	1984

193 | Design Workshop

1390 Lawrence Street, Suite 200
Denver, CO 80204
(303) 623-5186
www.designworkshop.com

WORLDWIDE REVENUE	$12,000,000
WORLDWIDE STAFF	80
HEADQUARTERS	Denver, CO
YEAR ESTABLISHED	1969

194 | Environetics

Environetics
Designing Environments That Work.

8530 Venice Boulevard
Los Angeles, CA 90034
(310) 287-2180
www.environetics.com

WORLDWIDE REVENUE	$11,975,000
WORLDWIDE STAFF	81
HEADQUARTERS	Los Angeles, CA
YEAR ESTABLISHED	1946

195 | Wakefield Beasley & Associates

5155 Peachtree Parkway, Suite 3220
Norcross, GA 30092
(770) 209-9393
www.wakefieldbeasley.com

WORLDWIDE REVENUE	$11,918,700
WORLDWIDE STAFF	80
HEADQUARTERS	Norcross, GA
YEAR ESTABLISHED	1980

196 | Orcutt I Winslow

3003 North Central Avenue, 16th Floor
Phoenix, AZ 85012
(602) 257-1764
www.owp.com

WORLDWIDE REVENUE	$11,811,600
WORLDWIDE STAFF	70
HEADQUARTERS	Phoenix, AZ
YEAR ESTABLISHED	1971

197 | Baker Barrios Architects

189 South Orange Avenue, Suite 1700
Orlando, FL 32801
(407) 926-3000
www.bakerbarrios.com

WORLDWIDE REVENUE	$11,777,940
WORLDWIDE STAFF	101-450
HEADQUARTERS	Orlando, FL
YEAR ESTABLISHED	1993

198 | Huntsman Architectural Group

50 California Street
San Francisco, CA 94111
(415) 394-1212
www.huntsmanag.com

WORLDWIDE REVENUE	$11,730,000
WORLDWIDE STAFF	70
HEADQUARTERS	San Francisco, CA
YEAR ESTABLISHED	1981

199 | Bermello Ajamil & Partners

2601 South Bayshore Drive, Suite 1000
Miami, FL 33133
(305) 859-2050
www.bamiami.com

WORLDWIDE REVENUE	$11,630,040
WORLDWIDE STAFF	21-100
HEADQUARTERS	Miami, FL
YEAR ESTABLISHED	1939

200 | VITETTA

4747 South Broad Street
Philadelphia, PA 19112
(215) 218-4747
www.vitetta.com

WORLDWIDE REVENUE	$11,580,060
WORLDWIDE STAFF	130
HEADQUARTERS	Philadelphia, PA
YEAR ESTABLISHED	1967

201 | Cooper, Robertson & Partners

311 West 43rd Street
New York, NY 10036
(212) 247-1717
www.cooperrobertson.com

WORLDWIDE REVENUE	$11,531,100
WORLDWIDE STAFF	21-100
HEADQUARTERS	New York, NY
YEAR ESTABLISHED	1979

202 | Overland Partners Architects

5101 Broadway
San Antonio, TX 78209
(210) 829-7003
www.overlandpartners.com

WORLDWIDE REVENUE	$11,373,000
WORLDWIDE STAFF	58
HEADQUARTERS	San Antonio, TX
YEAR ESTABLISHED	1987

203 | CDH Partners

675 Tower Road
Marietta, GA 30060
(770) 423-0016
www.cdhpartners.com

WORLDWIDE REVENUE	$11,300,000
WORLDWIDE STAFF	72
HEADQUARTERS	Marietta, GA
YEAR ESTABLISHED	1977

204 | KPS Group

2101 First Avenue North
Birmingham, AL 35203
(205) 458-3217
www.kpsgroup.com

WORLDWIDE REVENUE	$11,000,000
WORLDWIDE STAFF	50
HEADQUARTERS	Birmingham, AL
YEAR ESTABLISHED	1965

205 | FOX Architects

8444 Westpark Drive, Suite 120
McLean, VA 22102
(703) 821-7990
www.fox-architects.com

WORLDWIDE REVENUE	$10,900,000
WORLDWIDE STAFF	57
HEADQUARTERS	McLean, VA
YEAR ESTABLISHED	1993

206 | GGLO

1301 First Avenue, Suite 301
Seattle, WA 98101
(206) 467-5828
www.gglo.com

WORLDWIDE REVENUE	$10,800,000
WORLDWIDE STAFF	82
HEADQUARTERS	Seattle, WA
YEAR ESTABLISHED	1986

207 | MBH Architects

2470 Mariner Square Loop
Alameda, CA 94501
(510) 865-8663
www.mbharch.com

WORLDWIDE REVENUE	$10,782,420
WORLDWIDE STAFF	60
HEADQUARTERS	Alameda, CA
YEAR ESTABLISHED	1989

208 | Rosser International

1555 Peachtree Street Northeast
Atlanta, GA 30309
(404) 876-3800
www.rosser.com

WORLDWIDE REVENUE	$10,700,000
WORLDWIDE STAFF	85
HEADQUARTERS	Atlanta, GA
YEAR ESTABLISHED	1947

209 | Van Tilburg, Banvard & Soderbergh

1738 Berkeley Street
Santa Monica, CA 90404
(310) 394-0273
www.vtbs.com

WORLDWIDE REVENUE	$10,680,420
WORLDWIDE STAFF	105
HEADQUARTERS	Santa Monica, CA
YEAR ESTABLISHED	1994

210 | John Portman & Associates

303 Peachtree Center Avenue, Suite 575
Atlanta, GA 30303
(404) 614-5555
www.portmanusa.com

WORLDWIDE REVENUE	$10,460,100
WORLDWIDE STAFF	45
HEADQUARTERS	Atlanta, GA
YEAR ESTABLISHED	1953

211 | Bruner/Cott & Associates

130 Prospect Street
Cambridge, MA 02139
(617) 492-8400
www.brunercott.com

WORLDWIDE REVENUE	$10,404,000
WORLDWIDE STAFF	51
HEADQUARTERS	Cambridge, MA
YEAR ESTABLISHED	1972

212 | Rogers Marvel Architects

145 Hudson Street, Suite 300
New York, NY 10013
(212) 941-6718
www.rogersmarvel.com

WORLDWIDE REVENUE	$10,400,000
WORLDWIDE STAFF	52
HEADQUARTERS	New York, NY
YEAR ESTABLISHED	1992

213 | Bostwick Design Partnership

2729 Prospect Avenue
Cleveland, OH 44115
(216) 621-7900
www.bostwickdesign.com

WORLDWIDE REVENUE	$10,295,880
WORLDWIDE STAFF	35
HEADQUARTERS	Cleveland, OH
YEAR ESTABLISHED	1962

214 | Torti Gallas and Partners

1300 Spring Street
Silver Spring, MD 20910
(301) 588-4800
www.tortigallas.com

WORLDWIDE REVENUE	$10,174,500
WORLDWIDE STAFF	85
HEADQUARTERS	Silver Spring, MD
YEAR ESTABLISHED	1953

215 | GUND Partnership

47 Thorndike Street
Cambridge, MA 02141
(617) 250-6800
www.gundpartnership.com

WORLDWIDE REVENUE	$10,089,840
WORLDWIDE STAFF	21-100
HEADQUARTERS	Cambridge, MA
YEAR ESTABLISHED	1971

216 | Rossetti

Two Towne Square, Suite 200
Southfield, MI 48076
(248) 262-8300
www.rossetti.com

WORLDWIDE REVENUE	$9,996,000
WORLDWIDE STAFF	101-450
HEADQUARTERS	Detroit, MI
YEAR ESTABLISHED	1969

217 | Centerbrook Architects and Planners

67 Main Street, PO Box 955
Centerbrook, CT 06409
(860) 767-0175
www.centerbrook.com

WORLDWIDE REVENUE	$9,966,420
WORLDWIDE STAFF	21-100
HEADQUARTERS	Centerbrook, CT
YEAR ESTABLISHED	1975

218 | Thalden-Boyd-Emery Architects

1133 Olivette Executive Parkway
Olivette, MO 63132
(314) 727-7000
www.thaldenboyd.com

WORLDWIDE REVENUE	$9,835,350
WORLDWIDE STAFF	5-20
HEADQUARTERS	Olivette, MO
YEAR ESTABLISHED	1962

219 | Eskew+Dumez+Ripple

365 Canal Street, Suite 3150
New Orleans, LA 70130
(504) 561-8686
www.eskewdumezripple.com

WORLDWIDE REVENUE	$9,800,000
WORLDWIDE STAFF	45
HEADQUARTERS	New Orleans, LA
YEAR ESTABLISHED	1989

220 | Sherlock Smith & Adams

3047 Carter Hill Road
Montgomery, AL 36111
(334) 263-6481
www.ssainc.com

WORLDWIDE REVENUE	$9,714,225
WORLDWIDE STAFF	21-100
HEADQUARTERS	Montgomery, AL
YEAR ESTABLISHED	1946

221 | Merriman Associates/Architects

300 North Field Street
Dallas, TX 75202
(214) 987-1299
www.merrimanassociates.com

WORLDWIDE REVENUE	$9,690,000
WORLDWIDE STAFF	71
HEADQUARTERS	Dallas, TX
YEAR ESTABLISHED	1987

222 | Wank Adams Slavin Associates (WASA/Studio A)

740 Broadway
New York, NY 10003
(212) 420-1160
www.wasallp.com

WORLDWIDE REVENUE	$9,690,000
WORLDWIDE STAFF	70
HEADQUARTERS	New York, NY
YEAR ESTABLISHED	1889

223 | Hart Freeland Roberts

7101 Executive Center Drive
Brentwood, TN 37027
(615) 370-8500
www.hfrdesign.com

WORLDWIDE REVENUE	$9,544,650
WORLDWIDE STAFF	21-100
HEADQUARTERS	Nashville, TN
YEAR ESTABLISHED	1910

224 | Anderson Mason Dale Architects

3198 Speer Boulevard
Denver, CO 80211
(303) 294-9448
www.amdarchitects.com

WORLDWIDE REVENUE	$9,537,000
WORLDWIDE STAFF	40
HEADQUARTERS	Denver, CO
YEAR ESTABLISHED	1960

225 | SLATERPAULL Architects

1331 Nineteenth Street
Denver, CO 80202
(303) 607-0977
www.slaterpaull.com

WORLDWIDE REVENUE	$9,500,000
WORLDWIDE STAFF	37
HEADQUARTERS	Denver, CO
YEAR ESTABLISHED	1972

226 | Engberg Anderson

320 East Buffalo Street
Milwaukee, WI 53202
(414) 944-9000
www.engberganderson.com

WORLDWIDE REVENUE	$9,471,975
WORLDWIDE STAFF	45
HEADQUARTERS	Milwaukee, WI
YEAR ESTABLISHED	1988

227 | Hamilton Anderson Associates

1435 Randolph Street, Suite 200
Detroit, MI 48226
(313) 964-0270
www.hamilton-anderson.com

WORLDWIDE REVENUE	$9,444,865
WORLDWIDE STAFF	65
HEADQUARTERS	Detroit, MI
YEAR ESTABLISHED	1994

228 | Marshall Craft Associates

6112 York Road
Baltimore, MD 21212
(410) 532-3131
www.marshallcraft.com

WORLDWIDE REVENUE	$9,400,000
WORLDWIDE STAFF	36
HEADQUARTERS	Baltimore, MD
YEAR ESTABLISHED	1986

229 | H3 Hardy Collaboration Architecture

902 Broadway, 19th Floor
New York, NY 10010
(212) 677-6030
www.h3hc.com

WORLDWIDE REVENUE	$9,270,780
WORLDWIDE STAFF	35
HEADQUARTERS	New York, NY
YEAR ESTABLISHED	2004

230 | BCA

505 South Market Street
San Jose, CA 95113
(408) 588-3800
www.BCAarchitects.com

WORLDWIDE REVENUE	$9,180,000
WORLDWIDE STAFF	42
HEADQUARTERS	San Jose, CA
YEAR ESTABLISHED	1989

231 | Lehman Smith McLeish

1212 Banks
Washington, DC 20007
(202) 295-4800
www.lsm.com

WORLDWIDE REVENUE	$9,113,700
WORLDWIDE STAFF	35
HEADQUARTERS	Washington, DC
YEAR ESTABLISHED	1991

232 | CetraRuddy

584 Broadway
New York, NY 10012
(212) 941-9801
www.cetraruddy.com

WORLDWIDE REVENUE	$9,000,000
WORLDWIDE STAFF	55
HEADQUARTERS	New York, NY
YEAR ESTABLISHED	1987

233 | Forum Studio

2199 Innerbelt Business Center Drive
St. Louis, MO 63114
(314) 429-1010
www.forumstudio.com

WORLDWIDE REVENUE	$8,874,000
WORLDWIDE STAFF	37
HEADQUARTERS	St. Louis, MO
YEAR ESTABLISHED	1999

234 | Development Design Group

3700 O'Donnell Street
Baltimore, MD 21224
(410) 962-0505
www.ddg-usa.com

WORLDWIDE REVENUE	$8,843,400
WORLDWIDE STAFF	80
HEADQUARTERS	Baltimore, MD
YEAR ESTABLISHED	1979

235 | FWAJDB

400 Colony Square, Suite 400
Atlanta, GA 30361
(404) 879-6800
www.fwajdb.com

WORLDWIDE REVENUE	$8,823,000
WORLDWIDE STAFF	55
HEADQUARTERS	Atlanta, GA
YEAR ESTABLISHED	2006

236 | The Portico Group

1500 4th Avenue, 3rd Floor
Seattle, WA 98101
(206) 621-2196
www.porticogroup.com

WORLDWIDE REVENUE	$8,772,000
WORLDWIDE STAFF	52
HEADQUARTERS	Seattle, WA
YEAR ESTABLISHED	1984

237 | Morphosis

3440 Wesley Street
Culver City, CA 90232
(424) 258-6200
www.morphosis.com

WORLDWIDE REVENUE	$8,756,700
WORLDWIDE STAFF	21-100
HEADQUARTERS	Culver City, CA
YEAR ESTABLISHED	1972

238 | Research Facilities Design

3965 Fifth Avenue, Suite 400
San Diego, CA 92103
(619) 297-0159
www.rfd.com

WORLDWIDE REVENUE	$8,753,640
WORLDWIDE STAFF	31
HEADQUARTERS	San Diego, CA
YEAR ESTABLISHED	1984

239 | Rees Associates

92111 Lake Hefner Parkway, Suite 300
Oklahoma City, OK 73120
(888) 942-7337
www.rees.com

WORLDWIDE REVENUE	$8,700,000
WORLDWIDE STAFF	64
HEADQUARTERS	Oklahoma City, OK
YEAR ESTABLISHED	1975

240 | Bergmeyer Associates

51 Sleeper Street
Boston, MA 02210
(617) 542-1025
www.bergmeyer.com

WORLDWIDE REVENUE	$8,700,000
WORLDWIDE STAFF	55
HEADQUARTERS	Boston, MA
YEAR ESTABLISHED	1973

241 | SHoP Architects

11 Park Place, Penthouse
New York, NY 10007
(212) 889-9005
www.shoparc.com

WORLDWIDE REVENUE	$8,670,000
WORLDWIDE STAFF	60
HEADQUARTERS	New York, NY
YEAR ESTABLISHED	1996

Nick Merrick, Hedrich Blessing

Investment Firm, Dallas, TX | Staffelbach

242 | Machado and Silvetti Associates

560 Harrison Avenue, Suite 301
Boston, MA 02118
(617) 426-7070
www.machado-silvetti.com

WORLDWIDE REVENUE	$8,530,000
WORLDWIDE STAFF	29
HEADQUARTERS	Boston, MA
YEAR ESTABLISHED	1985

243 | JMZ Architects and Planners

190 Glen Street
Glens Falls, NY 12801
(518) 793-0786
www.jmzarchitects.com

WORLDWIDE REVENUE	$8,500,000
WORLDWIDE STAFF	27
HEADQUARTERS	Glen Falls, NY
YEAR ESTABLISHED	1977

244 | klipp

201 Broadway
Denver, CO 80203
(303) 893-1990
www.klipparch.com

WORLDWIDE REVENUE	$8,310,195
WORLDWIDE STAFF	45
HEADQUARTERS	Denver, CO
YEAR ESTABLISHED	1979

245 | Bearsch Compeau Knudson Architects & Engineers

41 Chenango Street
Binghamton, NY 13901
(607) 772-0007
www.bckpc.com

WORLDWIDE REVENUE	$8,291,500
WORLDWIDE STAFF	56
HEADQUARTERS	Binghamton, NY
YEAR ESTABLISHED	1976

246 | Staffelbach

STAFFELBACH

2525 McKinnon Street, Suite 800
Dallas, TX 75201
(214) 747-2511
www.staffelbach.com

WORLDWIDE REVENUE	$8,200,000
WORLDWIDE STAFF	78
HEADQUARTERS	Dallas, TX
YEAR ESTABLISHED	1966

247 | Wald, Ruhnke & Dost Architects

2340 Garden Road, Suite 100
Monterey, CA 93940
(831) 649-4642
www.wrdarch.com

WORLDWIDE REVENUE	$8,139,600
WORLDWIDE STAFF	38
HEADQUARTERS	Monterey, CA
YEAR ESTABLISHED	1990

248 | Workshop Architects

1736 North 2nd Street
Milwaukee, WI 53212
(414) 272-8822
www.workshoparchitects.com

WORLDWIDE REVENUE	$8,000,000
WORLDWIDE STAFF	17
HEADQUARTERS	Milwaukee, WI
YEAR ESTABLISHED	1996

249 | Cook + Fox Architects

641 Avenue of the Americas
New York, NY 10011
(212) 477-0287
www.cookplusfox.com

WORLDWIDE REVENUE	$7,889,700
WORLDWIDE STAFF	21-100
HEADQUARTERS	New York, NY
YEAR ESTABLISHED	2003

250 | KCBA Architects

8705 Germantown Avenue
Philadelphia, PA 19130
(215) 368-5806
www.kcba-architects.com

WORLDWIDE REVENUE	$7,810,140
WORLDWIDE STAFF	60
HEADQUARTERS	Philadelphia, PA
YEAR ESTABLISHED	1972

251 | GWWO

800 Wyman Park Drive, Suite 300
Baltimore, MD 21211
(410) 332-1009
www.gwwoinc.com

WORLDWIDE REVENUE	$7,800,000
WORLDWIDE STAFF	42
HEADQUARTERS	Baltimore, MD
YEAR ESTABLISHED	1990

252 | BLT Architects

1216 Arch Street
Philadelphia, PA 19107
(215) 563-3900
www.blta.com

WORLDWIDE REVENUE	$7,752,000
WORLDWIDE STAFF	32
HEADQUARTERS	Philadelphia, PA
YEAR ESTABLISHED	1961

253 | Bargmann Hendrie & Archetype

300 A Street
Boston, MA 02210
(617) 350-0450
www.bhplus.com

WORLDWIDE REVENUE	$7,742,310
WORLDWIDE STAFF	30
HEADQUARTERS	Boston, MA
YEAR ESTABLISHED	1980

254 | Bullock Tice Associates

909 East Cervantes Street
Pensacola, FL 32501
(850) 434-5444
www.bullocktice.com

WORLDWIDE REVENUE	$7,731,265
WORLDWIDE STAFF	26
HEADQUARTERS	Pensacola, FL
YEAR ESTABLISHED	1958

255 | Hawley Peterson & Snyder Architects

444 Castro Street, Suite 1000
Mountain View, CA 94041
(650) 968-2944
www.hpsarch.com

WORLDWIDE REVENUE	$7,672,950
WORLDWIDE STAFF	38
HEADQUARTERS	Mountain View, CA
YEAR ESTABLISHED	1957

256 | Elness Swenson Graham Architects

500 Washington Avenue, Suite 1080
Minneapolis, MN 55415
(612) 339-5508
www.esgarch.com

WORLDWIDE REVENUE	$7,662,000
WORLDWIDE STAFF	44
HEADQUARTERS	Minneapolis,MN
YEAR ESTABLISHED	1995

257 | Bignell Watkins Hasser Architects

One Park Place, Suite 250
Annapolis, MD 21401
(301) 261-8228
www.bigwaha.com

WORLDWIDE REVENUE	$7,650,000
WORLDWIDE STAFF	40
HEADQUARTERS	Annapolis,MD
YEAR ESTABLISHED	1977

258 | Holzman Moss Bottino Architecture

214 West 29th Street, 17th Floor
New York, NY 10001
(212) 465-0808
www.holzmanmoss.com

WORLDWIDE REVENUE	$7,609,200
WORLDWIDE STAFF	32
HEADQUARTERS	New York, NY
YEAR ESTABLISHED	2004

259 | Bennett Wagner & Grody Architects

1301 Wazee Street, Suite 100
Denver, CO 80204
(303) 623-7323
www.bwgarchitects.com

WORLDWIDE REVENUE	$7,604,752
WORLDWIDE STAFF	35
HEADQUARTERS	Denver, CO
YEAR ESTABLISHED	1989

260 | Field Paoli Architects

150 California Street, 7th Floor
San Francisco, CA 94111
(415) 788-6606
www.fieldpaoli.com

WORLDWIDE REVENUE	$7,585,816
WORLDWIDE STAFF	25
HEADQUARTERS	San Francisco, CA
YEAR ESTABLISHED	1986

261 | Hornberger + Worstell

170 Maiden Lane
San Francisco, CA 94108
(415) 391-1080
www.hornbergerworstell.com

WORLDWIDE REVENUE	$7,525,000
WORLDWIDE STAFF	42
HEADQUARTERS	San Francisco, CA
YEAR ESTABLISHED	1980

262 | JPC Architects

909 112th Avenue Northeast, Suite 206
Bellevue, WA 98004
(425) 641-9200
www.jpcarchitects.com

WORLDWIDE REVENUE	$7,500,000
WORLDWIDE STAFF	41
HEADQUARTERS	Bellevue, WA
YEAR ESTABLISHED	1986

263 | POLLACK Architecture

111 Maiden Lane, Suite 350
San Francisco, CA 94108
(415) 788-4400
www.pollackarch.com

WORLDWIDE REVENUE	$7,446,000
WORLDWIDE STAFF	41
HEADQUARTERS	San Francisco, CA
YEAR ESTABLISHED	1985

264 | JBHM Architects

308 East Pearl Street, Suite 300
Jackson, MS 39201
(601) 352-2699
www.jbhm.com

WORLDWIDE REVENUE	$7,375,000
WORLDWIDE STAFF	40
HEADQUARTERS	Tupelo, MS
YEAR ESTABLISHED	1970

265 | Stanley Beaman & Sears

180 Peachtree Street, Northwest, Suite 600
Atlanta, GA 30303
(404) 524-2200
www.stanleybeamansears.com

WORLDWIDE REVENUE	$7,242,000
WORLDWIDE STAFF	57
HEADQUARTERS	Atlanta, GA
YEAR ESTABLISHED	1991

266 | Levinson Alcoser Associates

1177 West Loop South, Suite 900	WORLDWIDE REVENUE	$7,200,000
Houston, TX 77027	WORLDWIDE STAFF	35
(713) 787-0000	HEADQUARTERS	Houston, TX
www.levinsonalcoser.com	YEAR ESTABLISHED	1992

267 | Yost Grube Hall Architecture

1211 Southwest 5th Avenue, Suite 2700	WORLDWIDE REVENUE	$7,165,500
Portland, OR 97204	WORLDWIDE STAFF	58
(503) 221-0150	HEADQUARTERS	Portland, OR
www.ygh.com	YEAR ESTABLISHED	1964

268 | Bohlin Cywinski Jackson

8 West Market Street, Suite 1200	WORLDWIDE REVENUE	$7,134,900
Wilkes-Barre, PA 18701	WORLDWIDE STAFF	185
(570) 825-8756	HEADQUARTERS	None
www.bcj.com	YEAR ESTABLISHED	1965

269 | JHP Architecture/Urban Design

8340 Meadow Road, Suite 150	WORLDWIDE REVENUE	$7,127,000
Dallas, TX 75231	WORLDWIDE STAFF	30
(214) 363-5687	HEADQUARTERS	Dallas, TX
www.jhparch.com	YEAR ESTABLISHED	1979

270 | Allied Works Architecture

1532 Southwest Morrison Street	WORLDWIDE REVENUE	$7,043,100
Portland, OR 97205	WORLDWIDE STAFF	40
(503) 227-1737	HEADQUARTERS	Portland, OR
www.alliedworks.com	YEAR ESTABLISHED	1994

271 | DiMella Shaffer

281 Summer Street	WORLDWIDE REVENUE	$7,038,000
Boston, MA 02210	WORLDWIDE STAFF	65
(617) 426-5004	HEADQUARTERS	Boston, MA
www.dimellashaffer.com	YEAR ESTABLISHED	1967

272 | Hodges & Associates Architects

13642 Omega
Dallas, TX 75244
(972) 387-1000
www.hodgesusa.com

WORLDWIDE REVENUE	$7,009,338
WORLDWIDE STAFF	30
HEADQUARTERS	Dallas, TX
YEAR ESTABLISHED	1977

273 | Helix Architecture + Design

1629 Walnut Street
Kansas City, MO 64108
(816) 300-0300
www.helixkc.com

WORLDWIDE REVENUE	$7,000,000
WORLDWIDE STAFF	29
HEADQUARTERS	Kansas City, MO
YEAR ESTABLISHED	1992

274 | Crawford Architects

1801 McGee, Suite 200
Kansas City, MO 64108
(816) 421-2640
www.crawfordarch.com

WORLDWIDE REVENUE	$6,836,040
WORLDWIDE STAFF	5-20
HEADQUARTERS	Kansas City, MO
YEAR ESTABLISHED	2001

275 | Ellenzweig

1280 Massachusetts Avenue
Cambridge, MA 02138
(617) 491-5575
www.ellenzweig.com

WORLDWIDE REVENUE	$6,780,960
WORLDWIDE STAFF	55
HEADQUARTERS	Cambridge, MA
YEAR ESTABLISHED	1965

276 | Margulies Perruzzi Architects

308 Congress Street
Boston, MA 02210
(617) 482-3232
www.mp-architects.com

WORLDWIDE REVENUE	$6,630,000
WORLDWIDE STAFF	31
HEADQUARTERS	Boston, MA
YEAR ESTABLISHED	1988

277 | MKC Associates

40 West 4th Street
Mansfield, OH 44902
(877) 652-1102
www.mkcinc.com

WORLDWIDE REVENUE	$6,619,800
WORLDWIDE STAFF	21-100
HEADQUARTERS	Mansfield, OH
YEAR ESTABLISHED	1924

278 | Northeast Collaborative Architects

38 Washington Square	WORLDWIDE REVENUE	$6,616,740
Newport, RI 02840	WORLDWIDE STAFF	25
(401) 846-9583	HEADQUARTERS	Newport, RI
www.ncarchitects.com	YEAR ESTABLISHED	1981

279 | Lindsay, Pope, Brayfield & Associates

344 West Pike Street	WORLDWIDE REVENUE	$6,593,535
Lawrenceville, GA 30046	WORLDWIDE STAFF	5-20
(770) 963-8989	HEADQUARTERS	Lawrenceville, GA
www.lpbatlanta.com	YEAR ESTABLISHED	1975

280 | Architects Delawie Wilkes Rodrigues Barker

2265 India Street	WORLDWIDE REVENUE	$6,554,520
San Diego, CA 92101	WORLDWIDE STAFF	21-100
(619) 299-6690	HEADQUARTERS	San Diego, CA
www.a-dwrb.com	YEAR ESTABLISHED	1961

281 | Polk Stanley Wilcox

2222 Cottondale Lane, Suite 100	WORLDWIDE REVENUE	$6,525,000
Little Rock, AR 72201	WORLDWIDE STAFF	40
(501) 378-0878	HEADQUARTERS	Little Rock, AR
www.polkstanleywilcox.com	YEAR ESTABLISHED	2009

282 | Stephen B. Jacobs Group/Andi Pepper Designs

381 Park Avenue South	WORLDWIDE REVENUE	$6,500,000
New York, NY 10016	WORLDWIDE STAFF	35
(212) 421-3712	HEADQUARTERS	New York, NY
www.sbjgroup.com	YEAR ESTABLISHED	1967

283 | ICON Architecture

38 Chauncy Street	WORLDWIDE REVENUE	$6,434,600
Boston, MA 02111	WORLDWIDE STAFF	32
(617) 451-3333	HEADQUARTERS	Boston, MA
www.iconarch.com	YEAR ESTABLISHED	1996

284 | Marks, Thomas Architects

1414 Key Highway, 2nd Floor
Baltimore, MD 21230
(410) 539-4300
www.marks-thomas.com

WORLDWIDE REVENUE	$6,384,180
WORLDWIDE STAFF	45
HEADQUARTERS	Baltimore, MD
YEAR ESTABLISHED	1967

285 | TR,i Architects

9812 Manchester Road
St. Louis, MO 63119
(314) 395-9750
www.triarchitects.com

WORLDWIDE REVENUE	$6,377,671
WORLDWIDE STAFF	16
HEADQUARTERS	St. Louis, MO
YEAR ESTABLISHED	1989

286 | Barker Rinker Seacat Architecture

3457 Ringsby Court, Unit 200
Denver, CO 80216
(303) 455-1366
www.brsarch.com

WORLDWIDE REVENUE	$6,376,020
WORLDWIDE STAFF	28
HEADQUARTERS	Denver, CO
YEAR ESTABLISHED	1975

287 | GSR Andrade Architects

4121 Commerce Street, Suite One
Dallas, TX 75226
(214) 824-7040
www.gsr-andrade.com

WORLDWIDE REVENUE	$6,300,000
WORLDWIDE STAFF	29
HEADQUARTERS	Dallas, TX
YEAR ESTABLISHED	1991

288 | Beame Architectural Partnership

3059 Grand Avenue, Suite 440
Coconut Grove, FL 33133
(305) 444-7100
www.bapdesign.com

WORLDWIDE REVENUE	$6,259,840
WORLDWIDE STAFF	30
HEADQUARTERS	Miami, FL
YEAR ESTABLISHED	1984

289 | DiGiorgio Associates

225 Friend Street
Boston, MA 02114
(617) 723-7100
www.dai-boston.com

WORLDWIDE REVENUE	$6,259,740
WORLDWIDE STAFF	21-100
HEADQUARTERS	Boston, MA
YEAR ESTABLISHED	1984

290 | Lantz-Boggio Architects

5650 DTC Parkway
Englewood, CO 80111
(303) 773-0436
www.lantz-boggio.com

WORLDWIDE REVENUE	$6,220,000
WORLDWIDE STAFF	25
HEADQUARTERS	Denver, CO
YEAR ESTABLISHED	1981

291 | Pfeiffer Partners Architects

811 West 7th Street, 7th Floor
Los Angeles, CA 90017
(213) 624-2775
www.pfeifferpartners.com

WORLDWIDE REVENUE	$6,201,600
WORLDWIDE STAFF	21-100
HEADQUARTERS	Los Angeles, CA
YEAR ESTABLISHED	2004

292 | BJAC

811 West Hargett Street
Raleigh, NC 27603
(919) 645-3224
www.bjac.com

WORLDWIDE REVENUE	$6,198,820
WORLDWIDE STAFF	25
HEADQUARTERS	Raleigh, NC
YEAR ESTABLISHED	1994

293 | Aguirre Roden

10670 North Central Expressway, 6th Floor
Dallas, TX 75231
(972) 788-1508
www.aguirreroden.com

WORLDWIDE REVENUE	$6,146,100
WORLDWIDE STAFF	64
HEADQUARTERS	Dallas, TX
YEAR ESTABLISHED	1960

294 | Manning Architects

650 Poydras Street, Suite 1250
New Orleans, LA 70130
(504) 412-2000
www.manningarchitects.com

WORLDWIDE REVENUE	$6,130,200
WORLDWIDE STAFF	34
HEADQUARTERS	New Orleans, LA
YEAR ESTABLISHED	1985

295 | Gromatzky Dupree & Associates

3090 Olive Street, Suite 500
Dallas, TX 75219
(214) 871-9078
www.gdainet.com

WORLDWIDE REVENUE	$6,120,000
WORLDWIDE STAFF	21-100
HEADQUARTERS	Dallas, TX
YEAR ESTABLISHED	1984

296 | Flansburgh Architects

77 North Washington Street	WORLDWIDE REVENUE	$6,114,900
Boston, MA 02114	WORLDWIDE STAFF	19
(617) 367-3970	HEADQUARTERS	Boston, MA
www.faiarchitects.com	YEAR ESTABLISHED	1963

297 | KYA Design Group

934 Pumehana Street	WORLDWIDE REVENUE	$6,100,000
Honolulu, HI 96826	WORLDWIDE STAFF	22
(808) 949-7770	HEADQUARTERS	Honolulu, HI
www.kyadesigngroup.com	YEAR ESTABLISHED	1972

298 | Hollis + Miller Architects

8205 West 108th Terrace	WORLDWIDE REVENUE	$6,000,000
Overland Park, KS 66210	WORLDWIDE STAFF	37
(913) 451-8886	HEADQUARTERS	Overland Park, KS
www.hollisandmiller.com	YEAR ESTABLISHED	1950

299 | Hardy McCullah/MLM Architects

12221 Merit Drive, Suite 280	WORLDWIDE REVENUE	$5,889,480
Dallas, TX 75251	WORLDWIDE STAFF	5-20
(972) 385-1900	HEADQUARTERS	Dallas, TX
www.hmmlmarchitects.com	YEAR ESTABLISHED	1967

300 | Rubeling & Associates

1104 Kenilworth Dr., Suite 500	WORLDWIDE REVENUE	$5,824,200
Towson, MD 21204	WORLDWIDE STAFF	25
(410) 337-2886	HEADQUARTERS	Baltimore, MD
www.rubeling.com	YEAR ESTABLISHED	1981

301 | Omniplan

1845 Woodall Rodgers Freeway, Suite 1500	WORLDWIDE REVENUE	$5,800,000
Dallas, TX 75201	WORLDWIDE STAFF	30
(214) 826-7080	HEADQUARTERS	Dallas, TX
www.omniplan.com	YEAR ESTABLISHED	1956

302 | Kann Partners

33 South Gay Street, Suite 400
Baltimore, MD 21202
(410) 234-0900
www.kannpartners.com

WORLDWIDE REVENUE	$5,724,240
WORLDWIDE STAFF	32
HEADQUARTERS	Baltimore, MD
YEAR ESTABLISHED	1974

303 | MOA Architecture

821 17th Street, Suite 400
Denver, CO 80202
(303) 308-1190
www.moaarch.com

WORLDWIDE REVENUE	$5,720,000
WORLDWIDE STAFF	24
HEADQUARTERS	Denver, CO
YEAR ESTABLISHED	1981

304 | IKM

One PPG Place
Pittsburgh, PA 15222
(412) 281-1337
www.ikminc.com

WORLDWIDE REVENUE	$5,700,000
WORLDWIDE STAFF	40
HEADQUARTERS	Pittsburgh, PA
YEAR ESTABLISHED	1911

305 | TowerPinkster

242 East Kalamazoo Avenue
Kalamazoo, MI 49007
(269) 343-6133
www.towerpinkster.com

WORLDWIDE REVENUE	$5,612,000
WORLDWIDE STAFF	45
HEADQUARTERS	Kalamazoo, MI
YEAR ESTABLISHED	1953

306 | Architectural Resources

505 Franklin Street
Buffalo, NY 14202
(716) 883-5566
www.archres.com

WORLDWIDE REVENUE	$5,598,780
WORLDWIDE STAFF	25
HEADQUARTERS	Buffalo, NY
YEAR ESTABLISHED	1991

307 | Peter Marino Architect

150 East 58th Street
New York, NY 10022
(212) 752-5444
www.petermarinoarchitect.com

WORLDWIDE REVENUE	$5,511,060
WORLDWIDE STAFF	125
HEADQUARTERS	New York, NY
YEAR ESTABLISHED	1978

308 | SB Architects

One Beach Street, Suite 301
San Francisco, CA 94133
(415) 673-8990
www.sb-architects.com

WORLDWIDE REVENUE	$5,510,652
WORLDWIDE STAFF	65
HEADQUARTERS	San Francisco, CA
YEAR ESTABLISHED	1960

309 | Design Partnership of Cambridge

500 Rutherford Avenue
Charlestown, MA 02129
(617) 241-9800
www.design-partnership.com

WORLDWIDE REVENUE	$5,510,142
WORLDWIDE STAFF	21-100
HEADQUARTERS	Charleston, MA
YEAR ESTABLISHED	1981

310 | Urban Design Associates

707 Grant Street, Gulf Tower, 31st Floor
Pittsburgh, PA 15219
(412) 263-5200
www.urbandesignassociates.com

WORLDWIDE REVENUE	$5,500,000
WORLDWIDE STAFF	25
HEADQUARTERS	Pittsburgh, PA
YEAR ESTABLISHED	1964

311 | Ohlson Lavoie Collaborative

616 East Speer Boulevard
Denver, CO 80203
(303) 294-9244
www.olcdesigns.com

WORLDWIDE REVENUE	$5,462,100
WORLDWIDE STAFF	21-100
HEADQUARTERS	Denver, CO
YEAR ESTABLISHED	1982

312 | Tsao & McKown Architects

20 Vandam Street
New York, NY 10013
(212) 337-3800
www.tsao-mckown.com

WORLDWIDE REVENUE	$5,375,400
WORLDWIDE STAFF	5-20
HEADQUARTERS	New York, NY
YEAR ESTABLISHED	1985

313 | Meyer, Scherer & Rockcastle

710 South 2nd Street, 8th Floor
Minneapolis, MN 55401
(612) 375-0336
www.msrltd.com

WORLDWIDE REVENUE	$5,355,000
WORLDWIDE STAFF	40
HEADQUARTERS	Minneapolis,MN
YEAR ESTABLISHED	1981

314 | Ferraro Choi and Associates

1240 Ala Moana Boulevard, Suite 510
Honolulu, HI 96814
(808) 533-8880
www.ferrarochoi.com

WORLDWIDE REVENUE	$5,329,500
WORLDWIDE STAFF	23
HEADQUARTERS	Honolulu, HI
YEAR ESTABLISHED	1988

315 | Dougherty + Dougherty Architects

3194D Airport Loop Drive
Costa Mesa, CA 92626
(714) 427-0277
www.ddarchitecture.com

WORLDWIDE REVENUE	$5,300,000
WORLDWIDE STAFF	35
HEADQUARTERS	Costa Mesa, CA
YEAR ESTABLISHED	1979

316 | Ann Beha Architects

33 Kingston Street
Boston, MA 02111
(617) 338-3000
www.annbeha.com

WORLDWIDE REVENUE	$5,262,180
WORLDWIDE STAFF	21-100
HEADQUARTERS	Boston, MA
YEAR ESTABLISHED	1977

317 | Architectural Resources Group

Pier 9, The Embarcadero, Suite 107
San Francisco, CA 94111
(415) 421-1680
www.argsf.com

WORLDWIDE REVENUE	$5,210,670
WORLDWIDE STAFF	21-100
HEADQUARTERS	San Francisco, CA
YEAR ESTABLISHED	1980

318 | M+A Architects

775 Yard Street, Suite 325
Columbus, OH 43212
(614) 764-0407
www.ma-architects.com

WORLDWIDE REVENUE	$5,207,100
WORLDWIDE STAFF	42
HEADQUARTERS	Dublin, OH
YEAR ESTABLISHED	1980

319 | Perry Dean Rogers | Partners Architects

177 Milk Street, Seventh Floor
Boston, MA 02109
(617) 423-0100
www.perrydean.com

WORLDWIDE REVENUE	$5,202,000
WORLDWIDE STAFF	30
HEADQUARTERS	Boston, MA
YEAR ESTABLISHED	1923

320 | Gilmore Group

91 Fifth Avenue, 7th Floor
New York, NY 10003
(212) 675-5122
www.gilmoregroup.com

WORLDWIDE REVENUE	$5,200,000
WORLDWIDE STAFF	40
HEADQUARTERS	New York, NY
YEAR ESTABLISHED	2003

321 | KDF Architecture

1310 North 16th Avenue
Yakima, WA 98902
(509) 575-5408
www.kdfarchitecture.com

WORLDWIDE REVENUE	$5,131,620
WORLDWIDE STAFF	26
HEADQUARTERS	Yakima, WA
YEAR ESTABLISHED	1976

322 | Daniel P. Coffey & Associates

233 South Wacker, Sears Tower, Suite 5750
Chicago, IL 60605
(312) 382-9898
www.dpcaltd.com

WORLDWIDE REVENUE	$5,100,000
WORLDWIDE STAFF	25
HEADQUARTERS	Chicago, IL
YEAR ESTABLISHED	1984

323 | Horty Elving

505 East Grant Street
Minneapolis, MN 55404
(612) 332-4422
www.hortyelving.com

WORLDWIDE REVENUE	$5,105,000
WORLDWIDE STAFF	30
HEADQUARTERS	Minneapolis, MN
YEAR ESTABLISHED	1955

324 | Boggs & Partners Architects

410 Severn Avenue, Suite 406
Annapolis, MD 21403
(410) 268-3797
www.boggspartners.com

WORLDWIDE REVENUE	$5,100,000
WORLDWIDE STAFF	10
HEADQUARTERS	Annapolis,MD
YEAR ESTABLISHED	1996

325 | Gantt Huberman Architects

500 North Tryon Street
Charlotte, NC 28202
(704) 334-6436
www.gantthuberman.com

WORLDWIDE REVENUE	$5,000,000
WORLDWIDE STAFF	26
HEADQUARTERS	Charlotte, NC
YEAR ESTABLISHED	1971

326 | HBRA (Hammond Beeby Rupert Ainge)

372 West Ontario Street, 2nd Floor
Chicago, IL 60654
(312) 527-3200
www.hbra-arch.com

WORLDWIDE REVENUE	$4,951,080
WORLDWIDE STAFF	21-100
HEADQUARTERS	Chicago, IL
YEAR ESTABLISHED	1961

327 | VBN Architects

560 14th Street
Oakland, CA 94612
(510) 763-1313
www.vbnarch.com

WORLDWIDE REVENUE	$4,941,900
WORLDWIDE STAFF	5-20
HEADQUARTERS	Oakland, CA
YEAR ESTABLISHED	1958

328 | Loebl Schlossman & Hackl

233 North Michigan Avenue, Suite 3000
Chicago, IL 60601
(312) 565-1800
www.lshdesign.com

WORLDWIDE REVENUE	$4,900,000
WORLDWIDE STAFF	36
HEADQUARTERS	Chicago, IL
YEAR ESTABLISHED	1925

329 | Slocum Platts Architects Design Studio

200 East New England Avenue, Suite 300
Winter Park, FL 32789
(407) 645-3019
www.slocumplatts.com

WORLDWIDE REVENUE	$4,748,100
WORLDWIDE STAFF	5-20
HEADQUARTERS	Winter Park, FL
YEAR ESTABLISHED	1994

330 | LCA Architects

245 Ygnacio Valley Road
Walnut Creek, CA 94596
(925) 944-1626
www.lca-architects.com

WORLDWIDE REVENUE	$4,737,900
WORLDWIDE STAFF	21-100
HEADQUARTERS	Walnut Creek, CA
YEAR ESTABLISHED	1973

331 | Emc2 Group Architects

1635 North Greenfield Road, Suite 144
Mesa, AZ 85205
(480) 830-3838
www.emc2architects.com

WORLDWIDE REVENUE	$4,471,380
WORLDWIDE STAFF	17
HEADQUARTERS	Mesa, AZ
YEAR ESTABLISHED	1978

332 | Champalimaud

One Union Square West, Suite 705
New York, NY 10003
(212) 807-8869
www.champalimauddesign.com

WORLDWIDE REVENUE	$4,462,500
WORLDWIDE STAFF	21-100
HEADQUARTERS	New York, NY
YEAR ESTABLISHED	1981

333 | Jova/Daniels/Busby

400 Colony Square, Suite 400
Atlanta, GA 30361
(404) 879-6800
www.jova.com

WORLDWIDE REVENUE	$4,386,000
WORLDWIDE STAFF	22
HEADQUARTERS	Atlanta, GA
YEAR ESTABLISHED	1967

2

**AMERICA'S LEADING
ARCHITECTURE & DESIGN FIRMS |**

This chapter features an alphabetical listing
of leading North American architecture and
design firms with data about the type of
services they offer; their size, headquarters,
and geography; the market segments they
work in; and metrics from the *DI Index*.

America's Leading Architecture & Design Firms 2013

This section of the *Almanac* features an alphabetical listing of leading North American architecture and design firms selected by the editors. Each year, *DesignIntelligence* polls architects and designers in North America regarding their firms' officers, firm size, primary services offered, market segments and geographical locations served, and the nature of their practices. The firms are invited to participate in additional research underwritten by the Design Futures Council, which includes surveys about trends and market shifts, compensation and fees, technology, mergers and acquisitions, and management strategies.

The key to interpreting the tables is featured below. Firm size, headquarters (HQ), firm type, and markets are determined by *DesignIntelligence* surveys or from record files. Although the concept of headquarters might be less normative than in the past, this convention is still often used for diagnostic purposes in many market-data studies. If your firm has no headquarters and we have listed one, please make sure to complete a survey next year at di.net. The list of services includes market segments and specific professional specializations. The DI Index was determined by survey responses, with further research conducted by *DesignIntelligence* and Greenway Group analysts. The criteria include geographic service coverage and reputation (awards as listed in the *Almanac of Architecture & Design* and recognition in professional and business publications). Of the five tiers, only firms in the top three (as represented by 3–5 stars) are included due to space considerations. Abbreviations were used in some firm names due to space constraints: architecture = Arch.; architects = Archts.; associates = Assoc.; construction = Const.; engineers = Engrs.

Principals of firms who want to be included in our next *Almanac* can obtain and/or fill in a survey at di.net; email the editor, Jane Wolford, at jwolford@di.net for a copy; or call *DesignIntelligence* at (678) 879-0929. Firms appearing in this *Almanac* can expect to receive a copy of next year's survey in the mail soon or can request a survey by contacting DI or the editor.

KEY

Rank
Refers to DI Ranking (chapter 1)

Size

	Small	20 employees or less
	Medium	21–100 employees
	Large	101–450 employees
	Extra Large	451+ employees

HQ
Listed by state, C (CAN) or Mexico (MEX)

Regions Served

E	East	C	Canada
M	Midwest	G	Global
S	South		
W	West		

Services Offered

A	Architecture	O	Other
E	Engineering		(inc. industrial design)
G	Graphic Design	P	Planning
I	Interior Design	S	Sustainability
L	Landscape Architecture	U	Urban Design

Market Segments

C	Corporate	M	Museum/Cultural
E	Higher Education	R	Religious
K	K-12	Rs	Residential-Single
G	Government	Rm	Residential-Multi.
Hc	Healthcare	Re	Retail/Commercial
H	Hospitality	S	Sports
I	Industrial/Tech.	O	Other

DI Brand Recognition Index

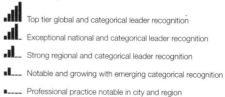

Top tier global and categorical leader recognition

Exceptional national and categorical leader recognition

Strong regional and categorical leader recognition

Notable and growing with emerging categorical recognition

Professional practice notable in city and region

Rank	Firm/Web	Size	HQ	Regions	Services	Markets	DI Index
	360 Architecture www.360architects.com	👥	MO	E M S W C G	A E G I L P S U O	C E K G Hc H I M R Rs Rm Rc S O	.ıll.
	4240 Architecture www.4240architecture.com	👥	CO	E M S W C G	A E G I L P S U O	C E K G Hc H I M R Rs Rm Rc S O	.ıl.
A	**A. Morton Thomas & Associates** www.amtengineering.com	👥	MD	E M S W C G	A E G I L P S U O	C E K G Hc H I M R Rs Rm Rc S O	.ıl.
	A4 Architecture www.a4arch.com	👤	RI	E M S W C G	A E G I L P S U O	C E K G Hc H I M R Rs Rm Rc S O	.ıll.
	Abell & Associates Architects www.jamesabell.com	👤	AZ	E M S W C G	A E G I L P S U O	C E K G Hc H I M R Rs Rm Rc S O	.ıll.
106	**AC Martin** www.acmartin.com	👥	CA	E M S W C G	A E G I L P S U O	C E K G Hc H I M R Rs Rm Rc S O	.ıll
	Acai Associates www.acaiworld.com	👥	FL	E M S W C G	A E G I L P S U O	C E K G Hc H I M R Rs Rm Rc S O	.ıl.
	ACI/Boland www.aci-boland.com	👥	MO	E M S W C G	A E G I L P S U O	C E K G Hc H I M R Rs Rm Rc S O	.ıl.
	Adache Group Architects www.adache.com	👥	FL	E M S W C G	A E G I L P S U O	C E K G Hc H I M R Rs Rm Rc S O	.ıl.
	Adamson Associates Architects www.adamson-associates.com	👥	CAN	E M S W C G	A E G I L P S U O	C E K G Hc H I M R Rs Rm Rc S O	.ıl.
138	**ADD Inc** www.addinc.com	👥	MA	E M S W C G	A E G I L P S U O	C E K G Hc H I M R Rs Rm Rc S O	.ıll
76	**Adrian Smith + Gordon Gill Architecture** www.smithgill.com	👥	IL	E M S W C G	A E G I L P S U O	C E K G Hc H I M R Rs Rm Rc S O	.ıll
2	**AECOM (Architecture)** www.aecom.com	👥	CA	E M S W C G	A E G I L P S U O	C E K G Hc H I M R Rs Rm Rc S O	.ıll
75	**Aedas** www.aedas.com	👥	NY	E M S W C G	A E G I L P S U O	C E K G Hc H I M R Rs Rm Rc S O	.ıl.
	AEDIS Architecture & Planning www.aedisgroup.com	👥	CA	E M S W C G	A E G I L P S U O	C E K G Hc H I M R Rs Rm Rc S O	.ıll
	Affiniti Architects www.affinitiarchitects.com	👥	FL	E M S W C G	A E G I L P S U O	C E K G Hc H I M R Rs Rm Rc S O	.ıl.
293	**Aguirre Roden** www.aguirreroden.com	👥	TX	E M S W C G	A E G I L P S U O	C E K G Hc H I M R Rs Rm Rc S O	.ıl.

Regions East (E), Midwest (M), South (S), West (W), Canada (C), Global (G)

Services Architecture (A), Engineering (E), Graphic Design (G), Interior Design (I), Landscape Architecture (L), Planning (P), Sustainability (S), Urban Design (U), Other-including Industrial Design (O)

Markets Corporate (C), Higher Ed. (E), K-12 (K), Government (G), Healthcare (Hc), Hospitality (H), Industrial/Tech. (I), Museum/Cultural (M), Religious (R), Residential-Single (Rs), Residential-Multi. (Rm), Retail/Commercial (Rc), Sports (S), Other (O)

Rank	Firm/Web	Size	HQ	Regions	Services	Markets	DI Index
	Aidlin Darling Design www.aidlin-darling-design.com	👤	CA	E M S W C G	A E G I L P S U O	C E K G Hc H I M R Rs Rm Rc S O	▪▮▮▮_
	Albert Kahn Associates www.albertkahn.com	👤👤👤	MI	E M S W C G	A E G I L P S U O	C E K G Hc H I M R Rs Rm Rc S O	▪▮▮▮_
	Alliance Architects www.alliancearch.com	👤	TX	E M S W C G	A E G I L P S U O	C E K G Hc H I M R Rs Rm Rc S O	▪▮▮__
270	**Allied Works Architecture** www.alliedworks.com	👤👤	OR	E M S W C G	A E G I L P S U O	C E K G Hc H I M R Rs Rm Rc S O	▪▮▮▮▮
192	**Altoon + Porter Architects** ALTOON PARTNERS www.altoonporter.com	👤👤	CA	E M S W C G	A E G I L P S U O	C E K G Hc H I M R Rs Rm Rc S O	▪▮▮▮_
	Ammon Heisler Sachs Architects www.ahsarch.com	👤	MD	E M S W C G	A E G I L P S U O	C E K G Hc H I M R Rs Rm Rc S O	▪▮▮__
	Anderson Brulé Architects www.aba-arch.com	👤	CA	E M S W C G	A E G I L P S U O	C E K G Hc H I M R Rs Rm Rc S O	▪▮▮__
224	**Anderson Mason Dale Architects** www.amdarchitects.com	👤👤	CO	E M S W C G	A E G I L P S U O	C E K G Hc H I M R Rs Rm Rc S O	▪▮▮▮_
	Ankrom Moisan Associated Architects www.amaa.com	👤👤	OR	E M S W C G	A E G I L P S U O	C E K G Hc H I M R Rs Rm Rc S O	▪▮▮__
316	**Ann Beha Architects** www.annbeha.com AnnBehaArchitects	👤👤	MA	E M S W C G	A E G I L P S U O	C E K G Hc H I M R Rs Rm Rc S O	▪▮▮▮_
	Anova Architects www.anovaarchitects.com	👤👤	CA	E M S W C G	A E G I L P S U O	C E K G Hc H I M R Rs Rm Rc S O	▪▮▮__
	Antinozzi Associates www.antinozzi.com	👤👤	CT	E M S W C G	A E G I L P S U O	C E K G Hc H I M R Rs Rm Rc S O	▪▮▮__
	Apostolou Associates www.apostolouassociates.com	👤	PA	E M S W C G	A E G I L P S U O	C E K G Hc H I M R Rs Rm Rc S O	▪▮▮__
	App Architecture www.app-arch.com	👤👤	OH	E M S W C G	A E G I L P S U O	C E K G Hc H I M R Rs Rm Rc S O	▪▮▮__
128	**ARC/Architectural Resources Cambridge** ARC www.arcusa.com	👤👤	MA	E M S W C G	A E G I L P S U O	C E K G Hc H I M R Rs Rm Rc S O	▪▮▮__
	Archicon www.archicon.com	👤👤	AZ	E M S W C G	A E G I L P S U O	C E K G Hc H I M R Rs Rm Rc S O	▪▮▮__
	Architects BCRA www.bcradesign.com	👤👤👤	WA	E M S W C G	A E G I L P S U O	C E K G Hc H I M R Rs Rm Rc S O	▪▮▮__

DI Brand Recognition Index

▪▮▮▮▮	Top tier global and categorical leader recognition
▪▮▮▮_	Exceptional national and categorical leader recognition
▪▮▮__	Strong regional and categorical leader recognition
▪▮___	Notable and growing with emerging categorical recognition
▪____	Professional practice notable in city and region

Rank	Firm/Web	Size	HQ	Regions	Services	Markets	DI Index
280	**Architects Delawie Wilkes Rodrigues Barker** www.a-dwrb.com	👥	CA	E M S W C G	A E G I L P S U O	C E K G Hc H I M R Rs Rm Rc S O	▪▪▮▪▫
188	**Architects Design Group** www.adgusa.org	👥	FL	E M S W C G	A E G I L P S U O	C E K G Hc H I M R Rs Rm Rc S O	▪▪▮▪▫
74	**Architects Hawaii** www.ahldesign.com	👥	HI	E M S W C G	A E G I L P S U O	C E K G Hc H I M R Rs Rm Rc S O	▪▪▮▪▫
	Architects In Partnership www.aipdesign.com	👤	FL	E M S W C G	A E G I L P S U O	C E K G Hc H I M R Rs Rm Rc S O	▪▪▮▪▫
	Architects Pacific www.architectspacificinc.com	👤	HI	E M S W C G	A E G I L P S U O	C E K G Hc H I M R Rs Rm Rc S O	▪▪▮▪▫
	Architects Studio www.architectsstudio.us	👤	HI	E M S W C G	A E G I L P S U O	C E K G Hc H I M R Rs Rm Rc S O	▪▪▮▪▫
	Architectural Alliance www.archalliance.com	👥	MN	E M S W C G	A E G I L P S U O	C E K G Hc H I M R Rs Rm Rc S O	▪▪▮▪▫
	Architectural Concepts www.arconcepts.com	👥	PA	E M S W C G	A E G I L P S U O	C E K G Hc H I M R Rs Rm Rc S O	▪▪▮▪▫
	Architectural Resource Team www.art-team.com	👤	AZ	E M S W C G	A E G I L P S U O	C E K G Hc H I M R Rs Rm Rc S O	▪▪▮▪▫
306	**Architectural Resources** www.archres.com	👥	NY	E M S W C G	A E G I L P S U O	C E K G Hc H I M R Rs Rm Rc S O	▪▪▮▪▫
317	**Architectural Resources Group** www.argsf.com	👥	CA	E M S W C G	A E G I L P S U O	C E K G Hc H I M R Rs Rm Rc S O	▪▪▮▪▫
	Architectural Resources Inc. www.arimn.com	👤	MN	E M S W C G	A E G I L P S U O	C E K G Hc H I M R Rs Rm Rc S O	▪▪▮▪▫
	Architectural Studio www.sbdassociates.com	👤	FL	E M S W C G	A E G I L P S U O	C E K G Hc H I M R Rs Rm Rc S O	▪▪▮▪▫
	Architecture, Inc. www.archinc.com	👤	VA	E M S W C G	A E G I L P S U O	C E K G Hc H I M R Rs Rm Rc S O	▪▪▮▪▫
	Architecture Incorporated www.architectureinc.com	👥	SD	E M S W C G	A E G I L P S U O	C E K G Hc H I M R Rs Rm Rc S O	▪▪▮▪▫
	ArchitectureIsFun www.architectureisfun.com	👤	IL	E M S W C G	A E G I L P S U O	C E K G Hc H I M R Rs Rm Rc S O	▪▪▮▪▫
	Architecture PML www.archpml.com	👤	CO	E M S W C G	A E G I L P S U O	C E K G Hc H I M R Rs Rm Rc S O	▪▪▮▪▮

Regions East (E), Midwest (M), South (S), West (W), Canada (C), Global (G)

Services Architecture (A), Engineering (E), Graphic Design (G), Interior Design (I), Landscape Architecture (L), Planning (P), Sustainability (S), Urban Design (U), Other-including Industrial Design (O)

Markets Corporate (C), Higher Ed. (E), K-12 (K), Government (G), Healthcare (Hc), Hospitality (H), Industrial/Tech. (I), Museum/Cultural (M), Religious (R), Residential-Single (Rs), Residential-Multi. (Rm), Retail/Commercial (Rc), Sports (S), Other (O)

Rank	Firm/Web	Size	HQ	Regions	Services	Markets	DI Index
	Architekton — ARCHITEKTON — www.architekton.com		AZ	E M S W C G	A E G I L P S U O	C E K G Hc H I M R Rs Rm Rc S O	
174	Arcturis www.arcturis.com		MO	E M S W C G	A E G I L P S U O	C E K G Hc H I M R Rs Rm Rc S O	
	ARIUMae www.ARIUMae.com		MD	E M S W C G	A E G I L P S U O	C E K G Hc H I M R Rs Rm Rc S O	
70	Arquitectonica — ARQUITECTONICA — www.arquitectonica.com		FL	E M S W C G	A E G I L P S U O	C E K G Hc H I M R Rs Rm Rc S O	
	Arrington Watkins Architects www.awarch.com		AZ	E M S W C G	A E G I L P S U O	C E K G Hc H I M R Rs Rm Rc S O	
94	Arrowstreet www.arrowstreet.com		MA	E M S W C G	A E G I L P S U O	C E K G Hc H I M R Rs Rm Rc S O	
185	Ascension Group Architects www.ascensiongroup.biz		TX	E M S W C G	A E G I L P S U O	C E K G Hc H I M R Rs Rm Rc S O	
153	ASD — A S D — www.asdnet.com		GA	E M S W C G	A E G I L P S U O	C E K G Hc H I M R Rs Rm Rc S O	
	Ashley McGraw Architects www.ashleymcgraw.com		NY	E M S W C G	A E G I L P S U O	C E K G Hc H I M R Rs Rm Rc S O	
110	Astorino www.astorino.com		PA	E M S W C G	A E G I L P S U O	C E K G Hc H I M R Rs Rm Rc S O	
	ATI Architects & Engineers www.atiae.com		CA	E M S W C G	A E G I L P S U O	C E K G Hc H I M R Rs Rm Rc S O	
	Austin Kuester www.austinkuester.com		VA	E M S W C G	A E G I L P S U O	C E K G Hc H I M R Rs Rm Rc S O	
67	Ayers Saint Gross www.asg-architects.com		MD	E M S W C G	A E G I L P S U O	C E K G Hc H I M R Rs Rm Rc S O	
B	Baird Sampson Neuert Architects www.bsnarchitects.com		CAN	E M S W C G	A E G I L P S U O	C E K G Hc H I M R Rs Rm Rc S O	
197	Baker Barrios Architects www.bakerbarrios.com		FL	E M S W C G	A E G I L P S U O	C E K G Hc H I M R Rs Rm Rc S O	
85	Ballinger — BALLINGER — www.ballinger-ae.com		PA	E M S W C G	A E G I L P S U O	C E K G Hc H I M R Rs Rm Rc S O	
	BAR Architects www.bararch.com		CA	E M S W C G	A E G I L P S U O	C E K G Hc H I M R Rs Rm Rc S O	

DI Brand Recognition Index

▪▪▪▪ Top tier global and categorical leader recognition	▪▪___ Notable and growing with emerging categorical recognition
▪▪▪_ Exceptional national and categorical leader recognition	▪____ Professional practice notable in city and region
▪▪__ Strong regional and categorical leader recognition	

Rank	Firm/Web	Size	HQ	Regions	Services	Markets	DI Index
253	**Bargmann Hendrie & Archetype** www.bhplus.com	👥	MA	E M S W C G	A E G I L P S U O	C E K G Hc H I M R Rs Rm Rc S O	
286	**Barker Rinker Seacat Architecture** www.brsarch.com	👥	CO	E M S W C G	A E G I L P S U O	C E K G Hc H I M R Rs Rm Rc S O	
	BartonPartners www.bartonpartners.com	👥	PA	E M S W C G	A E G I L P S U O	C E K G Hc H I M R Rs Rm Rc S O	
173	**Baskervill** www.baskervill.com	👥👥	VA	E M S W C G	A E G I L P S U O	C E K G Hc H I M R Rs Rm Rc S O	
	Bassetti Architects www.bassettiarch.com	👤	WA	E M S W C G	A E G I L P S U O	C E K G Hc H I M R Rs Rm Rc S O	
	BAUER Architects www.bauerandwiley.com	👤	CA	E M S W C G	A E G I L P S U O	C E K G Hc H I M R Rs Rm Rc S O	
	Bay Architects www.bayarchitects.com	👥	TX	E M S W C G	A E G I L P S U O	C E K G Hc H I M R Rs Rm Rc S O	
133	**BBG-BBGM** www.bbg-bbgm.com	👥👥	NY	E M S W C G	A E G I L P S U O	C E K G Hc H I M R Rs Rm Rc S O	
	BBL Architects www.bblarchitects.com	👥	OR	E M S W C G	A E G I L P S U O	C E K G Hc H I M R Rs Rm Rc S O	
230	**BCA** www.BCAarchitects.com	👥	CA	E M S W C G	A E G I L P S U O	C E K G Hc H I M R Rs Rm Rc S O	
	BC Architects www.bcarchitects.com	👤	FL	E M S W C G	A E G I L P S U O	C E K G Hc H I M R Rs Rm Rc S O	
	BEA International www.beai.com	👥	FL	E M S W C G	A E G I L P S U O	C E K G Hc H I M R Rs Rm Rc S O	
288	**Beame Architectural Partnership** www.bapdesign.com	👥	FL	E M S W C G	A E G I L P S U O	C E K G Hc H I M R Rs Rm Rc S O	
245	**Bearsch Compeau Knudson Architects & Engineers** www.bckpc.com	👥	NY	E M S W C G	A E G I L P S U O	C E K G Hc H I M R Rs Rm Rc S O	
	Beatty, Harvey, Coco Architects www.bhc-architects.com	👥	NY	E M S W C G	A E G I L P S U O	C E K G Hc H I M R Rs Rm Rc S O	
142	**Beck Group (Architecture), The** www.beckgroup.com	👥	TX	E M S W C G	A E G I L P S U O	C E K G Hc H I M R Rs Rm Rc S O	
	Becker & Becker Associates www.beckerandbecker.com	👤	CT	E M S W C G	A E G I L P S U O	C E K G Hc H I M R Rs Rm Rc S O	

Regions   East (E), Midwest (M), South (S), West (W), Canada (C), Global (G)

Services   Architecture (A), Engineering (E), Graphic Design (G), Interior Design (I), Landscape Architecture (L), Planning (P), Sustainability (S), Urban Design (U), Other-including Industrial Design (O)

Markets   Corporate (C), Higher Ed. (E), K-12 (K), Government (G), Healthcare (Hc), Hospitality (H), Industrial/Tech. (I), Museum/Cultural (M), Religious (R), Residential-Single (Rs), Residential-Multi. (Rm), Retail/Commercial (Rc), Sports (S), Other (O)

Coast at Lakeshore East, Chicago, IL | bKL Architects

GEMS World Academy, Phase 1, Chicago, IL | bKL Architects

Rank	Firm/Web	Size	HQ	Regions	Services	Markets	DI Index
	Benham Companies, The www.benham.com	†††	OK	E M S W C G	A E G I L P S U O	C E K G Hc H I M R Rs Rm Rc S O	
	Benjamin Woo Architects www.benwooarchitects.com	†	HI	E M S W C G	A E G I L P S U O	C E K G Hc H I M R Rs Rm Rc S O	
259	**Bennett Wagner & Grody Architects** www.bwgarchitects.com	††	CO	E M S W C G	A E G I L P S U O	C E K G Hc H I M R Rs Rm Rc S O	
	Bentel & Bentel Architects/Planners www.bentelandbentel.com	†	NY	E M S W C G	A E G I L P S U O	C E K G Hc H I M R Rs Rm Rc S O	
	Bergmann Associates www.bergmannpc.com	††	NY	E M S W C G	A E G I L P S U O	C E K G Hc H I M R Rs Rm Rc S O	
240	**Bergmeyer Associates** www.bergmeyer.com Bergmeyer	††	MA	E M S W C G	A E G I L P S U O	C E K G Hc H I M R Rs Rm Rc S O	
199	**Bermello Ajamil & Partners** www.bamiami.com	††	FL	E M S W C G	A E G I L P S U O	C E K G Hc H I M R Rs Rm Rc S O	
	Bernardon Haber Holloway www.bernardon.com	††	PA	E M S W C G	A E G I L P S U O	C E K G Hc H I M R Rs Rm Rc S O	
63	**Beyer Blinder Belle** www.beyerblinderbelle.com	†††	NY	E M S W C G	A E G I L P S U O	C E K G Hc H I M R Rs Rm Rc S O	
132	**BHDP Architecture** www.bhdp.com	†††	OH	E M S W C G	A E G I L P S U O	C E K G Hc H I M R Rs Rm Rc S O	
	Bialosky & Partners Architects www.bialosky.com	††	OH	E M S W C G	A E G I L P S U O	C E K G Hc H I M R Rs Rm Rc S O	
257	**Bignell Watkins Hasser Architects** www.bigwaha.com	††	MD	E M S W C G	A E G I L P S U O	C E K G Hc H I M R Rs Rm Rc S O	
	Bingham Hill Architects www.bharch.ca	†	BC	E M S W C G	A E G I L P S U O	C E K G Hc H I M R Rs Rm Rc S O	
	Bing Thom Architects www.bingthomarchitects.com	††	CAN	E M S W C G	A E G I L P S U O	C E K G Hc H I M R Rs Rm Rc S O	
292	**BJAC** www.bjac.com	††	NC	E M S W C G	A E G I L P S U O	C E K G Hc H I M R Rs Rm Rc S O	
	bKL Architects www.bklarch.com	††	IL	E M S W C G	A E G I L P S U O	C E K G Hc H I M R Rs Rm Rc S O	
	BKV Group www.bkvgroup.com	††	MN	E M S W C G	A E G I L P S U O	C E K G Hc H I M R Rs Rm Rc S O	

Regions   East (E), Midwest (M), South (S), West (W), Canada (C), Global (G)

Services   Architecture (A), Engineering (E), Graphic Design (G), Interior Design (I), Landscape Architecture (L), Planning (P), Sustainability (S), Urban Design (U), Other-including Industrial Design (O)

Markets   Corporate (C), Higher Ed. (E), K-12 (K), Government (G), Healthcare (Hc), Hospitality (H), Industrial/Tech. (I), Museum/Cultural (M), Religious (R), Residential-Single (Rs), Residential-Multi. (Rm), Retail/Commercial (Rc), Sports (S), Other (O)

Rank	Firm/Web	Size	HQ	Regions	Services	Markets	DI Index
	Blackburn Architects www.blackburnarchitects.com	👤	IN	E M S W C G	A E G I L P S U O	C E K G Hc H I M R Rs Rm Rc S O	▪▫▫▫
	Blackburn Architects www.blackburnarch.com	👤	DC	E M S W C G	A E G I L P S U O	C E K G Hc H I M R Rs Rm Rc S O	▪▪▫▫
	Blackney Hayes Architects www.blackneyhayes.com	👥	PA	E M S W C G	A E G I L P S U O	C E K G Hc H I M R Rs Rm Rc S O	▪▪▫▫
	Blackwell, Marlon, Architect www.marlonblackwell.com	👤	AR	E M S W C G	A E G I L P S U O	C E K G Hc H I M R Rs Rm Rc S O	▪▪▪▪
	Blankstudio Architecture www.blankspaces.net	👤	AZ	E M S W C G	A E G I L P S U O	C E K G Hc H I M R Rs Rm Rc S O	▪▪▫▫
252	**BLT Architects** www.blta.com	👥	PA	E M S W C G	A E G I L P S U O	C E K G Hc H I M R Rs Rm Rc S O	▪▪▫▫
	BMS Design Group www.bmsdesigngroup.com	👤	CA	E M S W C G	A E G I L P S U O	C E K G Hc H I M R Rs Rm Rc S O	▪▪▫▫
184	**BNIM Architects** www.bnim.com	👥👥	MO	E M S W C G	A E G I L P S U O	C E K G Hc H I M R Rs Rm Rc S O	▪▪▪▪
324	**Boggs & Partners Architects** www.boggspartners.com	👤	MD	E M S W C G	A E G I L P S U O	C E K G Hc H I M R Rs Rm Rc S O	▪▪▫▫
268	**Bohlin Cywinski Jackson** www.bcj.com	👥👥	PA	E M S W C G	A E G I L P S U O	C E K G Hc H I M R Rs Rm Rc S O	▪▪▪▪
187	**BOKA Powell** www.bokapowell.com	👥	TX	E M S W C G	A E G I L P S U O	C E K G Hc H I M R Rs Rm Rc S O	▪▪▫▫
155	**BOORA Architects** www.boora.com	👥	OR	E M S W C G	A E G I L P S U O	C E K G Hc H I M R Rs Rm Rc S O	▪▪▪▪
	Booth Hansen Associates www.boothhansen.com	👤	IL	E M S W C G	A E G I L P S U O	C E K G Hc H I M R Rs Rm Rc S O	▪▪▫▫
	Borrelli + Partners www.borrelliarchitects.com	👤	FL	E M S W C G	A E G I L P S U O	C E K G Hc H I M R Rs Rm Rc S O	▪▪▫▫
21	**Bostwick Design Partnership** www.bostwickdesign.com	👥	OH	E M S W C G	A E G I L P S U O	C E K G Hc H I M R Rs Rm Rc S O	▪▪▫▫
	Boulder Associates www.boulderassociates.com	👥	CO	E M S W C G	A E G I L P S U O	C E K G Hc H I M R Rs Rm Rc S O	▪▪▫▫
	Brand + Allen Architects www.brandallen.com	👥	TX	E M S W C G	A E G I L P S U O	C E K G Hc H I M R Rs Rm Rc S O	▪▪▫▫

DI Brand Recognition Index

▪▪▪▪ Top tier global and categorical leader recognition

▪▪▪▫ Exceptional national and categorical leader recognition

▪▪▫▫ Strong regional and categorical leader recognition

▪▪▫▫ Notable and growing with emerging categorical recognition

▪▫▫▫ Professional practice notable in city and region

Rank	Firm/Web	Size	HQ	Regions	Services	Markets	DI Index
	Brasher Design www.brasherdesign.com		MD	E M S W C G	A E G I L P S U O	C E K G Hc H I M R Rs Rm Rc S O	
	Braun & Steidl Architects www.bsa-net.com		OH	E M S W C G	A E G I L P S U O	C E K G Hc H I M R Rs Rm Rc S O	
	Brooks + Scarpa www.brooksscarpa.com		CA	E M S W C G	A E G I L P S U O	C E K G Hc H I M R Rs Rm Rc S O	
	Brown Craig Turner www.brownandcraig.com		MD	E M S W C G	A E G I L P S U O	C E K G Hc H I M R Rs Rm Rc S O	
	Browning Day Mullins Dierdorf Architects www.bdmd.com		IN	E M S W C G	A E G I L P S U O	C E K G Hc H I M R Rs Rm Rc S O	
	BRPH www.brph.com		FL	E M S W C G	A E G I L P S U O	C E K G Hc H I M R Rs Rm Rc S O	
	Bruce Mau Design www.brucemaudesign.com		CAN	E M S W C G	A E G I L P S U O	C E K G Hc H I M R Rs Rm Rc S O	
211	**Bruner/Cott & Associates** www.brunercott.com Bruner/Cott		MA	E M S W C G	A E G I L P S U O	C E K G Hc H I M R Rs Rm Rc S O	
	BSA Architects www.bsaarchitects.com		CA	E M S W C G	A E G I L P S U O	C E K G Hc H I M R Rs Rm Rc S O	
47	**BSA LifeStructures** www.bsals.com		IN	E M S W C G	A E G I L P S U O	C E K G Hc H I M R Rs Rm Rc S O	
254	**Bullock Tice Associates** www.bullocktice.com		FL	E M S W C G	A E G I L P S U O	C E K G Hc H I M R Rs Rm Rc S O	
	Bumpus & Associates www.bumpusandassociates.com		FL	E M S W C G	A E G I L P S U O	C E K G Hc H I M R Rs Rm Rc S O	
	Burgess & Niple www.burgessniple.com		OH	E M S W C G	A E G I L P S U O	C E K G Hc H I M R Rs Rm Rc S O	
	Burke Hogue Mills www.bhm.us.com		FL	E M S W C G	A E G I L P S U O	C E K G Hc H I M R Rs Rm Rc S O	
	Burkett Design www.burkettdesign.com		CO	E M S W C G	A E G I L P S U O	C E K G Hc H I M R Rs Rm Rc S O	
	Burns & McDonnell www.burnsmcd.com		MO	E M S W C G	A E G I L P S U O	C E K G Hc H I M R Rs Rm Rc S O	
	Butler Design Group www.butlerdesigngroup.com		AZ	E M S W C G	A E G I L P S U O	C E K G Hc H I M R Rs Rm Rc S O	

Regions — East (E), Midwest (M), South (S), West (W), Canada (C), Global (G)

Services — Architecture (A), Engineering (E), Graphic Design (G), Interior Design (I), Landscape Architecture (L), Planning (P), Sustainability (S), Urban Design (U), Other-including Industrial Design (O)

Markets — Corporate (C), Higher Ed. (E), K-12 (K), Government (G), Healthcare (Hc), Hospitality (H), Industrial/Tech. (I), Museum/Cultural (M), Religious (R), Residential-Single (Rs), Residential-Multi. (Rm), Retail/Commercial (Rc), Sports (S), Other (O)

Rank	Firm/Web	Size	HQ	Regions	Services	Markets	DI Index
	Butler Rogers Baskett Architects www.brb.com		NY	E M S W C G	A E G I L P S U O	C E K G Hc H I M R Rs Rm Rc S O	
90	**BWBR Architects** B|W|B|R www.bwbr.com		MN	E M S W C G	A E G I L P S U O	C E K G Hc H I M R Rs Rm Rc S O	
C	**C.N. Carley Associates** www.cncarley.com		NH	E M S W C G	A E G I L P S U O	C E K G Hc H I M R Rs Rm Rc S O	
	C.T. Hsu + Associates www.cthsu.com		FL	E M S W C G	A E G I L P S U O	C E K G Hc H I M R Rs Rm Rc S O	
	CADM Architectecture www.cadmarchitects.com		AR	E M S W C G	A E G I L P S U O	C E K G Hc H I M R Rs Rm Rc S O	
38	**Callison** www.callison.com		WA	E M S W C G	A E G I L P S U O	C E K G Hc H I M R Rs Rm Rc S O	
	CAMA www.camainc.com		CT	E M S W C G	A E G I L P S U O	C E K G Hc H I M R Rs Rm Rc S O	
99	**Cambridge Seven Associates** www.c7a.com		MA	E M S W C G	A E G I L P S U O	C E K G Hc H I M R Rs Rm Rc S O	
	Canin Associates www.canin.com		FL	E M S W C G	A E G I L P S U O	C E K G Hc H I M R Rs Rm Rc S O	
9	**Cannon Design** CANNON DESIGN www.cannondesign.com		N/A	E M S W C G	A E G I L P S U O	C E K G Hc H I M R Rs Rm Rc S O	
	Carde Ten Architects www.cardeten.com		CA	E M S W C G	A E G I L P S U O	C E K G Hc H I M R Rs Rm Rc S O	
	Cardinal Hardy Architects www.cardinal-hardy.ca		CAN	E M S W C G	A E G I L P S U O	C E K G Hc H I M R Rs Rm Rc S O	
163	**Carrier Johnson + CULTURE** carrierjohnson + CULTURE www.carrierjohnson.com		CA	E M S W C G	A E G I L P S U O	C E K G Hc H I M R Rs Rm Rc S O	
	Cascade Design Collaborative www.cascadedesigncollab.com		WA	E M S W C G	A E G I L P S U O	C E K G Hc H I M R Rs Rm Rc S O	
	CASCO www.cascocorp.com		MO	E M S W C G	A E G I L P S U O	C E K G Hc H I M R Rs Rm Rc S O	
	Cass | Sowatsky | Chapman + Associates www.csc-a.com		CA	E M S W C G	A E G I L P S U O	C E K G Hc H I M R Rs Rm Rc S O	
	CBLH Design www.cblhdesign.com		OH	E M S W C G	A E G I L P S U O	C E K G Hc H I M R Rs Rm Rc S O	

DI Brand Recognition Index

Top tier global and categorical leader recognition

Notable and growing with emerging categorical recognition

Exceptional national and categorical leader recognition

Professional practice notable in city and region

Strong regional and categorical leader recognition

Rank	Firm/Web	Size	HQ	Regions	Services	Markets	DI Index
	CBT www.cbtarchitects.com	👥👥	MA	E M S W C G	A E G I L P S U O	C E K G Hc H I M R Rs Rm Rc S O	▁▃▁
	CCBG Architects www.ccbg-arch.com	👤	AZ	E M S W C G	A E G I L P S U O	C E K G Hc H I M R Rs Rm Rc S O	▁▃▁
203	**CDH Partners** www.cdhpartners.com	👥👥	GA	E M S W C G	A E G I L P S U O	C E K G Hc H I M R Rs Rm Rc S O	▁▃▁
	CDI Corporation www.cdicorp.com	👥👥	PA	E M S W C G	A E G I L P S U O	C E K G Hc H I M R Rs Rm Rc S O	▁▃▁
	CDS International www.cdsintl.com	👤	HI	E M S W C G	A E G I L P S U O	C E K G Hc H I M R Rs Rm Rc S O	▁▃▁
	Cecil Baker + Partners www.cecilbakerpartners.com	👤	PA	E M S W C G	A E G I L P S U O	C E K G Hc H I M R Rs Rm Rc S O	▁▃▁
	Celli-Flynn Brennan Architects & Planners www.cfbarchitects.com	👤	PA	E M S W C G	A E G I L P S U O	C E K G Hc H I M R Rs Rm Rc S O	▁▃▁
217	**Centerbrook Architects and Planners** www.centerbrook.com	👥👥	CT	E M S W C G	A E G I L P S U O	C E K G Hc H I M R Rs Rm Rc S O	▁▃▅
232	**CetraRuddy** www.cetraruddy.com	👥👥	NY	E M S W C G	A E G I L P S U O	C E K G Hc H I M R Rs Rm Rc S O	▁▃▁
	Chambers, Murphy & Burge Architects www.cmbarchitects.com	👤	OH	E M S W C G	A E G I L P S U O	C E K G Hc H I M R Rs Rm Rc S O	▁▃▁
332	**Champalimaud** www.champalimaudesign.com	👥👥	NY	E M S W C G	A E G I L P S U O	C E K G Hc H I M R Rs Rm Rc S O	▁▃▅▇
	Champlin Architecture www.charchitects.com	👥👥	OH	E M S W C G	A E G I L P S U O	C E K G Hc H I M R Rs Rm Rc S O	▁▃▁
	Charlan Brock & Associates www.cbaarchitects.com	👤	FL	E M S W C G	A E G I L P S U O	C E K G Hc H I M R Rs Rm Rc S O	▁▃▁
	Childs Mascari Warner Architects www.childsmascariwarner.com	👥👥	CA	E M S W C G	A E G I L P S U O	C E K G Hc H I M R Rs Rm Rc S O	▁▃▁
	Chiodini Associates www.chiodini.com	👤	MO	E M S W C G	A E G I L P S U O	C E K G Hc H I M R Rs Rm Rc S O	▁▃▁
	Chipman Design Architecture chipmandesignarch.com	👥👥	IL	E M S W C G	A E G I L P S U O	C E K G Hc H I M R Rs Rm Rc S O	▁▃▁
	Cho Benn Holback + Associates www.cbhassociates.com	👥👥	MD	E M S W C G	A E G I L P S U O	C E K G Hc H I M R Rs Rm Rc S O	▁▃▁

Regions   East (E), Midwest (M), South (S), West (W), Canada (C), Global (G)

Services   Architecture (A), Engineering (E), Graphic Design (G), Interior Design (I), Landscape Architecture (L), Planning (P), Sustainability (S), Urban Design (U), Other-including Industrial Design (O)

Markets   Corporate (C), Higher Ed. (E), K-12 (K), Government (G), Healthcare (Hc), Hospitality (H), Industrial/Tech. (I), Museum/Cultural (M), Religious (R), Residential-Single (Rs), Residential-Multi. (Rm), Retail/Commercial (Rc), Sports (S), Other (O)

Rank	Firm/Web	Size	HQ	Regions	Services	Markets	DI Index
	Christner www.christnerinc.com	👥	MO	E M S W C G	A E G I L P S U O	C E K G Hc H I M R Rs Rm Rc S O	.il..
	Cibinel Architects www.cibinel.com	👤	CAN	E M S W C G	A E G I L P S U O	C E K G Hc H I M R Rs Rm Rc S O	.il..
	City Architecture www.cityarch.com	👥	OH	E M S W C G	A E G I L P S U O	C E K G Hc H I M R Rs Rm Rc S O	.il..
	CJS Group Architects www.cjsgrouparchitects.com	👤	HI	E M S W C G	A E G I L P S U O	C E K G Hc H I M R Rs Rm Rc S O	.il..
32	**Clark Nexsen** www.clarknexsen.com	👥👥👥	VA	E M S W C G	A E G I L P S U O	C E K G Hc H I M R Rs Rm Rc S O	.iil.
	CLC Associates www.clcassoc.com	👥	CO	E M S W C G	A E G I L P S U O	C E K G Hc H I M R Rs Rm Rc S O	.il..
168	**CMA** www.cmarch.com	👥👥	MN	E M S W C G	A E G I L P S U O	C E K G Hc H I M R Rs Rm Rc S O	.il..
	CMSS Architects www.cmssarchitects.com	👥	VA	E M S W C G	A E G I L P S U O	C E K G Hc H I M R Rs Rm Rc S O	.il..
95	**CO Architects** www.coarchitects.com	👥	CA	E M S W C G	A E G I L P S U O	C E K G Hc H I M R Rs Rm Rc S O	.il..
	Colimore Thoemke Architects www.colimorethoemke.com	👤	MD	E M S W C G	A E G I L P S U O	C E K G Hc H I M R Rs Rm Rc S O	.il..
	Collaborative Design Group www.collaborativedesigngroup.com	👥	MN	E M S W C G	A E G I L P S U O	C E K G Hc H I M R Rs Rm Rc S O	.il..
	Collective Invention www.collectiveinvention.com	👤	CA	E M S W C G	A E G I L P S U O	C E K G Hc H I M R Rs Rm Rc S O	.il..
	CollinsWoerman www.collinswoerman.com	👥	WA	E M S W C G	A E G I L P S U O	C E K G Hc H I M R Rs Rm Rc S O	.il..
	Colorado Architecture Partnership www.cyberarchitects.com	👤	CO	E M S W C G	A E G I L P S U O	C E K G Hc H I M R Rs Rm Rc S O	.il..
249	**Cook + Fox Architects** www.cookplusfox.com	👥	NY	E M S W C G	A E G I L P S U O	C E K G Hc H I M R Rs Rm Rc S O	.iil.
58	**Cooper Carry** www.coopercarry.com	👥👥👥	GA	E M S W C G	A E G I L P S U O	C E K G Hc H I M R Rs Rm Rc S O	.iil.
201	**Cooper, Robertson & Partners** www.cooperrobertson.com	👥	NY	E M S W C G	A E G I L P S U O	C E K G Hc H I M R Rs Rm Rc S O	.iil.

DI Brand Recognition Index

.iiil	Top tier global and categorical leader recognition
.iil	Exceptional national and categorical leader recognition
.il.	Strong regional and categorical leader recognition
.l__	Notable and growing with emerging categorical recognition
.___	Professional practice notable in city and region

Rank	Firm/Web	Size	HQ	Regions	Services	Markets	DI Index
	Corbin Design www.corbindesign.com	♟	MI	E M S W C G	A E G I L P S U O	C E K G Hc H I M R Rs Rm Rc S O	▂▃▄▅
	Cordogan, Clark and Associates www.cordoganclark.com	♟♟	IL	E M S W C G	A E G I L P S U O	C E K G Hc H I M R Rs Rm Rc S O	▂▃▁▁
	CORE Architecture + Design www.coredc.com	♟	DC	E M S W C G	A E G I L P S U O	C E K G Hc H I M R Rs Rm Rc S O	▂▃▁▁
29	**Corgan Associates** www.corgan.com	♟♟♟	TX	E M S W C G	A E G I L P S U O	C E K G Hc H I M R Rs Rm Rc S O	▂▃▁▁
	Crabtree, Rohrbaugh & Associates www.cra-architects.com	♟♟	PA	E M S W C G	A E G I L P S U O	C E K G Hc H I M R Rs Rm Rc S O	▂▃▄▁
	CR Architecture + Design www.cr-architects.com	♟♟	OH	E M S W C G	A E G I L P S U O	C E K G Hc H I M R Rs Rm Rc S O	▂▃▁▁
	Crafton Tull Sparks www.craftontullsparks.com	♟♟♟	AR	E M S W C G	A E G I L P S U O	C E K G Hc H I M R Rs Rm Rc S O	▂▃▄▁
	Craig Gaulden Davis www.cgdarch.com	♟	SC	E M S W C G	A E G I L P S U O	C E K G Hc H I M R Rs Rm Rc S O	▂▃▄▁
274	**Crawford Architects** www.crawfordarch.com	♟	MO	E M S W C G	A E G I L P S U O	C E K G Hc H I M R Rs Rm Rc S O	▂▃▄▁
107	**Cromwell Architects Engineers** www.cromwell.com	♟♟♟	AR	E M S W C G	A E G I L P S U O	C E K G Hc H I M R Rs Rm Rc S O	▂▃▄▁
	CSHQA www.cshqa.com	♟♟	ID	E M S W C G	A E G I L P S U O	C E K G Hc H I M R Rs Rm Rc S O	▂▃▄▁
	CSO Architects www.csoinc.net	♟♟	IN	E M S W C G	A E G I L P S U O	C E K G Hc H I M R Rs Rm Rc S O	▂▃▄▁
54	**CTA Architects Engineers** www.ctagroup.com	♟♟♟	MT	E M S W C G	A E G I L P S U O	C E K G Hc H I M R Rs Rm Rc S O	▂▃▄▅
	Cuhaci & Peterson www.c-p.com	♟♟	FL	E M S W C G	A E G I L P S U O	C E K G Hc H I M R Rs Rm Rc S O	▂▃▄▁
49	**Cuningham Group Architecture** www.cuningham.com	♟♟♟	MN	E M S W C G	A E G I L P S U O	C E K G Hc H I M R Rs Rm Rc S O	▂▃▄▅
	Cunningham I Quill Architects www.cunninghamquill.com	♟♟	DC	E M S W C G	A E G I L P S U O	C E K G Hc H I M R Rs Rm Rc S O	▂▃▄▁
	Cutler Associates www.cutlerassociatesinc.com	♟♟♟	MA	E M S W C G	A E G I L P S U O	C E K G Hc H I M R Rs Rm Rc S O	▂▃▄▁

Regions East (E), Midwest (M), South (S), West (W), Canada (C), Global (G)

Services Architecture (A), Engineering (E), Graphic Design (G), Interior Design (I), Landscape Architecture (L), Planning (P), Sustainability (S), Urban Design (U), Other-including Industrial Design (O)

Markets Corporate (C), Higher Ed. (E), K-12 (K), Government (G), Healthcare (Hc), Hospitality (H), Industrial/Tech. (I), Museum/Cultural (M), Religious (R), Residential-Single (Rs), Residential-Multi. (Rm), Retail/Commercial (Rc), Sports (S), Other (O)

Rank	Firm/Web	Size	HQ	Regions	Services	Markets	DI Index
D	**D2CA Architects** www.d2ca.com	👤	PA	E M S W C G	A E G I L P S U O	C E K G Hc H I M R Rs Rm Rc S O	▪ll_
	DAG Architects www.dagarchitects.com	👥	FL	E M S W C G	A E G I L P S U O	C E K G Hc H I M R Rs Rm Rc S O	▪ll_
	Dahlin Group www.dahlingroup.com	👥👤	CA	E M S W C G	A E G I L P S U O	C E K G Hc H I M R Rs Rm Rc S O	▪ll_
	Daly Genik www.dalygenik.com	👤	CA	E M S W C G	A E G I L P S U O	C E K G Hc H I M R Rs Rm Rc S O	▪lll_
322	**Daniel P. Coffey & Associates** www.dpcaltd.com	👥	IL	E M S W C G	A E G I L P S U O	C E K G Hc H I M R Rs Rm Rc S O	▪ll_
	Daniel Smith & Associates www.dsaarch.com	👤	CA	E M S W C G	A E G I L P S U O	C E K G Hc H I M R Rs Rm Rc S O	▪ll_
	Danielian Assoicates www.danielian.com	👥	CA	E M S W C G	A E G I L P S U O	C E K G Hc H I M R Rs Rm Rc S O	▪ll_
172	**Dattner Architects** www.dattner.com	👥	NY	E M S W C G	A E G I L P S U O	C E K G Hc H I M R Rs Rm Rc S O	▪ll_
	David M. Schwarz Architects www.dmsas.com	👥	DC	E M S W C G	A E G I L P S U O	C E K G Hc H I M R Rs Rm Rc S O	▪lll_
	David Oakey Designs www.davidoakeydesigns.com	👤	GA	E M S W C G	A E G I L P S U O	C E K G Hc H I M R Rs Rm Rc S O	▪lll_
	Davis www.thedavisexperience.com	👥	AZ	E M S W C G	A E G I L P S U O	C E K G Hc H I M R Rs Rm Rc S O	▪ll_
	Davis Brody Bond Aedus www.davisbrody.com	👥	NY	E M S W C G	A E G I L P S U O	C E K G Hc H I M R Rs Rm Rc S O	▪llll
144	**Davis Carter Scott** www.dcsdesign.com	👥	VA	E M S W C G	A E G I L P S U O	C E K G Hc H I M R Rs Rm Rc S O	▪ll_
88	**Davis Partnership Architects** www.davispartner.com	👥	CO	E M S W C G	A E G I L P S U O	C E K G Hc H I M R Rs Rm Rc S O	▪ll_
141	**Dekker/Perich/Sabatini** www.dpsdesign.org	👥👤	NM	E M S W C G	A E G I L P S U O	C E K G Hc H I M R Rs Rm Rc S O	▪ll_
159	**DES Architects + Engineers** www.des-ae.com	👥👤	CA	E M S W C G	A E G I L P S U O	C E K G Hc H I M R Rs Rm Rc S O	▪ll_
	Design Alliance Architects, The www.tda-architects.com	👥	PA	E M S W C G	A E G I L P S U O	C E K G Hc H I M R Rs Rm Rc S O	▪ll_

DI Brand Recognition Index

▪llll Top tier global and categorical leader recognition

▪lll_ Exceptional national and categorical leader recognition

▪ll_ Strong regional and categorical leader recognition

▪l___ Notable and growing with emerging categorical recognition

▪____ Professional practice notable in city and region

Rank	Firm/Web	Size	HQ	Regions	Services	Markets	DI Index
	Design Collective www.designcollective.com	♦♦♦	MD	E M S W C G	A E G I L P S U O	C E K G Hc H I M R Rs Rm Rc S O	
	Design Development www.designdevelopment.com	♦	NC	E M S W C G	A E G I L P S U O	C E K G Hc H I M R Rs Rm Rc S O	
	DesignGroup www.dgcolumbus.com	♦♦	OH	E M S W C G	A E G I L P S U O	C E K G Hc H I M R Rs Rm Rc S O	
	Design Partners www.designpartnersinc.com	♦	HI	E M S W C G	A E G I L P S U O	C E K G Hc H I M R Rs Rm Rc S O	
309	**Design Partnership of Cambridge** www.design-partnership.com	♦♦	MA	E M S W C G	A E G I L P S U O	C E K G Hc H I M R Rs Rm Rc S O	
193	**Design Workshop** www.designworkshop.com	♦♦	CO	E M S W C G	A E G I L P S U O	C E K G Hc H I M R Rs Rm Rc S O	
234	**Development Design Group** www.ddg-usa.com	♦♦	MD	E M S W C G	A E G I L P S U O	C E K G Hc H I M R Rs Rm Rc S O	
158	**Devenney Group Architects** www.devenneygroup.com	♦♦	AZ	E M S W C G	A E G I L P S U O	C E K G Hc H I M R Rs Rm Rc S O	
	Devrouax & Purnell Architects www.dp-architects.com	♦♦	DC	E M S W C G	A E G I L P S U O	C E K G Hc H I M R Rs Rm Rc S O	
22	**Dewberry (Architecture)** www.dewberry.com	♦♦♦♦♦	VA	E M S W C G	A E G I L P S U O	C E K G Hc H I M R Rs Rm Rc S O	
	Dialog www.designdialog.com	♦♦♦	CAN	E M S W C G	A E G I L P S U O	C E K G Hc H I M R Rs Rm Rc S O	
	Diamond + Schmitt www.dsai.ca	♦♦♦	CAN	E M S W C G	A E G I L P S U O	C E K G Hc H I M R Rs Rm Rc S O	
	Dick & Fritsche Design Group www.dfdg.com	♦♦	AZ	E M S W C G	A E G I L P S U O	C E K G Hc H I M R Rs Rm Rc S O	
	DiClemente Siegel Design www.dsdonline.com	♦	MI	E M S W C G	A E G I L P S U O	C E K G Hc H I M R Rs Rm Rc S O	
	Diedrich www.diedrichllc.com	♦	GA	E M S W C G	A E G I L P S U O	C E K G Hc H I M R Rs Rm Rc S O	
	Diekema Hamann Architecture + Engineering www.dhae.com	♦	MI	E M S W C G	A E G I L P S U O	C E K G Hc H I M R Rs Rm Rc S O	
289	**DiGiorgio Associates** www.dai-boston.com	♦♦	MA	E M S W C G	A E G I L P S U O	C E K G Hc H I M R Rs Rm Rc S O	

Regions East (E), Midwest (M), South (S), West (W), Canada (C), Global (G)

Services Architecture (A), Engineering (E), Graphic Design (G), Interior Design (I), Landscape Architecture (L), Planning (P), Sustainability (S), Urban Design (U), Other-including Industrial Design (O)

Markets Corporate (C), Higher Ed. (E), K-12 (K), Government (G), Healthcare (Hc), Hospitality (H), Industrial/Tech. (I), Museum/Cultural (M), Religious (R), Residential-Single (Rs), Residential-Multi. (Rm), Retail/Commercial (Rc), Sports (S), Other (O)

Kings County Superior Court, New Hansford Courthouse, Hansford, CA I DLR Group

Intern Joplin High School, Joplin, MO I DLR Group

Rank	Firm/Web	Size	HQ	Regions	Services	Markets	DI Index
271	**DiMella Shaffer** www.dimellashaffer.com	👥	MA	E M S W C G	A E G I L P S U O	C E K G Hc H I M R Rs Rm Rc S O	
	Dinmore and Cisco Architects www.konaarchitects.com	👤	HI	E M S W C G	A E G I L P S U O	C E K G Hc H I M R Rs Rm Rc S O	
21	**DLR Group** www.dlrgroup.com	👥👥	N/A	E M S W C G	A E G I L P S U O	C E K G Hc H I M R Rs Rm Rc S O	
	DMR www.dmrarchitects.com	👤	NJ	E M S W C G	A E G I L P S U O	C E K G Hc H I M R Rs Rm Rc S O	
	DNK Architects www.dnkarchitects.com	👤	OH	E M S W C G	A E G I L P S U O	C E K G Hc H I M R Rs Rm Rc S O	
	Domenech Hicks & Krockmalnic Architects www.dhkinc.com	👤	MA	E M S W C G	A E G I L P S U O	C E K G Hc H I M R Rs Rm Rc S O	
	Dominy + Associates Architects www.domusstudio.com	👤	CA	E M S W C G	A E G I L P S U O	C E K G Hc H I M R Rs Rm Rc S O	
	Domokur Architects www.domokur.com	👤	OH	E M S W C G	A E G I L P S U O	C E K G Hc H I M R Rs Rm Rc S O	
	Dorsky Yue Architects www.dorskyyue.com	👥	OH	E M S W C G	A E G I L P S U O	C E K G Hc H I M R Rs Rm Rc S O	
315	**Dougherty + Dougherty Architects** www.ddarchitecture.com	👥	CA	E M S W C G	A E G I L P S U O	C E K G Hc H I M R Rs Rm Rc S O	
	Douglas Cardinal Architect www.djcarchitect.com	👤	CAN	E M S W C G	A E G I L P S U O	C E K G Hc H I M R Rs Rm Rc S O	
	Dowler-Gruman Architects www.dgaonline.com	👤	CA	E M S W C G	A E G I L P S U O	C E K G Hc H I M R Rs Rm Rc S O	
	DRS Architects www.drsarchitects.com	👥	PA	E M S W C G	A E G I L P S U O	C E K G Hc H I M R Rs Rm Rc S O	
	Drummey Rosane Anderson www.draarchitects.com	👥	MA	E M S W C G	A E G I L P S U O	C E K G Hc H I M R Rs Rm Rc S O	
	DTJ Design www.dtjdesign.com	👥	CO	E M S W C G	A E G I L P S U O	C E K G Hc H I M R Rs Rm Rc S O	
	Duany Plater-Zyberk & Company (DPZ) www.dpz.com	👥	FL	E M S W C G	A E G I L P S U O	C E K G Hc H I M R Rs Rm Rc S O	
	Dubbe-Moulder Architects www.dubbe-moulder.com	👤	WY	E M S W C G	A E G I L P S U O	C E K G Hc H I M R Rs Rm Rc S O	

Regions East (E), Midwest (M), South (S), West (W), Canada (C), Global (G)

Services Architecture (A), Engineering (E), Graphic Design (G), Interior Design (I), Landscape Architecture (L), Planning (P), Sustainability (S), Urban Design (U), Other-including Industrial Design (O)

Markets Corporate (C), Higher Ed. (E), K-12 (K), Government (G), Healthcare (Hc), Hospitality (H), Industrial/Tech. (I), Museum/Cultural (M), Religious (R), Residential-Single (Rs), Residential-Multi. (Rm), Retail/Commercial (Rc), Sports (S), Other (O)

Renovation of Hugh Newell Jacobsen House, Nantucket, MA | Dujardin Design Associates

Rank	Firm/Web	Size	HQ	Regions	Services	Markets	DI Index
	Dujardin Design Associates www.dujardindesign.com	👤	CT	E M S W C G	A E G I L P S U O	C E K G Hc H I M R Rs Rm Rc S O	
	Dull Olson Weekes Architects www.dowa.com	👥	OR	E M S W C G	A E G I L P S U O	C E K G Hc H I M R Rs Rm Rc S O	
	DWL Architects + Planners www.dwlarchitects.com	👥	AZ	E M S W C G	A E G I L P S U O	C E K G Hc H I M R Rs Rm Rc S O	
	Dykeman Architects www.dykeman.net	👥	WA	E M S W C G	A E G I L P S U O	C E K G Hc H I M R Rs Rm Rc S O	
E	**Eckert Wordell** www.eckert-wordell.com	👥	MI	E M S W C G	A E G I L P S U O	C E K G Hc H I M R Rs Rm Rc S O	
	EDG Interior Architecture & Design www.edgdesign.com	👥	CA	E M S W C G	A E G I L P S U O	C E K G Hc H I M R Rs Rm Rc S O	
	Edge & Tinney Architects www.edge-tinney.com	👤	OH	E M S W C G	A E G I L P S U O	C E K G Hc H I M R Rs Rm Rc S O	
150	**EDI International** www.ediarchitecture.com	👥👥	TX	E M S W C G	A E G I L P S U O	C E K G Hc H I M R Rs Rm Rc S O	
66	**EDSA** www.edsaplan.com	👥👥	FL	E M S W C G	A E G I L P S U O	C E K G Hc H I M R Rs Rm Rc S O	
	Edwards + Hotchkiss Architects www.eandharch.com	👤	TN	E M S W C G	A E G I L P S U O	C E K G Hc H I M R Rs Rm Rc S O	
	EHDD www.ehdd.com	👥	CA	E M S W C G	A E G I L P S U O	C E K G Hc H I M R Rs Rm Rc S O	
	Eight, Inc. www.eightinc.com	👥	CA	E M S W C G	A E G I L P S U O	C E K G Hc H I M R Rs Rm Rc S O	
	Eisenman Architects www.eisenmanarchitects.com	👥	NY	E M S W C G	A E G I L P S U O	C E K G Hc H I M R Rs Rm Rc S O	
87	**Elkus Manfredi Architects** www.elkus-manfredi.com	👥👥	MA	E M S W C G	A E G I L P S U O	C E K G Hc H I M R Rs Rm Rc S O	
275	**Ellenzweig** www.ellenzweig.com	👥	MA	E M S W C G	A E G I L P S U O	C E K G Hc H I M R Rs Rm Rc S O	
256	**Elness Swenson Graham Architects** www.esgarch.com	👥	MN	E M S W C G	A E G I L P S U O	C E K G Hc H I M R Rs Rm Rc S O	
331	**Emc2 Group Architects** www.emc2architects.com	👤	AZ	E M S W C G	A E G I L P S U O	C E K G Hc H I M R Rs Rm Rc S O	

Regions East (E), Midwest (M), South (S), West (W), Canada (C), Global (G)

Services Architecture (A), Engineering (E), Graphic Design (G), Interior Design (I), Landscape Architecture (L), Planning (P), Sustainability (S), Urban Design (U), Other-including Industrial Design (O)

Markets Corporate (C), Higher Ed. (E), K-12 (K), Government (G), Healthcare (Hc), Hospitality (H), Industrial/Tech. (I), Museum/Cultural (M), Religious (R), Residential-Single (Rs), Residential-Multi. (Rm), Retail/Commercial (Rc), Sports (S), Other (O)

Quad 3, architects; Rich Waters Photography

Eat'n Park: Hello Bistro, Pittsburgh, PA | Fathom

Rank	Firm/Web	Size	HQ	Regions	Services	Markets	DI Index
	Emersion Design www.emersiondesign.com		OH	E M S W C G	A E G I L P S U O	C E K G Hc H I M R Rs Rm Rc S O	
226	**Engberg Anderson** www.engberganderson.com		WI	E M S W C G	A E G I L P S U O	C E K G Hc H I M R Rs Rm Rc S O	
37	**Ennead Architects** www.ennead.com		NY	E M S W C G	A E G I L P S U O	C E K G Hc H I M R Rs Rm Rc S O	
	ENTOS Design www.entosdesign.com		TX	E M S W C G	A E G I L P S U O	C E K G Hc H I M R Rs Rm Rc S O	
194	**Environetics** www.environetics.com		CA	E M S W C G	A E G I L P S U O	C E K G Hc H I M R Rs Rm Rc S O	
	Envision Design www.envisionsite.com		DC	E M S W C G	A E G I L P S U O	C E K G Hc H I M R Rs Rm Rc S O	
	Eppstein Uhen Architects www.eua.com		WI	E M S W C G	A E G I L P S U O	C E K G Hc H I M R Rs Rm Rc S O	
146	**Epstein** www.epsteinglobal.com		IL	E M S W C G	A E G I L P S U O	C E K G Hc H I M R Rs Rm Rc S O	
	ESI Design www.esidesign.com		NY	E M S W C G	A E G I L P S U O	C E K G Hc H I M R Rs Rm Rc S O	
219	**Eskew+Dumez+Ripple** www.eskewdumezripple.com		LA	E M S W C G	A E G I L P S U O	C E K G Hc H I M R Rs Rm Rc S O	
	ESP Associates www.espassociates.com		NC	E M S W C G	A E G I L P S U O	C E K G Hc H I M R Rs Rm Rc S O	
	Evans Group, The www.theevansgroup.com		FL	E M S W C G	A E G I L P S U O	C E K G Hc H I M R Rs Rm Rc S O	
33	**EwingCole** www.ewingcole.com		PA	E M S W C G	A E G I L P S U O	C E K G Hc H I M R Rs Rm Rc S O	
30	**EYP Architecture & Engineering** www.eypaedesign.com		NY	E M S W C G	A E G I L P S U O	C E K G Hc H I M R Rs Rm Rc S O	
F	**Facility Design Group** www.facilitygroup.com		GA	E M S W C G	A E G I L P S U O	C E K G Hc H I M R Rs Rm Rc S O	
68	**Fanning/Howey Associates** www.fhai.com		OH	E M S W C G	A E G I L P S U O	C E K G Hc H I M R Rs Rm Rc S O	
	Fathom www.gofathom.com		PA	E M S W C G	A E G I L P S U O	C E K G Hc H I M R Rs Rm Rc S O	

Regions East (E), Midwest (M), South (S), West (W), Canada (C), Global (G)

Services Architecture (A), Engineering (E), Graphic Design (G), Interior Design (I), Landscape Architecture (L), Planning (P), Sustainability (S), Urban Design (U), Other-including Industrial Design (O)

Markets Corporate (C), Higher Ed. (E), K-12 (K), Government (G), Healthcare (Hc), Hospitality (H), Industrial/Tech. (I), Museum/Cultural (M), Religious (R), Residential-Single (Rs), Residential-Multi. (Rm), Retail/Commercial (Rc), Sports (S), Other (O)

Jason A. Knowles © Fentress Architects

Sanford Consortium for Regenerative Medicine-West Facade, La Jolla CA | Fentress

Rank	Firm/Web	Size	HQ	Regions	Services	Markets	DI Index
31	**Fentress Architects** www.fentressarchitects.com		CO	E M S W C G	A E G I L P S U O	C E K G Hc H I M R Rs Rm Rc S O	
	Fergus Garber Group www.fgg-arch.com		CA	E M S W C G	A E G I L P S U O	C E K G Hc H I M R Rs Rm Rc S O	
	Ferguson Pape Baldwin Architects www.mbarch.com		CA	E M S W C G	A E G I L P S U O	C E K G Hc H I M R Rs Rm Rc S O	
	Ferguson & Shamamian Architects www.fergusonshamamian.com		NY	E M S W C G	A E G I L P S U O	C E K G Hc H I M R Rs Rm Rc S O	
314	**Ferraro Choi and Associates** www.ferrarochoi.com		HI	E M S W C G	A E G I L P S U O	C E K G Hc H I M R Rs Rm Rc S O	
92	**FFKR Architects** www.ffkr.com		UT	E M S W C G	A E G I L P S U O	C E K G Hc H I M R Rs Rm Rc S O	
	FGM Architects www.fgmarchitects.com		IL	E M S W C G	A E G I L P S U O	C E K G Hc H I M R Rs Rm Rc S O	
260	**Field Paoli Architects** www.fieldpaoli.com		CA	E M S W C G	A E G I L P S U O	C E K G Hc H I M R Rs Rm Rc S O	
	Finegold Alexander + Associates www.faainc.com		MA	E M S W C G	A E G I L P S U O	C E K G Hc H I M R Rs Rm Rc S O	
	FitzGerald Associates Architects www.fitzgeraldassociates.net		IL	E M S W C G	A E G I L P S U O	C E K G Hc H I M R Rs Rm Rc S O	
51	**FKP Architects** www.fkp.com		TX	E M S W C G	A E G I L P S U O	C E K G Hc H I M R Rs Rm Rc S O	
44	**Flad Architects** www.flad.com		WI	E M S W C G	A E G I L P S U O	C E K G Hc H I M R Rs Rm Rc S O	
296	**Flansburgh Architects** www.faiarchitects.com		MA	E M S W C G	A E G I L P S U O	C E K G Hc H I M R Rs Rm Rc S O	
	Fletcher Farr Ayotte www.ffadesign.com		OR	E M S W C G	A E G I L P S U O	C E K G Hc H I M R Rs Rm Rc S O	
160	**Fletcher Thompson** www.fletcherthompson.com		CT	E M S W C G	A E G I L P S U O	C E K G Hc H I M R Rs Rm Rc S O	
	Flewelling & Moody www.flewelling-moody.com		CA	E M S W C G	A E G I L P S U O	C E K G Hc H I M R Rs Rm Rc S O	
	Ford Powell & Carson www.fpcarch.com		TX	E M S W C G	A E G I L P S U O	C E K G Hc H I M R Rs Rm Rc S O	

Regions   East (E), Midwest (M), South (S), West (W), Canada (C), Global (G)

Services   Architecture (A), Engineering (E), Graphic Design (G), Interior Design (I), Landscape Architecture (L), Planning (P), Sustainability (S), Urban Design (U), Other-including Industrial Design (O)

Markets   Corporate (C), Higher Ed. (E), K-12 (K), Government (G), Healthcare (Hc), Hospitality (H), Industrial/Tech. (I), Museum/Cultural (M), Religious (R), Residential-Single (Rs), Residential-Multi. (Rm), Retail/Commercial (Rc), Sports (S), Other (O)

Rank	Firm/Web	Size	HQ	Regions		Services		Markets		DI Index
	Foreman Architects Engineers www.foremangroup.com	👥	PA	E M S W C G		A E G I L P S U O		C E K G Hc H I M R Rs Rm Rc S O		▂▃▁
	Forum Architecture & Interior Design www.forumarchitecture.com	👤	FL	E M S W C G		A E G I L P S U O		C E K G Hc H I M R Rs Rm Rc S O		▂▃▁
233	**Forum Studio** www.forumstudio.com	👥	MO	E M S W C G		A E G I L P S U O		C E K G Hc H I M R Rs Rm Rc S O		▄▅▃
	Foss Architecture & Interiors www.fossarch.com	👤	ND	E M S W C G		A E G I L P S U O		C E K G Hc H I M R Rs Rm Rc S O		▂▃▁
205	**FOX Architects** www.fox-architects.com	👥	VA	E M S W C G		A E G I L P S U O		C E K G Hc H I M R Rs Rm Rc S O		▄▅▃
100	**Francis Cauffman** Francis Cauffman www.franciscauffman.com	👥👥	PA	E M S W C G		A E G I L P S U O		C E K G Hc H I M R Rs Rm Rc S O		▃▄▂
	Frankel + Coleman www.frankelcoleman.com	👤	IL	E M S W C G		A E G I L P S U O		C E K G Hc H I M R Rs Rm Rc S O		▄▅▃
	Franklin Associates Architects www.franklinarch.com	👥	TN	E M S W C G		A E G I L P S U O		C E K G Hc H I M R Rs Rm Rc S O		▂▃▁
147	**FRCH Design Worldwide** FRCH www.frch.com	👥👥	OH	E M S W C G		A E G I L P S U O		C E K G Hc H I M R Rs Rm Rc S O		▄▅▃
	Frederick+ Frederick Architects www.f-farchitects.com	👤	SC	E M S W C G		A E G I L P S U O		C E K G Hc H I M R Rs Rm Rc S O		▂▃▁
	Freelon Group, The FREELON www.freelon.com	👥	NC	E M S W C G		A E G I L P S U O		C E K G Hc H I M R Rs Rm Rc S O		▄▅▆
140	**FreemanWhite** FreemanWhite www.freemanwhite.com	👥	NC	E M S W C G		A E G I L P S U O		C E K G Hc H I M R Rs Rm Rc S O		▄▅▃
	Freiheit & Ho Architects www.fhoarch.com	👤	WA	E M S W C G		A E G I L P S U O		C E K G Hc H I M R Rs Rm Rc S O		▂▃▁
	French Associates www.frenchaia.com	👥	MI	E M S W C G		A E G I L P S U O		C E K G Hc H I M R Rs Rm Rc S O		▂▃▁
	French + Ryan www.frenchryan.com	👤	DE	E M S W C G		A E G I L P S U O		C E K G Hc H I M R Rs Rm Rc S O		▂▃▁
	Friedmutter Group www.friedmuttergroup.com	👥👥	NV	E M S W C G		A E G I L P S U O		C E K G Hc H I M R Rs Rm Rc S O		▂▃▁
	Fugleberg Koch www.fuglebergkoch.com	👤	FL	E M S W C G		A E G I L P S U O		C E K G Hc H I M R Rs Rm Rc S O		▂▃▁

DI Brand Recognition Index

▅▆▇ Top tier global and categorical leader recognition

▃▄▅ Exceptional national and categorical leader recognition

▂▃▄ Strong regional and categorical leader recognition

▂▁▁ Notable and growing with emerging categorical recognition

▁▁▁ Professional practice notable in city and region

Rank	Firm/Web	Size	HQ	Regions	Services	Markets	DI Index
235	**FWAJDB** www.fwajdb.com	👥	GA	E M S W C G	A E G I L P S U O	C E K G Hc H I M R Rs Rm Rc S O	▂▃▄
80	**FXFOWLE Architects** FXFOWLE www.fxfowle.com	👥👥	NY	E M S W C G	A E G I L P S U O	C E K G Hc H I M R Rs Rm Rc S O	▂▃▄▅
G / 325	**Gantt Huberman Architects** GHA www.gantthuberman.com	👥	NC	E M S W C G	A E G I L P S U O	C E K G Hc H I M R Rs Rm Rc S O	4 ▂▃
	Garcia Stromberg www.garciastromberg.com	👤	FL	E M S W C G	A E G I L P S U O	C E K G Hc H I M R Rs Rm Rc S O	▂▃▁
	Gaudreau www.gaudreauinc.com	👤	MD	E M S W C G	A E G I L P S U O	C E K G Hc H I M R Rs Rm Rc S O	▂▃▁
	Gauthier, Alvarado & Associates www.gaa-ae.com	👥	VA	E M S W C G	A E G I L P S U O	C E K G Hc H I M R Rs Rm Rc S O	▂▃▁
	Gawron Turgeon Architects www.gawronturgeon.com	👤	ME	E M S W C G	A E G I L P S U O	C E K G Hc H I M R Rs Rm Rc S O	▂▃▁
86	**GBBN Architects** GBBN architects www.gbbn.com	👥👥	OH	E M S W C G	A E G I L P S U O	C E K G Hc H I M R Rs Rm Rc S O	▂▃▄▅
	GBD Architects www.gbdarchitects.com	👥	OR	E M S W C G	A E G I L P S U O	C E K G Hc H I M R Rs Rm Rc S O	▂▃▁
134	**Gehry Partners** www.foga.com	👥👥	CA	E M S W C G	A E G I L P S U O	C E K G Hc H I M R Rs Rm Rc S O	▂▃▄▅
1	**Gensler** Gensler www.gensler.com	👥👥	CA	E M S W C G	A E G I L P S U O	C E K G Hc H I M R Rs Rm Rc S O	▂▃▄▅
206	**GGLO** www.gglo.com	👥	WA	E M S W C G	A E G I L P S U O	C E K G Hc H I M R Rs Rm Rc S O	▂▃▄
	GH2 Architects www.gh2.com	👥	OK	E M S W C G	A E G I L P S U O	C E K G Hc H I M R Rs Rm Rc S O	▂▃▁
50	**GHAFARI** GHAFARI www.ghafari.com	👥👥	MI	E M S W C G	A E G I L P S U O	C E K G Hc H I M R Rs Rm Rc S O	▂▃▄▅
	Gibbs Gage Architects Gibbs Gage www.gibbsgage.com	👥👥	CAN	E M S W C G	A E G I L P S U O	C E K G Hc H I M R Rs Rm Rc S O	▂▃▁
	Giffin Bolte Jurgens www.gbjarch.com	👤	OR	E M S W C G	A E G I L P S U O	C E K G Hc H I M R Rs Rm Rc S O	▂▃▁
320	**Gilmore Group** www.gilmoregroup.com	👥	NY	E M S W C G	A E G I L P S U O	C E K G Hc H I M R Rs Rm Rc S O	▂▃▁

Regions East (E), Midwest (M), South (S), West (W), Canada (C), Global (G)

Services Architecture (A), Engineering (E), Graphic Design (G), Interior Design (I), Landscape Architecture (L), Planning (P), Sustainability (S), Urban Design (U), Other-including Industrial Design (O)

Markets Corporate (C), Higher Ed. (E), K-12 (K), Government (G), Healthcare (Hc), Hospitality (H), Industrial/Tech. (I), Museum/Cultural (M), Religious (R), Residential-Single (Rs), Residential-Multi. (Rm), Retail/Commercial (Rc), Sports (S), Other (O)

Rank	Firm/Web	Size	HQ	Regions		Services		Markets		DI Index
91	**gkkworks** www.gkkworks.com	†††	CA	E M S W C G		A E G I L P S U O		C E K G Hc H I M R Rs Rm Rc S O		.ıll
	Glidden Spina & Partners www.gsp-architects.com	†	FL	E M S W C G		A E G I L P S U O		C E K G Hc H I M R Rs Rm Rc S O		.ıl..
	Godsey Associates Architects www.godseyassociates.com	†	KY	E M S W C G		A E G I L P S U O		C E K G Hc H I M R Rs Rm Rc S O		.ıl.
104	**Goettsch Partners** www.gpchicago.com	††	IL	E M S W C G		A E G I L P S U O		C E K G Hc H I M R Rs Rm Rc S O		.ıll
161	**Good Fulton & Farrell** www.gff.com	††	TX	E M S W C G		A E G I L P S U O		C E K G Hc H I M R Rs Rm Rc S O		.ıll
189	**Goodwyn, Mills & Cawood** www.gmcnetwork.com	†††	AL	E M S W C G		A E G I L P S U O		C E K G Hc H I M R Rs Rm Rc S O		.ıl.
113	**Goody Clancy** www.goodyclancy.com	††	MA	E M S W C G		A E G I L P S U O		C E K G Hc H I M R Rs Rm Rc S O		.ıll
	Goshow Architects www.goshow.com	††	NY	E M S W C G		A E G I L P S U O		C E K G Hc H I M R Rs Rm Rc S O		.ıl.
120	**Gould Evans** www.gouldevans.com	†††	MO	E M S W C G		A E G I L P S U O		C E K G Hc H I M R Rs Rm Rc S O		.ıll
	Graham Landscape Architecture www.grahamlandarch.com	†	MD	E M S W C G		A E G I L P S U O		C E K G Hc H I M R Rs Rm Rc S O		.ıl.
	Grant & Sinclair Architects www.grantandsinclair.ca	††	CAN	E M S W C G		A E G I L P S U O		C E K G Hc H I M R Rs Rm Rc S O		.ıll
	GREC Architects www.grecstudio.com	†††	IL	E M S W C G		A E G I L P S U O		C E K G Hc H I M R Rs Rm Rc S O		.ıl.
83	**GreenbergFarrow** www.greenbergfarrow.com	†††	GA	E M S W C G		A E G I L P S U O		C E K G Hc H I M R Rs Rm Rc S O		.ıll
25	**Gresham, Smith and Partners** www.gspnet.com	††††	TN	E M S W C G		A E G I L P S U O		C E K G Hc H I M R Rs Rm Rc S O		.ıll
	Griffiths Rankin Cook Architects www.grcarchitects.com	†	CAN	E M S W C G		A E G I L P S U O		C E K G Hc H I M R Rs Rm Rc S O		.ıl.
137	**Grimm + Parker Architects** www.grimmandparker.com	††	MD	E M S W C G		A E G I L P S U O		C E K G Hc H I M R Rs Rm Rc S O		.ıl..
295	**Gromatzky Dupree & Associates** www.gdainet.com	††	TX	E M S W C G		A E G I L P S U O		C E K G Hc H I M R Rs Rm Rc S O		.ıl.

DI Brand Recognition Index

.ıll	Top tier global and categorical leader recognition
.ıll	Exceptional national and categorical leader recognition
.ıl.	Strong regional and categorical leader recognition
.ı__	Notable and growing with emerging categorical recognition
.___	Professional practice notable in city and region

Rank	Firm/Web	Size	HQ	Regions	Services	Markets	DI Index
	Group 70 International www.group70int.com	👤	HI	E M S W C G	A E G I L P S U O	C E K G Hc H I M R Rs Rm Rc S O	
	Group Mackenzie www.groupmackenzie.com	👥	OR	E M S W C G	A E G I L P S U O	C E K G Hc H I M R Rs Rm Rc S O	
180	**Gruen Associates** GRUEN ASSOCIATES www.gruenassociates.com	👥	CA	E M S W C G	A E G I L P S U O	C E K G Hc H I M R Rs Rm Rc S O	
	Gruzen Samton www.gruzensamton.com	👥	NY	E M S W C G	A E G I L P S U O	C E K G Hc H I M R Rs Rm Rc S O	
	GSBS Architects www.gsbsarchitects.com	👥	UT	E M S W C G	A E G I L P S U O	C E K G Hc H I M R Rs Rm Rc S O	
287	**GSR Andrade Architects** www.gsr-andrade.com	👥	TX	E M S W C G	A E G I L P S U O	C E K G Hc H I M R Rs Rm Rc S O	
215	**GUND Partnership** www.gundpartnership.com	👥	MA	E M S W C G	A E G I L P S U O	C E K G Hc H I M R Rs Rm Rc S O	
190	**Gwathmey Siegel & Associates Architects** www.gwathmey-siegel.com	👥	NY	E M S W C G	A E G I L P S U O	C E K G Hc H I M R Rs Rm Rc S O	
251	**GWWO** www.gwwoinc.com	👥	MD	E M S W C G	A E G I L P S U O	C E K G Hc H I M R Rs Rm Rc S O	
	GYA Architects www.gyaarchitects.com	👤	HI	E M S W C G	A E G I L P S U O	C E K G Hc H I M R Rs Rm Rc S O	
H 97	**H+L Architecture** www.hlarch.com	👥	CO	E M S W C G	A E G I L P S U O	C E K G Hc H I M R Rs Rm Rc S O	
	H2L2 www.h2l2.com	👤	PA	E M S W C G	A E G I L P S U O	C E K G Hc H I M R Rs Rm Rc S O	
229	**H3 Hardy Collaboration Architecture** www.h3hc.com	👥	NY	E M S W C G	A E G I L P S U O	C E K G Hc H I M R Rs Rm Rc S O	
227	**Hamilton Anderson Associates** www.hamilton-anderson.com	👥	MI	E M S W C G	A E G I L P S U O	C E K G Hc H I M R Rs Rm Rc S O	
170	**Hanbury Evans Wright Vlattas + Company** HANBURY EVANS WRIGHT VLATTAS www.hewv.com	👥	VA	E M S W C G	A E G I L P S U O	C E K G Hc H I M R Rs Rm Rc S O	
123	**Handel Architects** www.handelarchitects.com	👥	NY	E M S W C G	A E G I L P S U O	C E K G Hc H I M R Rs Rm Rc S O	
	Hardison Komatsu Ivelich & Tucker www.hkit.com	👥	CA	E M S W C G	A E G I L P S U O	C E K G Hc H I M R Rs Rm Rc S O	

Regions   East (E), Midwest (M), South (S), West (W), Canada (C), Global (G)

Services   Architecture (A), Engineering (E), Graphic Design (G), Interior Design (I), Landscape Architecture (L), Planning (P), Sustainability (S), Urban Design (U), Other-including Industrial Design (O)

Markets   Corporate (C), Higher Ed. (E), K-12 (K), Government (G), Healthcare (Hc), Hospitality (H), Industrial/Tech. (I), Museum/Cultural (M), Religious (R), Residential-Single (Rs), Residential-Multi. (Rm), Retail/Commercial (Rc), Sports (S), Other (O)

University of Boulder, JILA Addition, Boulder, CO I HDR Architecture, Inc.

Rank	Firm/Web	Size	HQ	Regions	Services	Markets	DI Index
299	**Hardy McCullah/MLM Architects** www.hmmlmarchitects.com	👤	TX	E M S W C G	A E G I L P S U O	C E K G Hc H I M R Rs Rm Rc S O	
	Hargreaves Associates www.hargreaves.com	👥	CA	E M S W C G	A E G I L P S U O	C E K G Hc H I M R Rs Rm Rc S O	
64	**Harley Ellis Devereaux** www.harleyellisdevereaux.com	👥👥	MI	E M S W C G	A E G I L P S U O	C E K G Hc H I M R Rs Rm Rc S O	
223	**Hart Freeland Roberts** www.hfrdesign.com	👥	TN	E M S W C G	A E G I L P S U O	C E K G Hc H I M R Rs Rm Rc S O	
118	**Hart | Howerton** HART HOWERTON www.harthowerton.com	👥	NY	E M S W C G	A E G I L P S U O	C E K G Hc H I M R Rs Rm Rc S O	
	Hartman Design Group www.hartmandesigngroup.com	👥	MD	E M S W C G	A E G I L P S U O	C E K G Hc H I M R Rs Rm Rc S O	
	Harvard Jolly Architecture www.harvardjolly.com	👤	FL	E M S W C G	A E G I L P S U O	C E K G Hc H I M R Rs Rm Rc S O	
	Hasenstab Architects www.hainc.cc	👥👥	OH	E M S W C G	A E G I L P S U O	C E K G Hc H I M R Rs Rm Rc S O	
	Hastings & Chivetta Architects www.hastingschivetta.com	👥	MO	E M S W C G	A E G I L P S U O	C E K G Hc H I M R Rs Rm Rc S O	
255	**Hawley Peterson & Snyder Architects** www.hpsarch.com	👥	CA	E M S W C G	A E G I L P S U O	C E K G Hc H I M R Rs Rm Rc S O	
	Hayes Architecture/Interiors www.hayesstudio.com	👤	AZ	E M S W C G	A E G I L P S U O	C E K G Hc H I M R Rs Rm Rc S O	
	HBA/Hirsch Bedner Associates www.hbadesign.com	👥👥	GA	E M S W C G	A E G I L P S U O	C E K G Hc H I M R Rs Rm Rc S O	
	HBE www.hbecorp.com	👥👥	MO	E M S W C G	A E G I L P S U O	C E K G Hc H I M R Rs Rm Rc S O	
326	**HBRA** **(Hammond Beeby Rupert Ainge)** www.hbra-arch.com	👥	IL	E M S W C G	A E G I L P S U O	C E K G Hc H I M R Rs Rm Rc S O	
	HBT Architects www.hbtarchitects.com	👤	NY	E M S W C G	A E G I L P S U O	C E K G Hc H I M R Rs Rm Rc S O	
	HDA Architects www.hd-architects.com	👤	AZ	E M S W C G	A E G I L P S U O	C E K G Hc H I M R Rs Rm Rc S O	
6	**HDR Architecture, Inc.** HDR www.hdrarchitecture.com	👥👥	NE	E M S W C G	A E G I L P S U O	C E K G Hc H I M R Rs Rm Rc S O	

Regions   East (E), Midwest (M), South (S), West (W), Canada (C), Global (G)

Services   Architecture (A), Engineering (E), Graphic Design (G), Interior Design (I), Landscape Architecture (L), Planning (P), Sustainability (S), Urban Design (U), Other-including Industrial Design (O)

Markets   Corporate (C), Higher Ed. (E), K-12 (K), Government (G), Healthcare (Hc), Hospitality (H), Industrial/Tech. (I), Museum/Cultural (M), Religious (R), Residential-Single (Rs), Residential-Multi. (Rm), Retail/Commercial (Rc), Sports (S), Other (O)

Lakewood Cemetery Garden Mausoleum, Minneapolis, MN | HGA Architects and Engineers

Rank	Firm/Web	Size	HQ	Regions	Services	Markets	DI Index
	Heery International HEERY www.heery.com	†††	GA	E M S W C G	A E G I L P S U O	C E K G Hc H I M R Rs Rm Rc S O	.il..
273	Helix Architecture + Design www.helixkc.com	††	MO	E M S W C G	A E G I L P S U O	C E K G Hc H I M R Rs Rm Rc S O	.il..
	Heller and Metzger www.hellerandmetzger.com	†	DC	E M S W C G	A E G I L P S U O	C E K G Hc H I M R Rs Rm Rc S O	.il..
	Heller Manus Architects www.hellermanus.com	††	CA	E M S W C G	A E G I L P S U O	C E K G Hc H I M R Rs Rm Rc S O	.ill.
108	Helman Hurley Charvat Peacock/Architects www.hhcp.com	††	FL	E M S W C G	A E G I L P S U O	C E K G Hc H I M R Rs Rm Rc S O	.il..
	Helpern Architects www.helpern.com	†	NY	E M S W C G	A E G I L P S U O	C E K G Hc H I M R Rs Rm Rc S O	.il..
	Herbert | Lewis | Kruse | Blunck Architecture www.hlkb.com	††	IA	E M S W C G	A E G I L P S U O	C E K G Hc H I M R Rs Rm Rc S O	.il..
	Herman Gibans Fodor www.hgfarchitects.com	†	OH	E M S W C G	A E G I L P S U O	C E K G Hc H I M R Rs Rm Rc S O	.il..
	Hermes Architects www.hermesarchitects.com	††	TX	E M S W C G	A E G I L P S U O	C E K G Hc H I M R Rs Rm Rc S O	.il..
14	HGA Architects and Engineers www.hga.com	††††	MN	E M S W C G	A E G I L P S U O	C E K G Hc H I M R Rs Rm Rc S O	.ill
	HH Architects www.hharchitects.com	††	TX	E M S W C G	A E G I L P S U O	C E K G Hc H I M R Rs Rm Rc S O	.il..
	Hickok Cole Architects www.hickokcole.com	††	DC	E M S W C G	A E G I L P S U O	C E K G Hc H I M R Rs Rm Rc S O	.il..
143	Highland Associates www.highlandassociates.com	††	PA	E M S W C G	A E G I L P S U O	C E K G Hc H I M R Rs Rm Rc S O	.ill.
126	Hixson www.hixson-inc.com	†††	OH	E M S W C G	A E G I L P S U O	C E K G Hc H I M R Rs Rm Rc S O	.il..
8	HKS, Inc. HKS www.hksinc.com	††††	TX	E M S W C G	A E G I L P S U O	C E K G Hc H I M R Rs Rm Rc S O	.ill
73	HLW International hlw www.hlw.com	†††	NY	E M S W C G	A E G I L P S U O	C E K G Hc H I M R Rs Rm Rc S O	.ill.
23	HMC Architects HMC Architects www.hmcarchitects.com	††††	CA	E M S W C G	A E G I L P S U O	C E K G Hc H I M R Rs Rm Rc S O	.ill

Regions   East (E), Midwest (M), South (S), West (W), Canada (C), Global (G)
Services   Architecture (A), Engineering (E), Graphic Design (G), Interior Design (I), Landscape Architecture (L), Planning (P), Sustainability (S), Urban Design (U), Other-including Industrial Design (O)
Markets   Corporate (C), Higher Ed. (E), K-12 (K), Government (G), Healthcare (Hc), Hospitality (H), Industrial/Tech. (I), Museum/Cultural (M), Religious (R), Residential-Single (Rs), Residential-Multi. (Rm), Retail/Commercial (Rc), Sports (S), Other (O)

King Abdullah University of Science and Technology, Thuwal, Saudi Arabia | HOK

Kaiserslautern Military Community Medical Center, Kaiserslautern, Germany | HOK

Rank	Firm/Web	Size	HQ	Regions	Services	Markets	DI Index
	HMFH Architects www.hmfh.com	👥	MA	E M S W C G	A E G I L P S U O	C E K G Hc H I M R Rs Rm Rc S O	
	Hnedak Bobo Group www.hbginc.com	👥	TN	E M S W C G	A E G I L P S U O	C E K G Hc H I M R Rs Rm Rc S O	
28	**HNTB (Architecture)**　HNTB www.hntb.com	👥	MO	E M S W C G	A E G I L P S U O	C E K G Hc H I M R Rs Rm Rc S O	
154	**Hobbs+Black Architects** www.hobbs-black.com	👥	MI	E M S W C G	A E G I L P S U O	C E K G Hc H I M R Rs Rm Rc S O	
272	**Hodges & Associates Architects** www.hodgesusa.com	👥	TX	E M S W C G	A E G I L P S U O	C E K G Hc H I M R Rs Rm Rc S O	
	Hoerr Schaudt Landscape Architects www.hoerrschaudt.com	👥	IL	E M S W C G	A E G I L P S U O	C E K G Hc H I M R Rs Rm Rc S O	
3	**HOK**　H+K www.hok.com	👥	MO	E M S W C G	A E G I L P S U O	C E K G Hc H I M R Rs Rm Rc S O	
	Holabird & Root　HOLABIRD & ROOT www.holabird.com	👥	IL	E M S W C G	A E G I L P S U O	C E K G Hc H I M R Rs Rm Rc S O	
	Holleran Duitsman Architects www.hdai.com	👤	MO	E M S W C G	A E G I L P S U O	C E K G Hc H I M R Rs Rm Rc S O	
298	**Hollis + Miller Architects** www.hollisandmiller.com	👥	KS	E M S W C G	A E G I L P S U O	C E K G Hc H I M R Rs Rm Rc S O	
258	**Holzman Moss Bottino Architecture** www.holzmanmoss.com	👥	NY	E M S W C G	A E G I L P S U O	C E K G Hc H I M R Rs Rm Rc S O	
102	**Hord Coplan Macht** www.hcm2.com	👥	MD	E M S W C G	A E G I L P S U O	C E K G Hc H I M R Rs Rm Rc S O	
261	**Hornberger + Worstell** www.hornbergerworstell.com	👥	CA	E M S W C G	A E G I L P S U O	C E K G Hc H I M R Rs Rm Rc S O	
323	**Horty Elving** www.hortyelving.com	👥	MN	E M S W C G	A E G I L P S U O	C E K G Hc H I M R Rs Rm Rc S O	
171	**Humphreys & Partners Architects** www.humphreys.com	👥	TX	E M S W C G	A E G I L P S U O	C E K G Hc H I M R Rs Rm Rc S O	
	Humphries Poli Architects www.hparch.com	👥	CO	E M S W C G	A E G I L P S U O	C E K G Hc H I M R Rs Rm Rc S O	
175	**Hunton Brady Architects** www.huntonbrady.com	👥	FL	E M S W C G	A E G I L P S U O	C E K G Hc H I M R Rs Rm Rc S O	

Regions　East (E), Midwest (M), South (S), West (W), Canada (C), Global (G)

Services　Architecture (A), Engineering (E), Graphic Design (G), Interior Design (I), Landscape Architecture (L), Planning (P), Sustainability (S), Urban Design (U), Other-including Industrial Design (O)

Markets　Corporate (C), Higher Ed. (E), K-12 (K), Government (G), Healthcare (Hc), Hospitality (H), Industrial/Tech. (I), Museum/Cultural (M), Religious (R), Residential-Single (Rs), Residential-Multi. (Rm), Retail/Commercial (Rc), Sports (S), Other (O)

Rank	Firm/Web	Size	HQ	Regions	Services	Markets	DI Index
198	**Huntsman Architectural Group** www.huntsmanag.com		NY	E M S W / C G	A E G I L / P S U O	C E K G Hc H I / M R Rs Rm Rc S O	
	Hutker Architects www.hutkerarchitects.com		MA	E M S W / C G	A E G I L / P S U O	C E K G Hc H I / M R Rs Rm Rc S O	
	HWH Architects Engineers Planners www.hwhaep.com		OH	E M S W / C G	A E G I L / P S U O	C E K G Hc H I / M R Rs Rm Rc S O	
I	**IA Interior Architects** www.interiorarchitects.com		CA	E M S W / C G	A E G I L / P S U O	C E K G Hc H I / M R Rs Rm Rc S O	
	IBI Group www.ibigroup.com		CAN	E M S W / C G	A E G I L / P S U O	C E K G Hc H I / M R Rs Rm Rc S O	
283	**ICON Architecture** www.iconarch.com		MA	E M S W / C G	A E G I L / P S U O	C E K G Hc H I / M R Rs Rm Rc S O	
	IDC Architects (a division of CH2M Hill) www.idcarchitects.com		OR	E M S W / C G	A E G I L / P S U O	C E K G Hc H I / M R Rs Rm Rc S O	
304	**IKM** www.ikminc.com		PA	E M S W / C G	A E G I L / P S U O	C E K G Hc H I / M R Rs Rm Rc S O	
	Indovina Associates Architects www.indovina.net		PA	E M S W / C G	A E G I L / P S U O	C E K G Hc H I / M R Rs Rm Rc S O	
	Integrated Design Solutions www.ids-troy.com		MI	E M S W / C G	A E G I L / P S U O	C E K G Hc H I / M R Rs Rm Rc S O	
	Interplan www.interplanllc.com		FL	E M S W / C G	A E G I L / P S U O	C E K G Hc H I / M R Rs Rm Rc S O	
	INVISION www.invisionarch.com		IA	E M S W / C G	A E G I L / P S U O	C E K G Hc H I / M R Rs Rm Rc S O	
	IR2 Interior Resource www.ir2.com		CA	E M S W / C G	A E G I L / P S U O	C E K G Hc H I / M R Rs Rm Rc S O	
	Ittner Architects www.ittnerarchitects.com		MO	E M S W / C G	A E G I L / P S U O	C E K G Hc H I / M R Rs Rm Rc S O	
J	**Jackson & Ryan Architects** www.jacksonryan.com		TX	E M S W / C G	A E G I L / P S U O	C E K G Hc H I / M R Rs Rm Rc S O	
5	**Jacobs (Architecture)** www.jacobs.com		CA	E M S W / C G	A E G I L / P S U O	C E K G Hc H I / M R Rs Rm Rc S O	
	James G. Rogers Architects www.jgr-architects.com		CT	E M S W / C G	A E G I L / P S U O	C E K G Hc H I / M R Rs Rm Rc S O	

DI Brand Recognition Index

- Top tier global and categorical leader recognition
- Exceptional national and categorical leader recognition
- Strong regional and categorical leader recognition
- Notable and growing with emerging categorical recognition
- Professional practice notable in city and region

Rank	Firm/Web	Size	HQ	Regions	Services	Markets	DI Index
264	**JBHM Architects** www.jbhm.com	👥	MS	E M S W / C G	A E G I L / P S U O	C E K G Hc H I / M R Rs Rm Rc S O	
82	**JCJ Architecture** www.jcj.com — JCJARCHITECT	👥👥	CT	E M S W / C G	A E G I L / P S U O	C E K G Hc H I / M R Rs Rm Rc S O	
	Jensen Architects www.jensen-architects.com	👥	CA	E M S W / C G	A E G I L / P S U O	C E K G Hc H I / M R Rs Rm Rc S O	
105	**Jerde** www.jerde.com — JERDE	👥👥	CA	E M S W / C G	A E G I L / P S U O	C E K G Hc H I / M R Rs Rm Rc S O	
	JG Johnson Architects www.jgjohnson.com	👤	CO	E M S W / C G	A E G I L / P S U O	C E K G Hc H I / M R Rs Rm Rc S O	
269	**JHP Architecture/Urban Design** www.jhparch.com	👥	TX	E M S W / C G	A E G I L / P S U O	C E K G Hc H I / M R Rs Rm Rc S O	
	JKR Partners www.jkrpartners.com	👥	PA	E M S W / C G	A E G I L / P S U O	C E K G Hc H I / M R Rs Rm Rc S O	
	JLG Architects www.jlgarchitects.com	👥	MN	E M S W / C G	A E G I L / P S U O	C E K G Hc H I / M R Rs Rm Rc S O	
	JMA www.jmaarch.com	👥	NV	E M S W / C G	A E G I L / P S U O	C E K G Hc H I / M R Rs Rm Rc S O	
243	**JMZ Architects and Planners** www.jmzarchitects.com	👥	NY	E M S W / C G	A E G I L / P S U O	C E K G Hc H I / M R Rs Rm Rc S O	
	John Ciardullo Associates www.jca-ny.com	👥	NY	E M S W / C G	A E G I L / P S U O	C E K G Hc H I / M R Rs Rm Rc S O	
	John Poe Architects www.johnpoe.com	👤	OH	E M S W / C G	A E G I L / P S U O	C E K G Hc H I / M R Rs Rm Rc S O	
210	**John Portman & Associates** www.portmanusa.com	👥	GA	E M S W / C G	A E G I L / P S U O	C E K G Hc H I / M R Rs Rm Rc S O	
	John Snyder Architects www.js-architects.com	👤	NY	E M S W / C G	A E G I L / P S U O	C E K G Hc H I / M R Rs Rm Rc S O	
	Johnsen Schmaling Architects www.johnsenschmaling.com	👤	WI	E M S W / C G	A E G I L / P S U O	C E K G Hc H I / M R Rs Rm Rc S O	
176	**Johnson Fain** www.johnsonfain.com	👥	CA	E M S W / C G	A E G I L / P S U O	C E K G Hc H I / M R Rs Rm Rc S O	
	Jonathan Nehmer + Associates www.nehmer.com	👥	DC	E M S W / C G	A E G I L / P S U O	C E K G Hc H I / M R Rs Rm Rc S O	

Regions East (E), Midwest (M), South (S), West (W), Canada (C), Global (G)

Services Architecture (A), Engineering (E), Graphic Design (G), Interior Design (I), Landscape Architecture (L), Planning (P), Sustainability (S), Urban Design (U), Other-including Industrial Design (O)

Markets Corporate (C), Higher Ed. (E), K-12 (K), Government (G), Healthcare (Hc), Hospitality (H), Industrial/Tech. (I), Museum/Cultural (M), Religious (R), Residential-Single (Rs), Residential-Multi. (Rm), Retail/Commercial (Rc), Sports (S), Other (O)

Rank	Firm/Web	Size	HQ	Regions	Services	Markets	DI Index
	Jonathan Segal www.jonathansegalarchitect.com	👤	CA	E M S W C G	A E G I L P S U O	C E K G Hc H I M R Rs Rm Rc S O	▂▃▅▆
	Jones I Haydu www.joneshaydu.com	👤	CA	E M S W C G	A E G I L P S U O	C E K G Hc H I M R Rs Rm Rc S O	▂▃▄▅
	Joseph Wong Design Associates www.jwdainc.com	👥	CA	E M S W C G	A E G I L P S U O	C E K G Hc H I M R Rs Rm Rc S O	▂▃▄▄
333	**Jova/Daniels/Busby** www.jova.com	👥	GA	E M S W C G	A E G I L P S U O	C E K G Hc H I M R Rs Rm Rc S O	▂▃▄▅
262	**JPC Architects** www.jpcarchitects.com	👥	WA	E M S W C G	A E G I L P S U O	C E K G Hc H I M R Rs Rm Rc S O	▂▃▄▄
	JSA www.jsainc.com	👥	NH	E M S W C G	A E G I L P S U O	C E K G Hc H I M R Rs Rm Rc S O	▂▃▄▅
	JSA Architecture Planning Engineering Interior Design www.jsa-architects.com	👤	PA	E M S W C G	A E G I L P S U O	C E K G Hc H I M R Rs Rm Rc S O	▂▃▄▄
	Julie Snow Architects www.juliesnowarchitects.com	👤	MN	E M S W C G	A E G I L P S U O	C E K G Hc H I M R Rs Rm Rc S O	▂▃▅▆
	JZMK Partners www.jzmkpartners.com	👤	CA	E M S W C G	A E G I L P S U O	C E K G Hc H I M R Rs Rm Rc S O	▂▃▄▄
K 165	**ka** www.kainc.com	👥👤	OH	E M S W C G	A E G I L P S U O	C E K G Hc H I M R Rs Rm Rc S O	▂▃▄▄
149	**Kahler Slater** www.kahlerslater.com	👥👤	WI	E M S W C G	A E G I L P S U O	C E K G Hc H I M R Rs Rm Rc S O	▂▃▄▅
	KAI Design & Build www.kai-db.com	👥	MO	E M S W C G	A E G I L P S U O	C E K G Hc H I M R Rs Rm Rc S O	▂▃▄▄
	Kallmann McKinnell & Wood Architects www.kmwarch.com	👥	MA	E M S W C G	A E G I L P S U O	C E K G Hc H I M R Rs Rm Rc S O	▂▃▄▄
302	**Kann Partners** www.kannpartners.com	👥	MD	E M S W C G	A E G I L P S U O	C E K G Hc H I M R Rs Rm Rc S O	▂▃▄▄
	Kanner Architects www.kannerarch.com	👥	CA	E M S W C G	A E G I L P S U O	C E K G Hc H I M R Rs Rm Rc S O	▂▃▄▄
36	**Kasian Architecture Interior Design and Planning** www.kasian.com	👥	CAN	E M S W C G	A E G I L P S U O	C E K G Hc H I M R Rs Rm Rc S O	▂▃▄▅
	KBJ Architects www.kbj.com	👥	FL	E M S W C G	A E G I L P S U O	C E K G Hc H I M R Rs Rm Rc S O	▂▃▄▄

DI Brand Recognition Index

▂▃▅▆ Top tier global and categorical leader recognition

▂▃▄▅ Exceptional national and categorical leader recognition

▂▃▄▄ Strong regional and categorical leader recognition

▂▃▁▁ Notable and growing with emerging categorical recognition

▂▁▁▁ Professional practice notable in city and region

Rank	Firm/Web	Size	HQ	Regions	Services	Markets	DI Index
250	**KCBA Architects** www.kcba-architects.com	††	PA	E M S W C G	A E G I L P S U O	C E K G Hc H I M R Rs Rm Rc S O	
321	**KDF Architecture** www.kdfarchitecture.com	††	WA	E M S W C G	A E G I L P S U O	C E K G Hc H I M R Rs Rm Rc S O	
	Kell Munoz Architects www.kellmunoz.com	††	TX	E M S W C G	A E G I L P S U O	C E K G Hc H I M R Rs Rm Rc S O	
	Kendall/Heaton Associates www.kendall-heaton.com	††	TX	E M S W C G	A E G I L P S U O	C E K G Hc H I M R Rs Rm Rc S O	
	Kerns Group Architects www.kernsgroup.com	†	VA	E M S W C G	A E G I L P S U O	C E K G Hc H I M R Rs Rm Rc S O	
	Kevin Roche John Dinkeloo & Associates www.krjda.com	††	CT	E M S W C G	A E G I L P S U O	C E K G Hc H I M R Rs Rm Rc S O	
	KieranTimberlake www.kierantimberlake.com	††	PA	E M S W C G	A E G I L P S U O	C E K G Hc H I M R Rs Rm Rc S O	
	Killefer Flammang Architects www.kfarchitects.com	†	CA	E M S W C G	A E G I L P S U O	C E K G Hc H I M R Rs Rm Rc S O	
	Kirkegaard Associates www.kirkegaard.com	††	IL	E M S W C G	A E G I L P S U O	C E K G Hc H I M R Rs Rm Rc S O	
135	**Kirksey** www.kirksey.com	†††	TX	E M S W C G	A E G I L P S U O	C E K G Hc H I M R Rs Rm Rc S O	
	Kitchen & Associates Architectural Services www.kitchenandassociates.com	†	NJ	E M S W C G	A E G I L P S U O	C E K G Hc H I M R Rs Rm Rc S O	
	KlingStubbins, a Jacobs Company www.klingstubbins.com	†††	PA	E M S W C G	A E G I L P S U O	C E K G Hc H I M R Rs Rm Rc S O	
244	**klipp** www.klipparch.com	††	CO	E M S W C G	A E G I L P S U O	C E K G Hc H I M R Rs Rm Rc S O	
	KMA Architecture & Engineering www.kma-ae.com	††	CA	E M S W C G	A E G I L P S U O	C E K G Hc H I M R Rs Rm Rc S O	
62	**KMD Architects** www.kmdarchitects.com	†††	CA	E M S W C G	A E G I L P S U O	C E K G Hc H I M R Rs Rm Rc S O	
	Knowles Blunck Architecture www.kba-studio.com	†	IA	E M S W C G	A E G I L P S U O	C E K G Hc H I M R Rs Rm Rc S O	
	Kodet Architectural Group www.kodet.com	†	MN	E M S W C G	A E G I L P S U O	C E K G Hc H I M R Rs Rm Rc S O	

Regions East (E), Midwest (M), South (S), West (W), Canada (C), Global (G)

Services Architecture (A), Engineering (E), Graphic Design (G), Interior Design (I), Landscape Architecture (L), Planning (P), Sustainability (S), Urban Design (U), Other-including Industrial Design (O)

Markets Corporate (C), Higher Ed. (E), K-12 (K), Government (G), Healthcare (Hc), Hospitality (H), Industrial/Tech. (I), Museum/Cultural (M), Religious (R), Residential-Single (Rs), Residential-Multi. (Rm), Retail/Commercial (Rc), Sports (S), Other (O)

H.G.Esch/ Courtesy of Kohn Pedersen Fox Associates (KPF)

Shanghai World Financial Center, Shanghai, China | Kohn Pedersen Fox

Rank	Firm/Web	Size	HQ	Regions	Services	Markets	DI Index
19	**Kohn Pedersen Fox** KPF www.kpf.com	👥👥	NY	E M S W C G	A E G I L P S U O	C E K G Hc H I M R Rs Rm Rc S O	
	Kondylis Architecture www.kondylis.com	👥	NY	E M S W C G	A E G I L P S U O	C E K G Hc H I M R Rs Rm Rc S O	
	Koning Eizenberg Architecture www.kearch.com	👤	CA	E M S W C G	A E G I L P S U O	C E K G Hc H I M R Rs Rm Rc S O	
204	**KPS Group** www.kpsgroup.com	👥	AL	E M S W C G	A E G I L P S U O	C E K G Hc H I M R Rs Rm Rc S O	
	Kromm Rikimaru and Johansen www.krjarch.com	👤	MO	E M S W C G	A E G I L P S U O	C E K G Hc H I M R Rs Rm Rc S O	
	KTGY Group www.ktgy.com	👤	CA	E M S W C G	A E G I L P S U O	C E K G Hc H I M R Rs Rm Rc S O	
	Kubala Washatko Architects www.tkwa.com	👤	WI	E M S W C G	A E G I L P S U O	C E K G Hc H I M R Rs Rm Rc S O	
	Kuhlman Design Group www.kdginc.com	👥👥	MO	E M S W C G	A E G I L P S U O	C E K G Hc H I M R Rs Rm Rc S O	
	Kurtz Associates Architects www.kurtzarch.com	👤	IL	E M S W C G	A E G I L P S U O	C E K G Hc H I M R Rs Rm Rc S O	
	Kwan Henmi www.kwanhenmi.com	👥	CA	E M S W C G	A E G I L P S U O	C E K G Hc H I M R Rs Rm Rc S O	
297	**KYA Design Group** www.kyadesigngroup.com	👥	HI	E M S W C G	A E G I L P S U O	C E K G Hc H I M R Rs Rm Rc S O	
	KZF Design www.kzf.com	👥	OH	E M S W C G	A E G I L P S U O	C E K G Hc H I M R Rs Rm Rc S O	
L 119	**L. R. Kimball (Architecture)** www.lrkimball.com	👥👥👥	PA	E M S W C G	A E G I L P S U O	C E K G Hc H I M R Rs Rm Rc S O	
	Laguarda Low Architects www.laguardalow.com	👤	TX	E M S W C G	A E G I L P S U O	C E K G Hc H I M R Rs Rm Rc S O	
	LAI Design Group www.laidesigngroup.com	👤	CO	E M S W C G	A E G I L P S U O	C E K G Hc H I M R Rs Rm Rc S O	
	Lake/Flato Architects LAKE | FLATO www.lakeflato.com	👥👥	TX	E M S W C G	A E G I L P S U O	C E K G Hc H I M R Rs Rm Rc S O	
	Lami Grubb Architects www.lamigrubb.com	👥	PA	E M S W C G	A E G I L P S U O	C E K G Hc H I M R Rs Rm Rc S O	

Regions   East (E), Midwest (M), South (S), West (W), Canada (C), Global (G)

Services   Architecture (A), Engineering (E), Graphic Design (G), Interior Design (I), Landscape Architecture (L), Planning (P), Sustainability (S), Urban Design (U), Other-including Industrial Design (O)

Markets   Corporate (C), Higher Ed. (E), K-12 (K), Government (G), Healthcare (Hc), Hospitality (H), Industrial/Tech. (I), Museum/Cultural (M), Religious (R), Residential-Single (Rs), Residential-Multi. (Rm), Retail/Commercial (Rc), Sports (S), Other (O)

Harbin Water Park Complex, Beijing, China | **LEO A DALY**

Rank	Firm/Web	Size	HQ	Regions	Services	Markets	DI Index
61	**Langdon Wilson International** www.langdonwilson.com		CA	E M S W / C G	A E G I L / P S U O	C E K G Hc H I / M R Rs Rm Rc S O	
290	**Lantz-Boggio Architects** www.lantz-boggio.com		CO	E M S W / C G	A E G I L / P S U O	C E K G Hc H I / M R Rs Rm Rc S O	
84	**Lawrence Group** www.thelawrencegroup.com		MO	E M S W / C G	A E G I L / P S U O	C E K G Hc H I / M R Rs Rm Rc S O	
	Lawson Group Architects www.lawsongroup.net		FL	E M S W / C G	A E G I L / P S U O	C E K G Hc H I / M R Rs Rm Rc S O	
330	**LCA Architects** www.lca-architects.com		CA	E M S W / C G	A E G I L / P S U O	C E K G Hc H I / M R Rs Rm Rc S O	
166	**Lee, Burkhart, Liu** www.lblarch.com		CA	E M S W / C G	A E G I L / P S U O	C E K G Hc H I / M R Rs Rm Rc S O	
	Lee Harris Pomeroy Architects www.lhparch.com		NY	E M S W / C G	A E G I L / P S U O	C E K G Hc H I / M R Rs Rm Rc S O	
191	**Legat Architects** LEGATARCHITECTS www.legat.com		IL	E M S W / C G	A E G I L / P S U O	C E K G Hc H I / M R Rs Rm Rc S O	
231	**Lehman Smith McLeish** www.lsm.com		DC	E M S W / C G	A E G I L / P S U O	C E K G Hc H I / M R Rs Rm Rc S O	
15	**LEO A DALY** LEO A DALY www.leodaly.com		NE	E M S W / C G	A E G I L / P S U O	C E K G Hc H I / M R Rs Rm Rc S O	
	Leotta Designers www.leottadesigners.com		FL	E M S W / C G	A E G I L / P S U O	C E K G Hc H I / M R Rs Rm Rc S O	
	Levin Porter Associates www.levin-porter.com		OH	E M S W / C G	A E G I L / P S U O	C E K G Hc H I / M R Rs Rm Rc S O	
	Levi + Wong Design Associates www.lwda.com		MA	E M S W / C G	A E G I L / P S U O	C E K G Hc H I / M R Rs Rm Rc S O	
266	**Levinson Alcoser Associates** www.levinsonalcoser.com		TX	E M S W / C G	A E G I L / P S U O	C E K G Hc H I / M R Rs Rm Rc S O	
	LHB Engineers & Architects www.lhbcorp.com		MN	E M S W / C G	A E G I L / P S U O	C E K G Hc H I / M R Rs Rm Rc S O	
	Lindsay Newman Architecture & Design www.lnarchitecture.com		NY	E M S W / C G	A E G I L / P S U O	C E K G Hc H I / M R Rs Rm Rc S O	
279	**Lindsay, Pope, Brayfield & Associates** www.lpbatlanta.com		GA	E M S W / C G	A E G I L / P S U O	C E K G Hc H I / M R Rs Rm Rc S O	

Regions East (E), Midwest (M), South (S), West (W), Canada (C), Global (G)

Services Architecture (A), Engineering (E), Graphic Design (G), Interior Design (I), Landscape Architecture (L), Planning (P), Sustainability (S), Urban Design (U), Other-including Industrial Design (O)

Markets Corporate (C), Higher Ed. (E), K-12 (K), Government (G), Healthcare (Hc), Hospitality (H), Industrial/Tech. (I), Museum/Cultural (M), Religious (R), Residential-Single (Rs), Residential-Multi. (Rm), Retail/Commercial (Rc), Sports (S), Other (O)

Rank	Firm/Web	Size	HQ	Regions	Services	Markets	DI Index
72	**Lionakis** www.lionakis.com	👥	CA	E M S W C G	A E G I L P S U O	C E K G Hc H I M R Rs Rm Rc S O	📊
46	**Little** LITTLE www.littleonline.com	👥👥	NC	E M S W C G	A E G I L P S U O	C E K G Hc H I M R Rs Rm Rc S O	📊
	LMN Architects www.lmnarchitects.com	👥👥	WA	E M S W C G	A E G I L P S U O	C E K G Hc H I M R Rs Rm Rc S O	📊
328	**Loebl Schlossman & Hackl** www.lshdesign.com	👥	IL	E M S W C G	A E G I L P S U O	C E K G Hc H I M R Rs Rm Rc S O	📊
	Lohan Anderson www.lohananderson.com	👤	IL	E M S W C G	A E G I L P S U O	C E K G Hc H I M R Rs Rm Rc S O	📊
78	**Lord, Aeck & Sargent** www.lordaecksargent.com	👥👥	GA	E M S W C G	A E G I L P S U O	C E K G Hc H I M R Rs Rm Rc S O	📊
	Lorenz + Williams www.lorenzwilliams.com	👥	OH	E M S W C G	A E G I L P S U O	C E K G Hc H I M R Rs Rm Rc S O	📊
43	**LPA** LPA www.lpainc.com	👥👥	CA	E M S W C G	A E G I L P S U O	C E K G Hc H I M R Rs Rm Rc S O	📊
	LPK www.lpkarchitects.com	👤	MS	E M S W C G	A E G I L P S U O	C E K G Hc H I M R Rs Rm Rc S O	📊
	LRS Architects www.lrsarchitects.com	👥	OR	E M S W C G	A E G I L P S U O	C E K G Hc H I M R Rs Rm Rc S O	📊
45	**LS3P Associates Ltd.** www.LS3P.com	👥👥	SC	E M S W C G	A E G I L P S U O	C E K G Hc H I M R Rs Rm Rc S O	📊
	LSW Architects www.lsw-architects.com	👤	WA	E M S W C G	A E G I L P S U O	C E K G Hc H I M R Rs Rm Rc S O	📊
	Lucas Schwering Architects www.lsarc.net	👤	KY	E M S W C G	A E G I L P S U O	C E K G Hc H I M R Rs Rm Rc S O	📊
	Lucchesi Galati Architects www.lgainc.com	👤	NV	E M S W C G	A E G I L P S U O	C E K G Hc H I M R Rs Rm Rc S O	📊
	LWPB Architecture www.lwpb.com	👥	OK	E M S W C G	A E G I L P S U O	C E K G Hc H I M R Rs Rm Rc S O	📊
	Lyman Davidson Dooley www.lddi-architects.com	👤	GA	E M S W C G	A E G I L P S U O	C E K G Hc H I M R Rs Rm Rc S O	📊
M 318	**M+A Architects** www.ma-architects.com	👥	OH	E M S W C G	A E G I L P S U O	C E K G Hc H I M R Rs Rm Rc S O	📊

DI Brand Recognition Index

📊 Top tier global and categorical leader recognition

📊 Exceptional national and categorical leader recognition

📊 Strong regional and categorical leader recognition

📊 Notable and growing with emerging categorical recognition

📊 Professional practice notable in city and region

Rank	Firm/Web	Size	HQ	Regions	Services	Markets	DI Index
	Macgregor Associates Architects www.macgregorassoc.com		GA	E M S W / C G	A E G I L / P S U O	C E K G Hc H I / M R Rs Rm Rc S O	
242	**Machado and Silvetti Associates** www.machado-silvetti.com		MA	E M S W / C G	A E G I L / P S U O	C E K G Hc H I / M R Rs Rm Rc S O	
	Mackey Mitchell Architects www.mackeymitchell.com		MO	E M S W / C G	A E G I L / P S U O	C E K G Hc H I / M R Rs Rm Rc S O	
	MacLachlan, Cornelius & Filoni Architects www.mcfarchitects.com		PA	E M S W / C G	A E G I L / P S U O	C E K G Hc H I / M R Rs Rm Rc S O	
	Maguire Group www.maguiregroup.com		MA	E M S W / C G	A E G I L / P S U O	C E K G Hc H I / M R Rs Rm Rc S O	
151	**Mahlum** www.mahlum.com		WA	E M S W / C G	A E G I L / P S U O	C E K G Hc H I / M R Rs Rm Rc S O	
	MAI design group www.mai-architects.com		CO	E M S W / C G	A E G I L / P S U O	C E K G Hc H I / M R Rs Rm Rc S O	
	Manasc Isaac Architects www.manascisaac.com		CAN	E M S W / C G	A E G I L / P S U O	C E K G Hc H I / M R Rs Rm Rc S O	
101	**Mancini - Duffy** www.manciniduffy.com		NY	E M S W / C G	A E G I L / P S U O	C E K G Hc H I / M R Rs Rm Rc S O	
294	**Manning Architects** www.manningarchitects.com		LA	E M S W / C G	A E G I L / P S U O	C E K G Hc H I / M R Rs Rm Rc S O	
276	**Margulies Perruzzi Architects** www.mp-architects.com		MA	E M S W / C G	A E G I L / P S U O	C E K G Hc H I / M R Rs Rm Rc S O	
	Mark Cavagnero Associates www.cavagnero.com		CA	E M S W / C G	A E G I L / P S U O	C E K G Hc H I / M R Rs Rm Rc S O	
284	**Marks, Thomas Architects** www.marks-thomas.com		MD	E M S W / C G	A E G I L / P S U O	C E K G Hc H I / M R Rs Rm Rc S O	
	Marmol Radziner www.marmol-radziner.com		CA	E M S W / C G	A E G I L / P S U O	C E K G Hc H I / M R Rs Rm Rc S O	
	Marnell Corrao Associates www.marnellcorrao.com		NV	E M S W / C G	A E G I L / P S U O	C E K G Hc H I / M R Rs Rm Rc S O	
228	**Marshall Craft Associates** www.marshallcraft.com		MD	E M S W / C G	A E G I L / P S U O	C E K G Hc H I / M R Rs Rm Rc S O	
	Marshall Tittemore Architects www.mtalink.com		CAN	E M S W / C G	A E G I L / P S U O	C E K G Hc H I / M R Rs Rm Rc S O	

Regions East (E), Midwest (M), South (S), West (W), Canada (C), Global (G)

Services Architecture (A), Engineering (E), Graphic Design (G), Interior Design (I), Landscape Architecture (L), Planning (P), Sustainability (S), Urban Design (U), Other-including Industrial Design (O)

Markets Corporate (C), Higher Ed. (E), K-12 (K), Government (G), Healthcare (Hc), Hospitality (H), Industrial/Tech. (I), Museum/Cultural (M), Religious (R), Residential-Single (Rs), Residential-Multi. (Rm), Retail/Commercial (Rc), Sports (S), Other (O)

Rank	Firm/Web	Size	HQ	Regions	Services	Markets	DI Index
	Martin Holub Architects www.mharchitects.com	👤	NY	E M S W C G	A E G I L P S U O	C E K G Hc H I M R Rs Rm Rc S O	▪▖▖
	Martinez + Cutri Architects www.mc-architects.com	👤	CA	E M S W C G	A E G I L P S U O	C E K G Hc H I M R Rs Rm Rc S O	▪▖▖
	Mason Architects www.masonarch.com	👥	HI	E M S W C G	A E G I L P S U O	C E K G Hc H I M R Rs Rm Rc S O	▪▖▖
	Matrix Spencer www.matrixdesigncompanies.com	👥	TX	E M S W C G	A E G I L P S U O	C E K G Hc H I M R Rs Rm Rc S O	▪▖▖
207	**MBH Architects** www.mbharch.com	👥	CA	E M S W C G	A E G I L P S U O	C E K G Hc H I M R Rs Rm Rc S O	▪▖▖
	MC Harry & Associates www.mcharry.com	👤	FL	E M S W C G	A E G I L P S U O	C E K G Hc H I M R Rs Rm Rc S O	▪▖▖
	MCA Architects www.mca-architects.com	👤	OR	E M S W C G	A E G I L P S U O	C E K G Hc H I M R Rs Rm Rc S O	▪▖▖
	McCall Design Group www.mccalldesign.com	👥	CA	E M S W C G	A E G I L P S U O	C E K G Hc H I M R Rs Rm Rc S O	▪▖▖
	McCarty Holsaple McCarty www.mhminc.com	👥	TN	E M S W C G	A E G I L P S U O	C E K G Hc H I M R Rs Rm Rc S O	▪▖▖
	MCG www.mcgarchitecture.com	👥👤	CA	E M S W C G	A E G I L P S U O	C E K G Hc H I M R Rs Rm Rc S O	▪▖▖
	McGranahan Architects www.mcgranahan.com	👥	WA	E M S W C G	A E G I L P S U O	C E K G Hc H I M R Rs Rm Rc S O	▪▖▖
	McKinley & Associates www.mckinleyassoc.com	👤	WV	E M S W C G	A E G I L P S U O	C E K G Hc H I M R Rs Rm Rc S O	▪▖▖
109	**McKissack & McKissack** www.mckissackdc.com	👥👤	DC	E M S W C G	A E G I L P S U O	C E K G Hc H I M R Rs Rm Rc S O	▪▪▖
	McLarand Vasquez Emsiek & Partners www.mve-architects.com	👥	CA	E M S W C G	A E G I L P S U O	C E K G Hc H I M R Rs Rm Rc S O	▪▖▖
	McMonigal Architects www.mcmonigal.com	👤	MN	E M S W C G	A E G I L P S U O	C E K G Hc H I M R Rs Rm Rc S O	▪▖▖
	Mead & Hunt www.meadhunt.com	👥	WI	E M S W C G	A E G I L P S U O	C E K G Hc H I M R Rs Rm Rc S O	▪▖▖
	Medical Design International www.mdiatlanta.com	👤	GA	E M S W C G	A E G I L P S U O	C E K G Hc H I M R Rs Rm Rc S O	▪▖▖

DI Brand Recognition Index

▪▮▮▮ Top tier global and categorical leader recognition

▪▪▮▮ Exceptional national and categorical leader recognition

▪▪▮ Strong regional and categorical leader recognition

▪▖▖▖ Notable and growing with emerging categorical recognition

▪▖▖▖ Professional practice notable in city and region

Rank	Firm/Web	Size	HQ	Regions	Services	Markets	DI Index
	Meeks + Partners www.meekspartners.com		TX	E M S W C G	A E G I L P S U O	C E K G Hc H I M R Rs Rm Rc S O	
	Mekus Tanager www.mekustanager.com		IL	E M S W C G	A E G I L P S U O	C E K G Hc H I M R Rs Rm Rc S O	
221	**Merriman Associates/Architects** www.merrimanassociates.com		TX	E M S W C G	A E G I L P S U O	C E K G Hc H I M R Rs Rm Rc S O	
31	**Meyer, Scherer & Rockcastle** www.msrltd.com		MN	E M S W C G	A E G I L P S U O	C E K G Hc H I M R Rs Rm Rc S O	
	MGA Architecture www.mgahawaii.com		HI	E M S W C G	A E G I L P S U O	C E K G Hc H I M R Rs Rm Rc S O	
	MGA Partners Architects www.mgapartners.com		PA	E M S W C G	A E G I L P S U O	C E K G Hc H I M R Rs Rm Rc S O	
	MGE Architects www.mgearchitects.com		FL	E M S W C G	A E G I L P S U O	C E K G Hc H I M R Rs Rm Rc S O	
	MHTN Architects www.mhtn.com		UT	E M S W C G	A E G I L P S U O	C E K G Hc H I M R Rs Rm Rc S O	
112	**Michael Graves & Associates** www.michaelgraves.com		NJ	E M S W C G	A E G I L P S U O	C E K G Hc H I M R Rs Rm Rc S O	
	Michael Willis Architects www.mwaarchitects.com		CA	E M S W C G	A E G I L P S U O	C E K G Hc H I M R Rs Rm Rc S O	
	Miller Dunwiddie Architects www.millerdunwiddie.com		MN	E M S W C G	A E G I L P S U O	C E K G Hc H I M R Rs Rm Rc S O	
179	**Miller Hull Partnership** www.millerhull.com		WA	E M S W C G	A E G I L P S U O	C E K G Hc H I M R Rs Rm Rc S O	
	Milton Glaser www.miltonglaser.com		NY	E M S W C G	A E G I L P S U O	C E K G Hc H I M R Rs Rm Rc S O	
	Mitchell Associates www.mitchellai.com		DE	E M S W C G	A E G I L P S U O	C E K G Hc H I M R Rs Rm Rc S O	
	Mitchell I Giurgola Architects www.mitchellgiurgola.com		NY	E M S W C G	A E G I L P S U O	C E K G Hc H I M R Rs Rm Rc S O	
182	**Mithun** **MITHŪN** www.mithun.com		WA	E M S W C G	A E G I L P S U O	C E K G Hc H I M R Rs Rm Rc S O	
277	**MKC Associates** www.mkcinc.com		OH	E M S W C G	A E G I L P S U O	C E K G Hc H I M R Rs Rm Rc S O	

Regions   East (E), Midwest (M), South (S), West (W), Canada (C), Global (G)

Services   Architecture (A), Engineering (E), Graphic Design (G), Interior Design (I), Landscape Architecture (L), Planning (P), Sustainability (S), Urban Design (U), Other-including Industrial Design (O)

Markets   Corporate (C), Higher Ed. (E), K-12 (K), Government (G), Healthcare (Hc), Hospitality (H), Industrial/Tech. (I), Museum/Cultural (M), Religious (R), Residential-Single (Rs), Residential-Multi. (Rm), Retail/Commercial (Rc), Sports (S), Other (O)

Rank	Firm/Web	Size	HQ	Regions	Services	Markets	DI Index
	MKTHINK www.mkthink.com		CA	E M S W C G	A E G I L P S U O	C E K G Hc H I M R Rs Rm Rc S O	
303	**MOA Architecture** www.moaarch.com		CO	E M S W C G	A E G I L P S U O	C E K G Hc H I M R Rs Rm Rc S O	
	Moeckel Carbonell Associates www.architectsde.com		DE	E M S W C G	A E G I L P S U O	C E K G Hc H I M R Rs Rm Rc S O	
	Mojo Stumer Architects www.mojostumer.com		NY	E M S W C G	A E G I L P S U O	C E K G Hc H I M R Rs Rm Rc S O	
	Montalba Architects www.montalbaarchitects.com		CA	E M S W C G	A E G I L P S U O	C E K G Hc H I M R Rs Rm Rc S O	
121	**Moody - Nolan** www.moodynolan.com		OH	E M S W C G	A E G I L P S U O	C E K G Hc H I M R Rs Rm Rc S O	
	Moon Mayoras Architects www.moonmayoras.com		CA	E M S W C G	A E G I L P S U O	C E K G Hc H I M R Rs Rm Rc S O	
	Moore Planning Group www.mooreplanninggroup.com		LA	E M S W C G	A E G I L P S U O	C E K G Hc H I M R Rs Rm Rc S O	
	Moore Ruble Yudell Architects & Planners *moore ruble yudell architects & planners* www.moorerubleyudell.com		CA	E M S W C G	A E G I L P S U O	C E K G Hc H I M R Rs Rm Rc S O	
	Moriyama & Teshima Architects www.mtarch.com		CAN	E M S W C G	A E G I L P S U O	C E K G Hc H I M R Rs Rm Rc S O	
237	**Morphosis** www.morphosis.com		CA	E M S W C G	A E G I L P S U O	C E K G Hc H I M R Rs Rm Rc S O	
130	**Morris Architects** MORRIS ARCHITECTS www.morrisarchitects.com		TX	E M S W C G	A E G I L P S U O	C E K G Hc H I M R Rs Rm Rc S O	
	Moseley Architects www.moseleyarchitects.com		VA	E M S W C G	A E G I L P S U O	C E K G Hc H I M R Rs Rm Rc S O	
	Moshe Safdie and Associates www.msafdie.com		MA	E M S W C G	A E G I L P S U O	C E K G Hc H I M R Rs Rm Rc S O	
	Mount Vernon Group Architects www.mvgarchitects.com		MA	E M S W C G	A E G I L P S U O	C E K G Hc H I M R Rs Rm Rc S O	
	MRI Architectural Group www.mriarchitects.com		FL	E M S W C G	A E G I L P S U O	C E K G Hc H I M R Rs Rm Rc S O	
	MSA Architects www.msaarch.com		OH	E M S W C G	A E G I L P S U O	C E K G Hc H I M R Rs Rm Rc S O	

DI Brand Recognition Index

Top tier global and categorical leader recognition

Exceptional national and categorical leader recognition

Strong regional and categorical leader recognition

Notable and growing with emerging categorical recognition

Professional practice notable in city and region

Rank	Firm/Web	Size	HQ	Regions		Services		Markets		DI Index
	MSTSD www.mstsd.com	👥	GA	E M S W C G		A E G I L P S U O		C E K G Hc H I M R Rs Rm Rc S O		▂▃▁
41	**MulvannyG2 Architecture** www.mulvannyg2.com　MULVANNY G2	👥👥	WA	E M S W C G		A E G I L P S U O		C E K G Hc H I M R Rs Rm Rc S O		▂▄▆█
	Munger Munger + Associates www.mungermunger.com	👤	OH	E M S W C G		A E G I L P S U O		C E K G Hc H I M R Rs Rm Rc S O		▂▃▁
	Murphy and Dittenhafer www.murphdittarch.com	👥	MD	E M S W C G		A E G I L P S U O		C E K G Hc H I M R Rs Rm Rc S O		▂▂▁
77	**Murphy/Jahn** www.murphyjahn.com	👥	IL	E M S W C G		A E G I L P S U O		C E K G Hc H I M R Rs Rm Rc S O		▂▄▆█
N 96	**NAC|Architecture** www.nacarchitecture.com	👥👥	WA	E M S W C G		A E G I L P S U O		C E K G Hc H I M R Rs Rm Rc S O		▂▃▁
	Nacht & Lewis Architects www.nlarch.com	👥	CA	E M S W C G		A E G I L P S U O		C E K G Hc H I M R Rs Rm Rc S O		▂▃▁
164	**Nadel** www.nadelarc.com	👥	CA	E M S W C G		A E G I L P S U O		C E K G Hc H I M R Rs Rm Rc S O		▂▃▁
	Nagle Hartray Danker Kagan McKay Penny www.nhdkmp.com	👤	IL	E M S W C G		A E G I L P S U O		C E K G Hc H I M R Rs Rm Rc S O		▂▄▆█
	nArchitects www.narchitects.com	👤	NY	E M S W C G		A E G I L P S U O		C E K G Hc H I M R Rs Rm Rc S O		▂▃▁
11	**NBBJ** www.nbbj.com　*nbbj*	👥👥	WA	E M S W C G		A E G I L P S U O		C E K G Hc H I M R Rs Rm Rc S O		▂▄▆█
35	**NELSON** www.nelsononline.com　NELSON	👥👥	PA	E M S W C G		A E G I L P S U O		C E K G Hc H I M R Rs Rm Rc S O		▂▃▁
	Neumann Smith & Associates www.neumannsmith.com	👥	MI	E M S W C G		A E G I L P S U O		C E K G Hc H I M R Rs Rm Rc S O		▂▃▁
125	**Niles Bolton Associates** www.nilesbolton.com	👥	GA	E M S W C G		A E G I L P S U O		C E K G Hc H I M R Rs Rm Rc S O		▂▃▁
	NORR Architects Planners www.noorlimited.com	👥	CAN	E M S W C G		A E G I L P S U O		C E K G Hc H I M R Rs Rm Rc S O		▂▃▁
	Norris Design www.norris-design.com	👥	CO	E M S W C G		A E G I L P S U O		C E K G Hc H I M R Rs Rm Rc S O		▂▃▁
278	**Northeast Collaborative Architects** www.ncarchitects.com	👥	RI	E M S W C G		A E G I L P S U O		C E K G Hc H I M R Rs Rm Rc S O		▂▃▁

Regions　East (E), Midwest (M), South (S), West (W), Canada (C), Global (G)

Services　Architecture (A), Engineering (E), Graphic Design (G), Interior Design (I), Landscape Architecture (L), Planning (P), Sustainability (S), Urban Design (U), Other-including Industrial Design (O)

Markets　Corporate (C), Higher Ed. (E), K-12 (K), Government (G), Healthcare (Hc), Hospitality (H), Industrial/Tech. (I), Museum/Cultural (M), Religious (R), Residential-Single (Rs), Residential-Multi. (Rm), Retail/Commercial (Rc), Sports (S), Other (O)

Rank	Firm/Web	Size	HQ	Regions	Services	Markets	DI Index
59	**NTD Architecture** www.ntd.com	†††	CA	E M S W C G	A E G I L P S U O	C E K G Hc H I M R Rs Rm Rc S O	▂▄▆█
	Nudell Architects www.jhn.com	††	MI	E M S W C G	A E G I L P S U O	C E K G Hc H I M R Rs Rm Rc S O	▂▄__
O	**O'Brien/Atkins Associates** www.obrienatkins.com	††	NC	E M S W C G	A E G I L P S U O	C E K G Hc H I M R Rs Rm Rc S O	▂▄__
	O'Connell Robertson & Associates www.oconnellrobertson.com	††	TX	E M S W C G	A E G I L P S U O	C E K G Hc H I M R Rs Rm Rc S O	▂▄__
	Obata, Kiku, & Company www.kikuobata.com	†	MO	E M S W C G	A E G I L P S U O	C E K G Hc H I M R Rs Rm Rc S O	▂▄__
	OBM International www.obmi.com	†††	FL	E M S W C G	A E G I L P S U O	C E K G Hc H I M R Rs Rm Rc S O	▂▄__
	Odell www.odell.com	††	NC	E M S W C G	A E G I L P S U O	C E K G Hc H I M R Rs Rm Rc S O	▂▄▆_
311	**Ohlson Lavoie Collaborative** www.olcdesigns.com	††	CO	E M S W C G	A E G I L P S U O	C E K G Hc H I M R Rs Rm Rc S O	▂▄__
	OLIN www.theolinstudio.com	††	PA	E M S W C G	A E G I L P S U O	C E K G Hc H I M R Rs Rm Rc S O	▂▄▆█
	Oliver Design Group www.odg-architects.com	†	FL	E M S W C G	A E G I L P S U O	C E K G Hc H I M R Rs Rm Rc S O	▂▄__
	Olivieri, Shousky & Kiss www.olivieriarchitects.com	†	NJ	E M S W C G	A E G I L P S U O	C E K G Hc H I M R Rs Rm Rc S O	▂▄__
	Olson Kundig Architects www.olsonkundigarchitects.com	††	WA	E M S W C G	A E G I L P S U O	C E K G Hc H I M R Rs Rm Rc S O	▂▄▆█
301	**Omniplan** www.omniplan.com	††	TX	E M S W C G	A E G I L P S U O	C E K G Hc H I M R Rs Rm Rc S O	▂▄__
	Opsis Architecture www.opsisarch.com	††	OR	E M S W C G	A E G I L P S U O	C E K G Hc H I M R Rs Rm Rc S O	▂▄__
	Opus Architects & Engineers www.opus-group.com	††	MN	E M S W C G	A E G I L P S U O	C E K G Hc H I M R Rs Rm Rc S O	▂▄__
196	**Orcutt I Winslow** www.owp.com	††	AZ	E M S W C G	A E G I L P S U O	C E K G Hc H I M R Rs Rm Rc S O	▂▄__
	OTAK www.otak.com	†††	OR	E M S W C G	A E G I L P S U O	C E K G Hc H I M R Rs Rm Rc S O	▂▄▆█

DI Brand Recognition Index

▂▄▆█ Top tier global and categorical leader recognition

▂▄▆ Exceptional national and categorical leader recognition

▂▄ Strong regional and categorical leader recognition

▂▄___ Notable and growing with emerging categorical recognition

▂____ Professional practice notable in city and region

Rank	Firm/Web	Size	HQ	Regions	Services	Markets	DI Index
	Otis Koglin Wilson Architects www.okwarchitects.com	†††	OR	E M S W C G	A E G I L P S U O	C E K G Hc H I M R Rs Rm Rc S O	
	Oudens Knoop Knoop + Sachs Architects www.okarch.com	††	MD	E M S W C G	A E G I L P S U O	C E K G Hc H I M R Rs Rm Rc S O	
202	**Overland Partners Architects** www.overlandpartners.com	††	TX	E M S W C G	A E G I L P S U O	C E K G Hc H I M R Rs Rm Rc S O	
103	**OZ Architecture** www.ozarch.com	†††	CO	E M S W C G	A E G I L P S U O	C E K G Hc H I M R Rs Rm Rc S O	
P	**Pacific Architects** www.pacarchitects.com	††	HI	E M S W C G	A E G I L P S U O	C E K G Hc H I M R Rs Rm Rc S O	
27	**PageSoutherlandPage** www.pspaec.com	†††	TX	E M S W C G	A E G I L P S U O	C E K G Hc H I M R Rs Rm Rc S O	
	Partners & Sirny Architects www.partnersandsirny.com	†	MN	E M S W C G	A E G I L P S U O	C E K G Hc H I M R Rs Rm Rc S O	
	Partridge Architects www.partridgearch.com	†	PA	E M S W C G	A E G I L P S U O	C E K G Hc H I M R Rs Rm Rc S O	
	Paulett Taggart Architects www.ptarc.com	†	CA	E M S W C G	A E G I L P S U O	C E K G Hc H I M R Rs Rm Rc S O	
	Paulsen Architectural Design www.paulsenarchitects.com	†	MN	E M S W C G	A E G I L P S U O	C E K G Hc H I M R Rs Rm Rc S O	
65	**Payette** www.payette.com	†††	MA	E M S W C G	A E G I L P S U O	C E K G Hc H I M R Rs Rm Rc S O	
	pb2 Architecture & Engineering www.pb2ae.com	†	AR	E M S W C G	A E G I L P S U O	C E K G Hc H I M R Rs Rm Rc S O	
	PBK www.pbk.com	†††	TX	E M S W C G	A E G I L P S U O	C E K G Hc H I M R Rs Rm Rc S O	
	PBR Hawaii www.pbrhawaii.com	††	HI	E M S W C G	A E G I L P S U O	C E K G Hc H I M R Rs Rm Rc S O	
	Peckham & Wright Architects www.pwarchitects.com	†	MO	E M S W C G	A E G I L P S U O	C E K G Hc H I M R Rs Rm Rc S O	
	Peckham Guyton Albers & Viets www.pgav.com	†††	MO	E M S W C G	A E G I L P S U O	C E K G Hc H I M R Rs Rm Rc S O	
122	**Pei Cobb Freed & Partners Architects** www.pcf-p.com	††	NY	E M S W C G	A E G I L P S U O	C E K G Hc H I M R Rs Rm Rc S O	

Regions East (E), Midwest (M), South (S), West (W), Canada (C), Global (G)

Services Architecture (A), Engineering (E), Graphic Design (G), Interior Design (I), Landscape Architecture (L), Planning (P), Sustainability (S), Urban Design (U), Other-including Industrial Design (O)

Markets Corporate (C), Higher Ed. (E), K-12 (K), Government (G), Healthcare (Hc), Hospitality (H), Industrial/Tech. (I), Museum/Cultural (M), Religious (R), Residential-Single (Rs), Residential-Multi. (Rm), Retail/Commercial (Rc), Sports (S), Other (O)

Devon Energy Center, Oklahoma City, OK | Pickard Chilton

Rank	Firm/Web	Size	HQ	Regions	Services	Markets	DI Index
	Pelli Clarke Pelli Architects www.pcparch.com		CT	E M S W C G	A E G I L P S U O	C E K G Hc H I M R Rs Rm Rc S O	
	Pellow + Associates Architects www.pellowarchitects.com		CAN	E M S W C G	A E G I L P S U O	C E K G Hc H I M R Rs Rm Rc S O	
	Perfido Weiskopf Wagstaff + Goettel www.pwwgarch.com		PA	E M S W C G	A E G I L P S U O	C E K G Hc H I M R Rs Rm Rc S O	
4	**Perkins+Will** PERKINS +WILL www.perkinswill.com		N/A	E M S W C G	A E G I L P S U O	C E K G Hc H I M R Rs Rm Rc S O	
16	**Perkins Eastman** Perkins Eastman www.perkinseastman.com		NY	E M S W C G	A E G I L P S U O	C E K G Hc H I M R Rs Rm Rc S O	
57	**Perkowitz+Ruth Architects** www.prarchitects.com Perkowitz+Ruth		CA	E M S W C G	A E G I L P S U O	C E K G Hc H I M R Rs Rm Rc S O	
319	**Perry Dean Rogers	Partners Architects** www.perrydean.com		MA	E M S W C G	A E G I L P S U O	C E K G Hc H I M R Rs Rm Rc S O	
	Peter Chermayeff www.peterchermayeff.com		MA	E M S W C G	A E G I L P S U O	C E K G Hc H I M R Rs Rm Rc S O	
	Peter Henry Architects www.chebucto.ns.ca/Business/PHARCH		CAN	E M S W C G	A E G I L P S U O	C E K G Hc H I M R Rs Rm Rc S O	
307	**Peter Marino Architect** www.petermarinoarchitect.com		NY	E M S W C G	A E G I L P S U O	C E K G Hc H I M R Rs Rm Rc S O	
	Peter Vincent Architects www.pva.com		HI	E M S W C G	A E G I L P S U O	C E K G Hc H I M R Rs Rm Rc S O	
291	**Pfeiffer Partners Architects** PFEIFFER PARTNERS www.pfeifferpartners.com		CA	E M S W C G	A E G I L P S U O	C E K G Hc H I M R Rs Rm Rc S O	
	PGAL www.pgal.com		TX	E M S W C G	A E G I L P S U O	C E K G Hc H I M R Rs Rm Rc S O	
	Phillips Partnership www.phillipspart.com		GA	E M S W C G	A E G I L P S U O	C E K G Hc H I M R Rs Rm Rc S O	
	Philo Wilke Partnership www.pwarch.com		TX	E M S W C G	A E G I L P S U O	C E K G Hc H I M R Rs Rm Rc S O	
	Pica + Sullivan Architects www.picasullivan.com		CA	E M S W C G	A E G I L P S U O	C E K G Hc H I M R Rs Rm Rc S O	
	Pickard Chilton PICKARD CHILTON www.pickardchilton.com		CT	E M S W C G	A E G I L P S U O	C E K G Hc H I M R Rs Rm Rc S O	

Regions   East (E), Midwest (M), South (S), West (W), Canada (C), Global (G)

Services   Architecture (A), Engineering (E), Graphic Design (G), Interior Design (I), Landscape Architecture (L), Planning (P), Sustainability (S), Urban Design (U), Other-including Industrial Design (O)

Markets   Corporate (C), Higher Ed. (E), K-12 (K), Government (G), Healthcare (Hc), Hospitality (H), Industrial/Tech. (I), Museum/Cultural (M), Religious (R), Residential-Single (Rs), Residential-Multi. (Rm), Retail/Commercial (Rc), Sports (S), Other (O)

Rank	Firm/Web	Size	HQ	Regions	Services	Markets	DI Index
183	**Pieper O'Brien Herr Architects** www.poharchitects.com	👥	GA	E M S W C G	A E G I L P S U O	C E K G Hc H I M R Rs Rm Rc S O	▁▃▅▁
	Pinnacle Architects www.pinnaclearchitects.com	👤	OH	E M S W C G	A E G I L P S U O	C E K G Hc H I M R Rs Rm Rc S O	▁▃▅▁
	Plant Architect www.branchplant.com	👤	CAN	E M S W C G	A E G I L P S U O	C E K G Hc H I M R Rs Rm Rc S O	▁▃▅▁
	Platt Byard Dovell White Architects www.pbdw.com	👥	NY	E M S W C G	A E G I L P S U O	C E K G Hc H I M R Rs Rm Rc S O	▁▃▅▁
	Poggemeyer Design Group www.poggemeyer.com	👥👤	OH	E M S W C G	A E G I L P S U O	C E K G Hc H I M R Rs Rm Rc S O	▁▃▅▁
281	**Polk Stanley Wilcox** www.polkstanleywilcox.com	👥	AR	E M S W C G	A E G I L P S U O	C E K G Hc H I M R Rs Rm Rc S O	▁▃▅▁
263	**POLLACK Architecture** www.pollackarch.com	👥	CA	E M S W C G	A E G I L P S U O	C E K G Hc H I M R Rs Rm Rc S O	▁▃▅▁
	Pope Associates www.popearch.com	👥	MN	E M S W C G	A E G I L P S U O	C E K G Hc H I M R Rs Rm Rc S O	▁▃▅▁
24	**Populous** POPULOUS www.populous.com	👥👤	MO	E M S W C G	A E G I L P S U O	C E K G Hc H I M R Rs Rm Rc S O	▃▅▇▇
	Port City Architecture www.portcityarch.com	👤	ME	E M S W C G	A E G I L P S U O	C E K G Hc H I M R Rs Rm Rc S O	▁▃▅▁
236	**Portico Group, The** www.porticogroup.com	👥	WA	E M S W C G	A E G I L P S U O	C E K G Hc H I M R Rs Rm Rc S O	▁▃▅▁
	PositivEnergy Practice www.pepractice.com	👥	IL	E M S W C G	A E G I L P S U O	C E K G Hc H I M R Rs Rm Rc S O	▁▃▅▁
	Preston Partnership, The www.theprestonpartnership.com	👥👤	GA	E M S W C G	A E G I L P S U O	C E K G Hc H I M R Rs Rm Rc S O	▁▃▅▁
	PS & S Architecture & Engineering www.psands.com	👥	NJ	E M S W C G	A E G I L P S U O	C E K G Hc H I M R Rs Rm Rc S O	▁▃▅▁
	Pyatok Architects www.pyatok.com	👤	CA	E M S W C G	A E G I L P S U O	C E K G Hc H I M R Rs Rm Rc S O	▁▃▅▁
Q	**Quinn Evans Architects** www.quinnevans.com	👤	DC	E M S W C G	A E G I L P S U O	C E K G Hc H I M R Rs Rm Rc S O	▁▃▅▁
	Quorum Architects www.quorumarchitects.com	👤	WI	E M S W C G	A E G I L P S U O	C E K G Hc H I M R Rs Rm Rc S O	▁▃▅▁

DI Brand Recognition Index

▁▃▅▇ Top tier global and categorical leader recognition

▁▃▅▁ Exceptional national and categorical leader recognition

▁▃▅▁ Strong regional and categorical leader recognition

▁▃▁▁ Notable and growing with emerging categorical recognition

▁▁▁▁ Professional practice notable in city and region

Rank	Firm/Web	Size	HQ	Regions	Services	Markets	DI Index
R 26	**Rafael Viñoly Architects** www.rvapc.com	👤👤👤👤	NY	E M S W C G	A E G I L P S U O	C E K G Hc H I M R Rs Rm Rc S O	
	Randall Stout Architects www.stoutarc.com	👤	CA	E M S W C G	A E G I L P S U O	C E K G Hc H I M R Rs Rm Rc S O	
	Randy Brown Architects R3A www.randybrownarchitects.com	👤	NE	E M S W C G	A E G I L P S U O	C E K G Hc H I M R Rs Rm Rc S O	
169	**Ratcliff** RATCLIFF www.ratcliffarch.com	👤👤	CA	E M S W C G	A E G I L P S U O	C E K G Hc H I M R Rs Rm Rc S O	
162	**RATIO Architects** www.ratioarchitects.com	👤👤	IN	E M S W C G	A E G I L P S U O	C E K G Hc H I M R Rs Rm Rc S O	
152	**RBB Architects** www.rbbinc.com	👤👤	CA	E M S W C G	A E G I L P S U O	C E K G Hc H I M R Rs Rm Rc S O	
79	**RDG Planning & Design** RDg www.rdgusa.com	👤👤👤	IA	E M S W C G	A E G I L P S U O	C E K G Hc H I M R Rs Rm Rc S O	
239	**Rees Associates** www.rees.com	👤👤	OK	E M S W C G	A E G I L P S U O	C E K G Hc H I M R Rs Rm Rc S O	
	Renaissance 3 Architects www.r3a.com	👤	PA	E M S W C G	A E G I L P S U O	C E K G Hc H I M R Rs Rm Rc S O	
238	**Research Facilities Design** www.rfd.com	👤👤	CA	E M S W C G	A E G I L P S U O	C E K G Hc H I M R Rs Rm Rc S O	
	Richard Fleischman + Partners Architects www.studiorfa.com	👤👤	OH	E M S W C G	A E G I L P S U O	C E K G Hc H I M R Rs Rm Rc S O	
	Richard Matsunaga & Associates Architects www.rmaia-architects.com	👤👤	HI	E M S W C G	A E G I L P S U O	C E K G Hc H I M R Rs Rm Rc S O	
111	**Richard Meier & Partners Architects** www.richardmeier.com	👤👤👤	NY	E M S W C G	A E G I L P S U O	C E K G Hc H I M R Rs Rm Rc S O	
	richärd+bauer www.richard-bauer.com	👤	AZ	E M S W C G	A E G I L P S U O	C E K G Hc H I M R Rs Rm Rc S O	
	Rick Ryniak Architects www.ryniak.com	👤	HI	E M S W C G	A E G I L P S U O	C E K G Hc H I M R Rs Rm Rc S O	
	Riecke Sunnland Kono Architects www.rskarchitects.com	👤	HI	E M S W C G	A E G I L P S U O	C E K G Hc H I M R Rs Rm Rc S O	
	Risinger + Associates www.risingerassociates.com	👤	IL	E M S W C G	A E G I L P S U O	C E K G Hc H I M R Rs Rm Rc S O	

Regions East (E), Midwest (M), South (S), West (W), Canada (C), Global (G)

Services Architecture (A), Engineering (E), Graphic Design (G), Interior Design (I), Landscape Architecture (L), Planning (P), Sustainability (S), Urban Design (U), Other-including Industrial Design (O)

Markets Corporate (C), Higher Ed. (E), K-12 (K), Government (G), Healthcare (Hc), Hospitality (H), Industrial/Tech. (I), Museum/Cultural (M), Religious (R), Residential-Single (Rs), Residential-Multi. (Rm), Retail/Commercial (Rc), Sports (S), Other (O)

© Frank Ooms

US Department of Energy's Research Support Facillity at the National Renewable Energy Laboratory, Golden, CO | RNL

Rank	Firm/Web	Size	HQ	Regions	Services	Markets	DI Index
	RJC Architects www.rjcarch.com	👤	CA	E M S W C G	A E G I L P S U O	C E K G Hc H I M R Rs Rm Rc S O	
	RLPS Architects www.rlps.com	👤	PA	E M S W C G	A E G I L P S U O	C E K G Hc H I M R Rs Rm Rc S O	
18	**RMJM** www.rmjm.com		NY	E M S W C G	A E G I L P S U O	C E K G Hc H I M R Rs Rm Rc S O	
157	**RMW architecture & interiors** www.rmw.com		CA	E M S W C G	A E G I L P S U O	C E K G Hc H I M R Rs Rm Rc S O	
117	**RNL** www.rnldesign.com		CO	E M S W C G	A E G I L P S U O	C E K G Hc H I M R Rs Rm Rc S O	
	Rob Wellington Quigley www.robquigley.com	👤	CA	E M S W C G	A E G I L P S U O	C E K G Hc H I M R Rs Rm Rc S O	
39	**Robert A.M. Stern Architects** www.ramsa.com		NY	E M S W C G	A E G I L P S U O	C E K G Hc H I M R Rs Rm Rc S O	
	Robert Kubicek Architects and Associates www.rkaa.com		AZ	E M S W C G	A E G I L P S U O	C E K G Hc H I M R Rs Rm Rc S O	
	Robert M. Swedroe Architects www.swedroe.com	👤	FL	E M S W C G	A E G I L P S U O	C E K G Hc H I M R Rs Rm Rc S O	
	Robert P. Madison International www.rpmadison.com		OH	E M S W C G	A E G I L P S U O	C E K G Hc H I M R Rs Rm Rc S O	
	Robertson Loia Roof www.rlrpc.com		GA	E M S W C G	A E G I L P S U O	C E K G Hc H I M R Rs Rm Rc S O	
	Rockwell Group www.rockwellgroup.com		NY	E M S W C G	A E G I L P S U O	C E K G Hc H I M R Rs Rm Rc S O	
	Rodriguez and Quiroga Architects Chartered www.rodriguezquiroga.com	👤	FL	E M S W C G	A E G I L P S U O	C E K G Hc H I M R Rs Rm Rc S O	
	Roesling Nakamura Terada Architects www.rntarchitects.com		CA	E M S W C G	A E G I L P S U O	C E K G Hc H I M R Rs Rm Rc S O	
69	**Roger Ferris + Partners** www.ferrisarch.com		CT	E M S W C G	A E G I L P S U O	C E K G Hc H I M R Rs Rm Rc S O	
212	**Rogers Marvel Architects** www.rogersmarvel.com		NY	E M S W C G	A E G I L P S U O	C E K G Hc H I M R Rs Rm Rc S O	
	Ross Schonder Sterzinger Cupcheck www.rsscarch.com	👤	PA	E M S W C G	A E G I L P S U O	C E K G Hc H I M R Rs Rm Rc S O	

Regions   East (E), Midwest (M), South (S), West (W), Canada (C), Global (G)

Services   Architecture (A), Engineering (E), Graphic Design (G), Interior Design (I), Landscape Architecture (L), Planning (P), Sustainability (S), Urban Design (U), Other-including Industrial Design (O)

Markets   Corporate (C), Higher Ed. (E), K-12 (K), Government (G), Healthcare (Hc), Hospitality (H), Industrial/Tech. (I), Museum/Cultural (M), Religious (R), Residential-Single (Rs), Residential-Multi. (Rm), Retail/Commercial (Rc), Sports (S), Other (O)

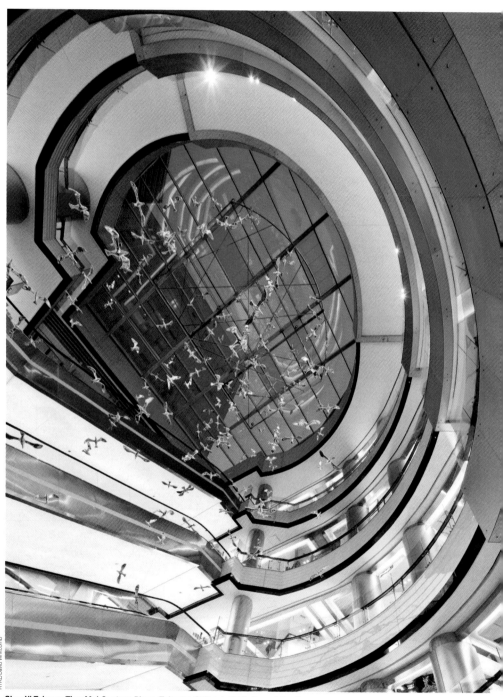

RTKL/David Whitcomb

ShanXi Taiyuan Tian Mei Century Plaza, Taiyuan, China | RTKL Associates Inc.

Rank	Firm/Web	Size	HQ	Regions	Services	Markets	DI Index
208	**Rosser International** www.rosser.com		GA	E M S W C G	A E G I L P S U O	C E K G Hc H I M R Rs Rm Rc S O	
216	**Rossetti** ROSSETTI www.rossetti.com		MI	E M S W C G	A E G I L P S U O	C E K G Hc H I M R Rs Rm Rc S O	
52	**RSP Architects** RSP ARCHITECTS www.rsparch.com		MN	E M S W C G	A E G I L P S U O	C E K G Hc H I M R Rs Rm Rc S O	
10	**RTKL Associates Inc.** RTKL www.rtkl.com		MD	E M S W C G	A E G I L P S U O	C E K G Hc H I M R Rs Rm Rc S O	
300	**Rubeling & Associates** www.rubeling.com		MD	E M S W C G	A E G I L P S U O	C E K G Hc H I M R Rs Rm Rc S O	
	RWA Architects www.rwaarchitects.com		OH	E M S W C G	A E G I L P S U O	C E K G Hc H I M R Rs Rm Rc S O	
S	**Salerno/Livingston Architects** www.slarchitects.com		CA	E M S W C G	A E G I L P S U O	C E K G Hc H I M R Rs Rm Rc S O	
	Salmela Architects www.salmelaarchitect.com		MN	E M S W C G	A E G I L P S U O	C E K G Hc H I M R Rs Rm Rc S O	
	Sandvick Architects www.sandvickarchitects.com		OH	E M S W C G	A E G I L P S U O	C E K G Hc H I M R Rs Rm Rc S O	
	Sarah Nettleton Architects www.sarah-architects.com		MN	E M S W C G	A E G I L P S U O	C E K G Hc H I M R Rs Rm Rc S O	
42	**Sasaki Associates, Inc.** SASAKI www.sasaki.com		MA	E M S W C G	A E G I L P S U O	C E K G Hc H I M R Rs Rm Rc S O	
	Saucier & Flynn www.saucierflynn.com		NH	E M S W C G	A E G I L P S U O	C E K G Hc H I M R Rs Rm Rc S O	
	Saucier and Perrotte Architects www.saucierperrotte.com		CAN	E M S W C G	A E G I L P S U O	C E K G Hc H I M R Rs Rm Rc S O	
	SaylorGregg Architects www.saylorgregg.com		PA	E M S W C G	A E G I L P S U O	C E K G Hc H I M R Rs Rm Rc S O	
308	**SB Architects** www.sb-architects.com		CA	E M S W C G	A E G I L P S U O	C E K G Hc H I M R Rs Rm Rc S O	
	SchenkelShultz www.schenkelshultz.com		IN	E M S W C G	A E G I L P S U O	C E K G Hc H I M R Rs Rm Rc S O	
	Schoenhardt Architecture www.schoenhardt.com		CT	E M S W C G	A E G I L P S U O	C E K G Hc H I M R Rs Rm Rc S O	

Regions East (E), Midwest (M), South (S), West (W), Canada (C), Global (G)

Services Architecture (A), Engineering (E), Graphic Design (G), Interior Design (I), Landscape Architecture (L), Planning (P), Sustainability (S), Urban Design (U), Other-including Industrial Design (O)

Markets Corporate (C), Higher Ed. (E), K-12 (K), Government (G), Healthcare (Hc), Hospitality (H), Industrial/Tech. (I), Museum/Cultural (M), Religious (R), Residential-Single (Rs), Residential-Multi. (Rm), Retail/Commercial (Rc), Sports (S), Other (O)

Rank	Firm/Web	Size	HQ	Regions	Services	Markets	DI Index
	Schooley Caldwell Associates www.sca-ae.com		OH	E M S W C G	A E G I L P S U O	C E K G Hc H I M R Rs Rm Rc S O	
	Schwartz/Silver Architects www.schwartzsilver.com		MA	E M S W C G	A E G I L P S U O	C E K G Hc H I M R Rs Rm Rc S O	
	Scott Partnership Architecture www.scottarchitects.com		FL	E M S W C G	A E G I L P S U O	C E K G Hc H I M R Rs Rm Rc S O	
	Seaver Franks Architects www.seaverfranks.com		AZ	E M S W C G	A E G I L P S U O	C E K G Hc H I M R Rs Rm Rc S O	
	SEM Architects www.semarchitects.com		CO	E M S W C G	A E G I L P S U O	C E K G Hc H I M R Rs Rm Rc S O	
	Semple Brown Design www.sbdesign-pc.com		CO	E M S W C G	A E G I L P S U O	C E K G Hc H I M R Rs Rm Rc S O	
	SGPA Architecture and Planning www.sgpa.com		CA	E M S W C G	A E G I L P S U O	C E K G Hc H I M R Rs Rm Rc S O	
	SH Architecture www.sh-architecture.com		NV	E M S W C G	A E G I L P S U O	C E K G Hc H I M R Rs Rm Rc S O	
148	**Shalom Baranes Associates** www.sbaranes.com		DC	E M S W C G	A E G I L P S U O	C E K G Hc H I M R Rs Rm Rc S O	
	Shea Architects www.shealink.com		MN	E M S W C G	A E G I L P S U O	C E K G Hc H I M R Rs Rm Rc S O	
	Shepherd Resources www.sriarchitect.com		CO	E M S W C G	A E G I L P S U O	C E K G Hc H I M R Rs Rm Rc S O	
71	**Shepley Bulfinch Richardson and Abbott** www.shepleybulfinch.com		MA	E M S W C G	A E G I L P S U O	C E K G Hc H I M R Rs Rm Rc S O	
220	**Sherlock Smith & Adams** www.ssainc.com		AL	E M S W C G	A E G I L P S U O	C E K G Hc H I M R Rs Rm Rc S O	
	Sheward Partnership, The www.theshewardpartnership.com		PA	E M S W C G	A E G I L P S U O	C E K G Hc H I M R Rs Rm Rc S O	
	Shlemmer+Algaze+Associates www.saaia.com		CA	E M S W C G	A E G I L P S U O	C E K G Hc H I M R Rs Rm Rc S O	
241	**SHoP Architects** www.shoparc.com		NY	E M S W C G	A E G I L P S U O	C E K G Hc H I M R Rs Rm Rc S O	
	Shore Point Architecture www.shorepointarch.com		NJ	E M S W C G	A E G I L P S U O	C E K G Hc H I M R Rs Rm Rc S O	

DI Brand Recognition Index

Top tier global and categorical leader recognition

Exceptional national and categorical leader recognition

Strong regional and categorical leader recognition

Notable and growing with emerging categorical recognition

Professional practice notable in city and region

Rank	Firm/Web	Size	HQ	Regions	Services	Markets	DI Index
139	SHP Leading Design www.shp.com		OH	E M S W C G	A E G I L P S U O	C E K G Hc H I M R Rs Rm Rc S O	
167	Shremshock Architects www.shremshock.com		OH	E M S W C G	A E G I L P S U O	C E K G Hc H I M R Rs Rm Rc S O	
	Shultz & Associates www.thearchitectfirm.com		ND	E M S W C G	A E G I L P S U O	C E K G Hc H I M R Rs Rm Rc S O	
34	SHW Group SHWGROUP www.shwgroup.com		TX	E M S W C G	A E G I L P S U O	C E K G Hc H I M R Rs Rm Rc S O	
	Sink Combs Dethlefs www.sinkcombs.com		CO	E M S W C G	A E G I L P S U O	C E K G Hc H I M R Rs Rm Rc S O	
	Sizemore Group www.sizemoregroup.com		GA	E M S W C G	A E G I L P S U O	C E K G Hc H I M R Rs Rm Rc S O	
7	Skidmore, Owings & Merrill SOM www.som.com		IL	E M S W C G	A E G I L P S U O	C E K G Hc H I M R Rs Rm Rc S O	
	Slack Alost Architecture www.slackalostarchitecture.com		LA	E M S W C G	A E G I L P S U O	C E K G Hc H I M R Rs Rm Rc S O	
56	SLAM Collaborative, The www.slamcoll.com		CT	E M S W C G	A E G I L P S U O	C E K G Hc H I M R Rs Rm Rc S O	
225	SLATERPAULL Architects www.slaterpaull.com		CO	E M S W C G	A E G I L P S U O	C E K G Hc H I M R Rs Rm Rc S O	
89	SLCE Architects www.slcearch.com		NY	E M S W C G	A E G I L P S U O	C E K G Hc H I M R Rs Rm Rc S O	
	Slifer Designs www.sliferdesigns.com		CO	E M S W C G	A E G I L P S U O	C E K G Hc H I M R Rs Rm Rc S O	
329	Slocum Platts Architects Design Studio www.slocumplatts.com		FL	E M S W C G	A E G I L P S U O	C E K G Hc H I M R Rs Rm Rc S O	
114	Smallwood, Reynolds, Stewart, Stewart & Associates www.srssa.com		GA	E M S W C G	A E G I L P S U O	C E K G Hc H I M R Rs Rm Rc S O	
	Smith Carter Smith Carter www.smithcarter.com		CAN	E M S W C G	A E G I L P S U O	C E K G Hc H I M R Rs Rm Rc S O	
	Smith Consulting Architects www.sca-sd.com		CA	E M S W C G	A E G I L P S U O	C E K G Hc H I M R Rs Rm Rc S O	
13	SmithGroupJJR SMITHGROUPJJR www.smithgroupjjr.com		N/A	E M S W C G	A E G I L P S U O	C E K G Hc H I M R Rs Rm Rc S O	

Regions   East (E), Midwest (M), South (S), West (W), Canada (C), Global (G)

Services   Architecture (A), Engineering (E), Graphic Design (G), Interior Design (I), Landscape Architecture (L), Planning (P), Sustainability (S), Urban Design (U), Other-including Industrial Design (O)

Markets   Corporate (C), Higher Ed. (E), K-12 (K), Government (G), Healthcare (Hc), Hospitality (H), Industrial/Tech. (I), Museum/Cultural (M), Religious (R), Residential-Single (Rs), Residential-Multi. (Rm), Retail/Commercial (Rc), Sports (S), Other (O)

Rank	Firm/Web	Size	HQ	Regions	Services	Markets	DI Index
	Soderstrom Architects www.sdra.com	👤	OR	E M S W C G	A E G I L P S U O	C E K G Hc H I M R Rs Rm Rc S O	▄▃▂
93	**Solomon Cordwell Buenz** www.scb.com	👥	IL	E M S W C G	A E G I L P S U O	C E K G Hc H I M R Rs Rm Rc S O	▄▃▂
	Southern A&E www.southernae.com	👤	GA	E M S W C G	A E G I L P S U O	C E K G Hc H I M R Rs Rm Rc S O	▄▃▂
	Sowinski Sullivan Architects www.sowinskisullivan.com	👥	NJ	E M S W C G	A E G I L P S U O	C E K G Hc H I M R Rs Rm Rc S O	▄▃▂
	SpaceSmith www.spacesmith.com	👤	NY	E M S W C G	A E G I L P S U O	C E K G Hc H I M R Rs Rm Rc S O	▄▃▂
	Spector Group Architects www.spectorgroup.com	👤	NY	E M S W C G	A E G I L P S U O	C E K G Hc H I M R Rs Rm Rc S O	▄▃▂
	spg www.spg3.com	👤	PA	E M S W C G	A E G I L P S U O	C E K G Hc H I M R Rs Rm Rc S O	▄▃▂
	SRG Partnership www.srgpartnership.com	👥	WA	E M S W C G	A E G I L P S U O	C E K G Hc H I M R Rs Rm Rc S O	▄▃▂
17	**SSOE Group** www.ssoe.com	👥	OH	E M S W C G	A E G I L P S U O	C E K G Hc H I M R Rs Rm Rc S O	▄▃▂
246	**Staffelbach** www.staffelbach.com	👥	TX	E M S W C G	A E G I L P S U O	C E K G Hc H I M R Rs Rm Rc S O	▄▃▂
265	**Stanley Beaman & Sears** www.stanleybeamansears.com	👥	GA	E M S W C G	A E G I L P S U O	C E K G Hc H I M R Rs Rm Rc S O	▄▃▂
	Stanley Love-Stanley www.stanleylove-stanleypc.com	👤	GA	E M S W C G	A E G I L P S U O	C E K G Hc H I M R Rs Rm Rc S O	▄▃▂
12	**Stantec Architecture (US)** www.stantec.com	👥	CA	E M S W C G	A E G I L P S U O	C E K G Hc H I M R Rs Rm Rc S O	▄▃▂
115	**Steelman Partners** www.steelmanpartners.com	👥	NV	E M S W C G	A E G I L P S U O	C E K G Hc H I M R Rs Rm Rc S O	▄▃▂
127	**Steffian Bradley Architects** www.steffian.com	👥	MA	E M S W C G	A E G I L P S U O	C E K G Hc H I M R Rs Rm Rc S O	▄▃▂
	Steinberg Architects www.steinbergarchitects.com	👥	CA	E M S W C G	A E G I L P S U O	C E K G Hc H I M R Rs Rm Rc S O	▄▃▂
282	**Stephen B. Jacobs Group/ Andi Pepper Designs** www.sbjgroup.com	👥	NY	E M S W C G	A E G I L P S U O	C E K G Hc H I M R Rs Rm Rc S O	▄▃▂

DI Brand Recognition Index

▄▃▂ Top tier global and categorical leader recognition

▄▃▂ Exceptional national and categorical leader recognition

▄▃▂ Strong regional and categorical leader recognition

▪▬ Notable and growing with emerging categorical recognition

▪▬ Professional practice notable in city and region

Rank	Firm/Web	Size	HQ	Regions	Services	Markets	DI Index
	Steven Holl Architects www.stevenholl.com		NY	E M S W C G	A E G I L P S U O	C E K G Hc H I M R Rs Rm Rc S O	
177	**Stevens & Wilkinson** www.stevenswilkinson.com		GA	E M S W C G	A E G I L P S U O	C E K G Hc H I M R Rs Rm Rc S O	
	STG Design www.stgdesign.com		TX	E M S W C G	A E G I L P S U O	C E K G Hc H I M R Rs Rm Rc S O	
	Strada Architecture www.stradallc.com		PA	E M S W C G	A E G I L P S U O	C E K G Hc H I M R Rs Rm Rc S O	
	Strekalovsky Architecture www.strekalovskyarchitecture.com		MA	E M S W C G	A E G I L P S U O	C E K G Hc H I M R Rs Rm Rc S O	
	Studio 2030 www.studio2030.com		MN	E M S W C G	A E G I L P S U O	C E K G Hc H I M R Rs Rm Rc S O	
	Studio Gang STUDIO/GANG/ARCHITECTS www.studiogang.net		IL	E M S W C G	A E G I L P S U O	C E K G Hc H I M R Rs Rm Rc S O	
	Studio Meng Strazzara www.studioms.com		WA	E M S W C G	A E G I L P S U O	C E K G Hc H I M R Rs Rm Rc S O	
53	**STUDIOS Architecture** STUDIOS architecture www.studiosarchitecture.com		DC	E M S W C G	A E G I L P S U O	C E K G Hc H I M R Rs Rm Rc S O	
	STV Group www.stvinc.com		NY	E M S W C G	A E G I L P S U O	C E K G Hc H I M R Rs Rm Rc S O	
	Susanka Studios www.susanka.com		MN	E M S W C G	A E G I L P S U O	C E K G Hc H I M R Rs Rm Rc S O	
	Swaback Partners www.swabackpartners.com		AZ	E M S W C G	A E G I L P S U O	C E K G Hc H I M R Rs Rm Rc S O	
55	**Swanke Hayden Connell Architects** www.shca.com		NY	E M S W C G	A E G I L P S U O	C E K G Hc H I M R Rs Rm Rc S O	
116	**Symmes Maini & McKee Associates** www.smma.com		MA	E M S W C G	A E G I L P S U O	C E K G Hc H I M R Rs Rm Rc S O	
T	**TAYLOR** www.wearetaylor.com		CA	E M S W C G	A E G I L P S U O	C E K G Hc H I M R Rs Rm Rc S O	
	tBP/Architecture www.tbparchitecture.com		CA	E M S W C G	A E G I L P S U O	C E K G Hc H I M R Rs Rm Rc S O	
	TCF Architecture www.tcfarchitecture.com		WA	E M S W C G	A E G I L P S U O	C E K G Hc H I M R Rs Rm Rc S O	

Regions East (E), Midwest (M), South (S), West (W), Canada (C), Global (G)

Services Architecture (A), Engineering (E), Graphic Design (G), Interior Design (I), Landscape Architecture (L), Planning (P), Sustainability (S), Urban Design (U), Other-including Industrial Design (O)

Markets Corporate (C), Higher Ed. (E), K-12 (K), Government (G), Healthcare (Hc), Hospitality (H), Industrial/Tech. (I), Museum/Cultural (M), Religious (R), Residential-Single (Rs), Residential-Multi. (Rm), Retail/Commercial (Rc), Sports (S), Other (O)

Rank	Firm/Web	Size	HQ	Regions	Services	Markets	DI Index
	TDA Architecture www.thendesign.com	●	OH	E M S W C G	A E G I L P S U O	C E K G Hc H I M R Rs Rm Rc S O	.ıl..
	Tecton Architects www.tectonarchitects.com	●●	CT	E M S W C G	A E G I L P S U O	C E K G Hc H I M R Rs Rm Rc S O	.ıl..
	TEN Arquitectos TEN ARQUITECTOS www.ten-arquitectos.com	●●	MEX	E M S W C G	A E G I L P S U O	C E K G Hc H I M R Rs Rm Rc S O	.ııll
	Terence Williams Architect www.twarchitect.ca	●	CAN	E M S W C G	A E G I L P S U O	C E K G Hc H I M R Rs Rm Rc S O	.ıl..
	Tessier Associates www.tessierarchitects.com	●	MA	E M S W C G	A E G I L P S U O	C E K G Hc H I M R Rs Rm Rc S O	.ıl..
218	**Thalden-Boyd-Emery Architects** www.thaldenboyd.com	●	MO	E M S W C G	A E G I L P S U O	C E K G Hc H I M R Rs Rm Rc S O	.ıl..
	Thomas Biro Associates www.thomasbiro.com	●	NJ	E M S W C G	A E G I L P S U O	C E K G Hc H I M R Rs Rm Rc S O	.ıl..
	Thompson & Litton www.t-l.com	●●●	VA	E M S W C G	A E G I L P S U O	C E K G Hc H I M R Rs Rm Rc S O	.ıl..
	Threshold Acoustics www.thresholdacoustics.com	●	IL	E M S W C G	A E G I L P S U O	C E K G Hc H I M R Rs Rm Rc S O	.ıl..
178	**THW Design** www.thw.com	●●	GA	E M S W C G	A E G I L P S U O	C E K G Hc H I M R Rs Rm Rc S O	.ıl..
	Tigerman McCurry Architects www.tigerman-mccurry.com	●	IL	E M S W C G	A E G I L P S U O	C E K G Hc H I M R Rs Rm Rc S O	.ııll
	TMP Associates www.tmp-architecture.com	●●●	MI	E M S W C G	A E G I L P S U O	C E K G Hc H I M R Rs Rm Rc S O	.ıl..
	Tod Williams Billie Tsien Architects www.twbta.com	●●	NY	E M S W C G	A E G I L P S U O	C E K G Hc H I M R Rs Rm Rc S O	.ııll
	Todd & Associates www.toddassoc.com	●	AZ	E M S W C G	A E G I L P S U O	C E K G Hc H I M R Rs Rm Rc S O	.ıl..
214	**Torti Gallas and Partners** www.tortigallas.com	●●	MD	E M S W C G	A E G I L P S U O	C E K G Hc H I M R Rs Rm Rc S O	.ıll.
	Tower Design Group www.towerhawaii.com	●	HI	E M S W C G	A E G I L P S U O	C E K G Hc H I M R Rs Rm Rc S O	.ıl..
305	**TowerPinkster** www.towerpinkster.com	●●	MI	E M S W C G	A E G I L P S U O	C E K G Hc H I M R Rs Rm Rc S O	.ıl..

DI Brand Recognition Index

.ııll Top tier global and categorical leader recognition

.ııl. Exceptional national and categorical leader recognition

.ıl.. Strong regional and categorical leader recognition

.ı___ Notable and growing with emerging categorical recognition

.____ Professional practice notable in city and region

Rank	Firm/Web	Size	HQ	Regions	Services	Markets	DI Index
285	**TR,i Architects** www.triarchitects.com	👤	MO	E M S W C G	A E G I L P S U O	C E K G Hc H I M R Rs Rm Rc S O	▂▃▁
	TRA Architects www.traarchitects.com	👤	FL	E M S W C G	A E G I L P S U O	C E K G Hc H I M R Rs Rm Rc S O	▂▃▁
	Trivers Associates www.trivers.com	👥	MO	E M S W C G	A E G I L P S U O	C E K G Hc H I M R Rs Rm Rc S O	▂▃▁
81	**TRO Jung | Brannen** TRO JB www.trojungbrannen.com	👥👤	MA	E M S W C G	A E G I L P S U O	C E K G Hc H I M R Rs Rm Rc S O	▃▄▅
	TruexCullins www.truexcullins.com	👥👤	VT	E M S W C G	A E G I L P S U O	C E K G Hc H I M R Rs Rm Rc S O	▂▃▁
	Tryba Architects www.trybaarchitects.com	👤	CO	E M S W C G	A E G I L P S U O	C E K G Hc H I M R Rs Rm Rc S O	▂▃▁
312	**Tsao & McKown Architects** www.tsao-mckown.com	👤	NY	E M S W C G	A E G I L P S U O	C E K G Hc H I M R Rs Rm Rc S O	▂▃▁
181	**Tsoi/Kobus & Associates** www.tka-architects.com	👥	MA	E M S W C G	A E G I L P S U O	C E K G Hc H I M R Rs Rm Rc S O	▃▄▅
186	**TSP** www.teamtsp.com	👥👤	SD	E M S W C G	A E G I L P S U O	C E K G Hc H I M R Rs Rm Rc S O	▂▃▁
	Tucker Sadler Architects www.tuckersadler.com	👥	CA	E M S W C G	A E G I L P S U O	C E K G Hc H I M R Rs Rm Rc S O	▂▃▁
	Tushie Montgomery Architects www.tmiarchitects.com	👤	MN	E M S W C G	A E G I L P S U O	C E K G Hc H I M R Rs Rm Rc S O	▂▃▁
	TVA Architects www.tvaarchitects.com	👥	OR	E M S W C G	A E G I L P S U O	C E K G Hc H I M R Rs Rm Rc S O	▂▃▁
60	**tvsdesign** [t] www.tvs-design.com	👥👤	GA	E M S W C G	A E G I L P S U O	C E K G Hc H I M R Rs Rm Rc S O	▃▄▅
U	**Urbahn Architects** www.urbahn.com	👤	NY	E M S W C G	A E G I L P S U O	C E K G Hc H I M R Rs Rm Rc S O	▂▃▁
310	**Urban Design Associates** www.urbandesignassociates.com	👥	PA	E M S W C G	A E G I L P S U O	C E K G Hc H I M R Rs Rm Rc S O	▃▄▅
	USKH www.uskh.com	👥	AK	E M S W C G	A E G I L P S U O	C E K G Hc H I M R Rs Rm Rc S O	▂▃▁
V	**Van H. Gilbert Architect** www.vhgarchitect.com	👥	NM	E M S W C G	A E G I L P S U O	C E K G Hc H I M R Rs Rm Rc S O	▂▃▁

Regions East (E), Midwest (M), South (S), West (W), Canada (C), Global (G)

Services Architecture (A), Engineering (E), Graphic Design (G), Interior Design (I), Landscape Architecture (L), Planning (P), Sustainability (S), Urban Design (U), Other-including Industrial Design (O)

Markets Corporate (C), Higher Ed. (E), K-12 (K), Government (G), Healthcare (Hc), Hospitality (H), Industrial/Tech. (I), Museum/Cultural (M), Religious (R), Residential-Single (Rs), Residential-Multi. (Rm), Retail/Commercial (Rc), Sports (S), Other (O)

Rank	Firm/Web	Size	HQ	Regions	Services	Markets	DI Index
209	**Van Tilburg, Banvard & Soderbergh** www.vtbs.com	👤👤👤	CA	E M S W C G	A E G I L P S U O	C E K G Hc H I M R Rs Rm Rc S O	▪▪▫▫
	Van Valkenburgh, Michael, Associates www.mvvainc.com	👤👤	NY	E M S W C G	A E G I L P S U O	C E K G Hc H I M R Rs Rm Rc S O	▪▪▪▪
	Vasquez + Marshall & Associates www.vmarch.net	👤	CA	E M S W C G	A E G I L P S U O	C E K G Hc H I M R Rs Rm Rc S O	▪▪▫▫
327	**VBN Architects** www.vbnarch.com	👤	CA	E M S W C G	A E G I L P S U O	C E K G Hc H I M R Rs Rm Rc S O	▪▪▫▫
	VEBH Architects www.vebh.com	👤	PA	E M S W C G	A E G I L P S U O	C E K G Hc H I M R Rs Rm Rc S O	▪▪▫▫
	Venturi, Scott, Brown and Associates www.vsba.com	👤	PA	E M S W C G	A E G I L P S U O	C E K G Hc H I M R Rs Rm Rc S O	▪▪▪▪
	Vision 3 Architects www.vision3architects.com	👤👤	RI	E M S W C G	A E G I L P S U O	C E K G Hc H I M R Rs Rm Rc S O	▪▪▫▫
	Visions in Architecture www.viarchitecture.com	👤	NE	E M S W C G	A E G I L P S U O	C E K G Hc H I M R Rs Rm Rc S O	▪▪▫▫
200	**VITETTA** VITETTA www.vitetta.com	👤👤👤	PA	E M S W C G	A E G I L P S U O	C E K G Hc H I M R Rs Rm Rc S O	▪▪▪▫
	VJAA VJAA www.vjaa.com	👤	MN	E M S W C G	A E G I L P S U O	C E K G Hc H I M R Rs Rm Rc S O	▪▪▪▪
	VLK Architects www.vlkarchitects.com	👤	TX	E M S W C G	A E G I L P S U O	C E K G Hc H I M R Rs Rm Rc S O	▪▪▫▫
48	**VOA Associates** VOA www.voa.com	👤👤👤	IL	E M S W C G	A E G I L P S U O	C E K G Hc H I M R Rs Rm Rc S O	▪▪▪▪
	VPS Architecture www.vpsarch.com	👤	IN	E M S W C G	A E G I L P S U O	C E K G Hc H I M R Rs Rm Rc S O	▪▪▫▫
W	**W Architecture & Landscape Architecture** www.w-architecture.com	👤	NY	E M S W C G	A E G I L P S U O	C E K G Hc H I M R Rs Rm Rc S O	▪▪▫▫
195	**Wakefield Beasley & Associates** www.wakefieldbeasley.com	👤👤	GA	E M S W C G	A E G I L P S U O	C E K G Hc H I M R Rs Rm Rc S O	▪▪▫▫
247	**Wald, Ruhnke & Dost Architects** www.wrdarch.com	👤👤	CA	E M S W C G	A E G I L P S U O	C E K G Hc H I M R Rs Rm Rc S O	▪▪▫▫
156	**Wallace Roberts & Todd** www.wrtdesign.com	👤👤👤	PA	E M S W C G	A E G I L P S U O	C E K G Hc H I M R Rs Rm Rc S O	▪▪▪▫

DI Brand Recognition Index

▪▪▪▪ Top tier global and categorical leader recognition

▪▪▪▫ Exceptional national and categorical leader recognition

▪▪▫▫ Strong regional and categorical leader recognition

▪▫▫▫ Notable and growing with emerging categorical recognition

▪▫▫▫ Professional practice notable in city and region

Rank	Firm/Web	Size	HQ	Regions	Services	Markets	DI Index
	Walsh Bishop Associates www.walshbishop.com		MN	E M S W C G	A E G I L P S U O	C E K G Hc H I M R Rs Rm Rc S O	
222	**Wank Adams Slavin Associates (WASA/Studio A)** WASA www.wasallp.com		NY	E M S W C G	A E G I L P S U O	C E K G Hc H I M R Rs Rm Rc S O	
	Ware Malcomb www.waremalcomb.com		CA	E M S W C G	A E G I L P S U O	C E K G Hc H I M R Rs Rm Rc S O	
	Waterleaf Architecture & Interiors www.waterleaf.com		OR	E M S W C G	A E G I L P S U O	C E K G Hc H I M R Rs Rm Rc S O	
	WBCM www.wbcm.com		MD	E M S W C G	A E G I L P S U O	C E K G Hc H I M R Rs Rm Rc S O	
	WD Partners wd PARTNERS www.wdpartners.com		OH	E M S W C G	A E G I L P S U O	C E K G Hc H I M R Rs Rm Rc S O	
136	**WDG Architecture** www.wdgarch.com		DC	E M S W C G	A E G I L P S U O	C E K G Hc H I M R Rs Rm Rc S O	
	Weiss/Manfredi Architects www.weissmanfredi.com		NY	E M S W C G	A E G I L P S U O	C E K G Hc H I M R Rs Rm Rc S O	
	Westlake Reed Leskosky Westlake Reed Leskosky www.wrldesign.com		OH	E M S W C G	A E G I L P S U O	C E K G Hc H I M R Rs Rm Rc S O	
98	**WHR Architects** WHR ARCHITECTS www.whrarchitects.com		TX	E M S W C G	A E G I L P S U O	C E K G Hc H I M R Rs Rm Rc S O	
	Widseth Smith Nolting & Associates www.wsn-mn.com		MN	E M S W C G	A E G I L P S U O	C E K G Hc H I M R Rs Rm Rc S O	
129	**Wight & Company** www.wightco.com		IL	E M S W C G	A E G I L P S U O	C E K G Hc H I M R Rs Rm Rc S O	
	William McDonough + Partners www.mcdonoughpartners.com		VA	E M S W C G	A E G I L P S U O	C E K G Hc H I M R Rs Rm Rc S O	
	William Nicholas Bodouva + Associates www.bodouva.com		NY	E M S W C G	A E G I L P S U O	C E K G Hc H I M R Rs Rm Rc S O	
145	**William Rawn Associates, Architects, Inc.** www.rawnarch.com		MA	E M S W C G	A E G I L P S U O	C E K G Hc H I M R Rs Rm Rc S O	
	Williams Blackstock Architects www.wba-architects.com		AL	E M S W C G	A E G I L P S U O	C E K G Hc H I M R Rs Rm Rc S O	
	Wilson Architectural Group www.wilsonargroup.com		TX	E M S W C G	A E G I L P S U O	C E K G Hc H I M R Rs Rm Rc S O	

Regions　East (E), Midwest (M), South (S), West (W), Canada (C), Global (G)

Services　Architecture (A), Engineering (E), Graphic Design (G), Interior Design (I), Landscape Architecture (L), Planning (P), Sustainability (S), Urban Design (U), Other-including Industrial Design (O)

Markets　Corporate (C), Higher Ed. (E), K-12 (K), Government (G), Healthcare (Hc), Hospitality (H), Industrial/Tech. (I), Museum/Cultural (M), Religious (R), Residential-Single (Rs), Residential-Multi. (Rm), Retail/Commercial (Rc), Sports (S), Other (O)

John E. Jaqua Academic Center for Student Athletes, University of Oregon, Eugene, OR | ZGF Architects

Rank	Firm/Web	Size	HQ	Regions	Services	Markets	DI Index
124	**Wilson Associates** WILSON /// ASSOCIATES www.wilsonassociates.com	👤👤👤	TX	E M S W C G	A E G I L P S U O	C E K G Hc H I M R Rs Rm Rc S O	▁▃▅▇
40	**Wimberly Allison Tong & Goo (WATG)** WATG www.watg.com	👤👤👤	CA	E M S W C G	A E G I L P S U O	C E K G Hc H I M R Rs Rm Rc S O	▁▃▅▇
	Wold Architects & Engineers www.woldae.com	👤👤👤	MN	E M S W C G	A E G I L P S U O	C E K G Hc H I M R Rs Rm Rc S O	▁▃▅
	Wolfberg Alvarez & Partners www.wolfbergalvarez.com	👤	FL	E M S W C G	A E G I L P S U O	C E K G Hc H I M R Rs Rm Rc S O	▁▃▅
	Woolpert www.woolpert.com	👤👤👤👤	OH	E M S W C G	A E G I L P S U O	C E K G Hc H I M R Rs Rm Rc S O	▁▃▅
248	**Workshop Architects** www.workshoparchitects.com	👤	WI	E M S W C G	A E G I L P S U O	C E K G Hc H I M R Rs Rm Rc S O	▁▃▅
	Worn Jerabek Architects www.wjaworks.com	👤	IL	E M S W C G	A E G I L P S U O	C E K G Hc H I M R Rs Rm Rc S O	▁▃▅
	WorthGroup Architects www.worthgroup.com	👤👤	CO	E M S W C G	A E G I L P S U O	C E K G Hc H I M R Rs Rm Rc S O	▁▃▅
	WTW Architects www.wtwarchitects.com	👤👤	PA	E M S W C G	A E G I L P S U O	C E K G Hc H I M R Rs Rm Rc S O	▁▃▅
X	**XTEN Architecture** www.xtenarchitecture.com	👤	CA	E M S W C G	A E G I L P S U O	C E K G Hc H I M R Rs Rm Rc S O	▁▃▅
Y	**YFH Architects** www.yfharchitects.com	👤	HI	E M S W C G	A E G I L P S U O	C E K G Hc H I M R Rs Rm Rc S O	▁▃▅
267	**Yost Grube Hall Architecture** www.ygh.com	👤👤	OR	E M S W C G	A E G I L P S U O	C E K G Hc H I M R Rs Rm Rc S O	▁▃▅
Z	**Zeidler Partnership Architects** www.zeidlerpartnership.com	👤👤👤	CAN	E M S W C G	A E G I L P S U O	C E K G Hc H I M R Rs Rm Rc S O	▁▃▅
20	**ZGF Architects** ZGF www.zgf.com	👤👤👤	OR	E M S W C G	A E G I L P S U O	C E K G Hc H I M R Rs Rm Rc S O	▁▃▅▇
	Ziegler Cooper Architects www.zieglercooper.com	👤👤	TX	E M S W C G	A E G I L P S U O	C E K G Hc H I M R Rs Rm Rc S O	▁▃▅
	Ziger/Snead Architects www.zigersnead.com	👤	MD	E M S W C G	A E G I L P S U O	C E K G Hc H I M R Rs Rm Rc S O	▁▃▅
	Zyscovich www.zyscovich.com	👤👤👤	FL	E M S W C G	A E G I L P S U O	C E K G Hc H I M R Rs Rm Rc S O	▁▃▅

Regions East (E), Midwest (M), South (S), West (W), Canada (C), Global (G)

Services Architecture (A), Engineering (E), Graphic Design (G), Interior Design (I), Landscape Architecture (L), Planning (P), Sustainability (S), Urban Design (U), Other-including Industrial Design (O)

Markets Corporate (C), Higher Ed. (E), K-12 (K), Government (G), Healthcare (Hc), Hospitality (H), Industrial/Tech. (I), Museum/Cultural (M), Religious (R), Residential-Single (Rs), Residential-Multi. (Rm), Retail/Commercial (Rc), Sports (S), Other (O)

BUILDING TYPES |

Listings of architecturally significant airports, aquariums, art museums, convention centers, and sports stadiums, with their requisite architectural statistics, are available in this chapter.

Airports: 1990–2012

Airports have evolved over the past century from small, utilitarian structures to sprawling multi-purpose complexes. Engineering challenges, the popularity of regional airlines, the need to accommodate larger jets, and expansion in Asia have resulted in the construction of countless new airport terminals since 1990. Many of those noteworthy for their architecture or engineering are listed in the following chart.

Airport	Location	Architect	Opened
Astana International Airport (KZT), Passenger Terminal	Astana, Kazakhstan	Kisho Kurokawa Architect & Associates (Japan)	2005
Barcelona International Airport (BCN), T1	Barcelona, Spain	Taller de Arquitectura (Spain)	2009
Barcelona International Airport (BCN), South Terminal	Barcelona, Spain	Taller de Arquitectura (Spain)	2005
Beihai Fucheng Airport (BHY), Domestic Terminal	Beihai, Guangxi, China	Llewelyn-Davies Ltd. (UK)	2000
Beijing Capital International Airport (PEK), Terminal 3	Beijing, China	Foster + Partners (UK) with Beijing Institute of Architectural Design (China)	2008
Ben Gurion Airport (TLV), Airside Complex, Terminal 3	Tel Aviv, Israel	Moshe Safdie and Associates and TRA Architects—a joint venture	2004
Ben Gurion Airport (TLV), Landside Complex, Terminal 3	Tel Aviv, Israel	Skidmore, Owings & Merrill; Moshe Safdie and Associates; Karmi Associates (Israel); Lissar Eldar Architects (Israel)—a joint venture	2002
Bilbao Airport (BIO), Terminal Building	Bilbao, Spain	Santiago Calatrava (Spain)	2000
Buffalo Niagara International Airport (BUF), Passenger Terminal	Cheektowaga, NY	Cannon Design; William Nicholas Bodouva + Associates; Kohn Pedersen Fox—a joint venture	1997
Carrasco International Airport (MVD), New Terminal	Montevideo, Uruguay	Rafael Viñoly Architects with Carla Bechelli Arquitectos (Argentina)	2009
Central Japan International Airport (NGO)	Tokoname City, Aichi Prefecture, Japan	Nikken Sekkei (Japan); Azusa Sekkei (Japan); Hellmuth, Obata & Kassabaum/Arup (UK)—a joint venture	2005
Changi Airport (SIN), Terminal 3	Singapore	CPG Corporation (Singapore); Skidmore, Owings & Merrill	2008
Charles de Gaulle Airport (CDG), Terminal 2E	Paris, France	Aéroports de Paris (France)	2003
Charles de Gaulle Airport (CDG), Terminal 2F	Paris, France	Aéroports de Paris (France)	1998
Chicago-O'Hare International Airport (ORD), Terminal 5	Chicago, IL	Perkins+Will with Heard & Associates	1994

Airports: 1990–2012

Airport	Location	Architect	Opened
Chongqing Jiangbei International Airport (CKG)	Chongqing, China	Llewelyn-Davies Ltd. (UK) with Arup (UK)	2004
Cologne/Bonn Airport (CGN), Terminal 2	Cologne, Germany	Murphy/Jahn	2000
Copenhagen International Airport (CPH), Terminal 3	Copenhagen, Denmark	Vilhelm Lauritzen AS (Denmark)	1998
Dallas-Fort Worth International Airport (DFW), Terminal D	Dallas/Fort Worth, TX	HNTB Architecture; HKS, Inc.; Corgan	2005
Denver International Airport (DEN)	Denver, CO	Fentress Bradburn Architects	1995
Detroit Metropolitan Wayne County Airport (DTW), North Terminal	Romulus, MI	Gensler; GHAFARI; Hamilton Anderson Associates	2008
Detroit Metropolitan Wayne County Airport (DTW), McNamara Terminal	Romulus, MI	SmithGroup	2002
Dubai International Airport (DXB), Terminal 3	Dubai, UAE	Paul Andreu Architecte (France)	2007
Dusseldorf International Airport (DUS)	Dusseldorf, Germany	JSK Architekten (Germany); Perkins+Will	2001–2003
Enfidha – Zine el Abidine Ben Ali Airport (NBE)	Enfidha, Tunisia	ADPi Designers & Planners (France)	2009
EuroAirport Basel-Mulhouse-Freiburg (BSL), South Terminal	Saint Louis Cédex, France	Aegerter and Bosshardt (Switzerland)	2005
Frankfurt Airport (FRA), Terminal 2	Frankfurt, Germany	Perkins+Will; JSK Architekten (Germany)	1994
Fukuoka International Airport (FUK), International Terminal	Hakata-ku, Fukuoka City, Japan	Hellmuth, Obata & Kassabaum; Azusa Sekkei (Japan); Mishima Architects (Japan); MHS Planners, Architects & Engineers Co. (Japan)	1999
Gardermoen Airport (GEN)	Oslo, Norway	AVIAPLAN (Norway); Niels Torp Architects (Norway)	1998
Graz International Airport (GRZ), Passenger Terminal	Graz, Austria	Pittino & Ortner Architekturbüro (Austria)	2005
Graz International Airport (GRZ), Passenger Terminal expansion	Graz, Austria	Riegler Riewe Architekten (Austria)	1994
Guangzhou Baiyun International Airport (CAN)	Guangdong, China	Parsons Brinckerhoff with URS Corporation	2004
Hamburg Airport (HAM), New Terminal 1	Hamburg, Germany	gmp Architekten (Germany) with von Gerkan, Marg & Partner Architekten (Germany)	2005
Hamburg Airport (HAM), Terminal 4 (now Terminal 2)	Hamburg, Germany	von Gerkan, Marg & Partner Architekten (Germany)	1991

Airport	Location	Architect	Opened
Haneda Airport (HND), New International Terminal	Tokyo, Japan	Unknown	2010
Haneda Airport (HND), Terminal 2	Tokyo, Japan	Cesar Pelli & Associates; Jun Mitsui & Associates Inc. Architects (Japan)	2004
Heathrow Airport (LHR), Terminal 5	London, UK	Richard Rogers Partnership (UK)	2008
Heathrow Airport (LHR), Pier 4A	London, UK	Nicholas Grimshaw & Partners (UK)	1993
Heathrow Airport (LHR), Europier	London, UK	Richard Rogers Partnership (UK)	1992
Hong Kong International Airport (HKG)	Hong Kong, China	Foster + Partners (UK)	1998
Incheon International Airport (ICN), Integrated Transportation Center	Seoul, South Korea	Terry Farrell and Partners (UK)	2002
Incheon International Airport (ICN)	Seoul, South Korea	Fentress Bradburn Architects with BHJW and Korean Architects Collaborative International (South Korea)	2001
Indianapolis Airport (IND), Passenger Terminal	Indianapolis, IN	Hellmuth, Obata & Kassabaum	2008
Indira Ghandi International Airport (DEL), Terminal 3	New Delhi, India	Hellmuth, Obata & Kassabaum with Mott MacDonald Group (UK)	2010
Jinan International Airport (TNA)	Jinan, China	Integrated Design Associates	2005
John F. Kennedy International Airport (JFK), Terminal 5	Jamaica, NY	Gensler	2008
John F. Kennedy International Airport (JFK), American Airlines Terminal, Phase 1	Jamaica, NY	DMJM Harris | AECOM	2005–2007
John F. Kennedy International Airport (JFK), Terminal 4	Jamaica, NY	Skidmore, Owings & Merrill	2001
John F. Kennedy International Airport (JFK), Terminal 1	Jamaica, NY	William Nicholas Bodouva + Associates	1998
Jorge Chávez International Airport (LIM), New Terminal	Lima, Peru	Arquitectonica	2005
Kansai International Airport (KIA)	Osaka Bay, Japan	Renzo Piano Building Workshop (Italy) with Nikken Sekkei (Japan), Aéroports de Paris (France), Japan Airport Consultants Inc. (Japan)	1994
King Fahd International Airport (DMM)	Dammam, Saudi Arabia	Minoru Yamasaki Associates (Japan)	1999
King Shaka International Airport (DUR)	Durban, South Africa	Osmond Lange Architects and Planners (South Africa)	2010

Airports: 1990–2012

Airport	Location	Architect	Opened
Kuala Lumpur International Airport (KUL)	Kuala Lumpur, Malaysia	Kisho Kurokawa Architect & Associates (Japan) with Akitek Jururancang (Malaysia)	1998
Learmonth International Airport (LEA)	Exeter, Australia	JCY Architects and Urban Designers (Australia)	1999
Lester B. Pearson International Airport (YYZ), Pier F at Terminal 1	Toronto, ON, Canada	Architects Canada; Moshe Safdie and Associates; Skidmore, Owings & Merrill; Adamson Associates Architects (Canada)	2007
Lester B. Pearson International Airport (YYZ), New Terminal 1	Toronto, ON, Canada	Skidmore, Owings & Merrill; Moshe Safdie and Associates; Adamson Associates Architects (Canada)	2004
Logan International Airport (BOS), Terminal A	Boston, MA	Hellmuth, Obata & Kassabaum with C&R/ Rizvi, Inc.	2005
Madrid Barajas International Airport (MAD), Terminal 3	Madrid, Spain	Richard Rogers Partnership (UK) with Estudio Lamela (Spain)	2005
Málaga Airport (AGP), Terminal 3	Malaga, Spain	Bruce S. Fairbanks (Spain)	2010
Malaga Airport (AGP), Pablo Ruiz Picasso Terminal	Malaga, Spain	Taller de Arquitectura (Spain)	1991
McCarran International Airport (LAS), Satellite D	Las Vegas, NV	LEO A DALY; Tate & Snyder	1998
Mineta San José International Airport (SJC), Terminals A and B	San Jose, CA	Fentress Architects	2010
Mineta San José International Airport (SJC), Terminals A and B Concourses	San Jose, CA	Gensler	2010
Ministro Pistarini International Airport (EZE), Terminal A	Buenos Aires, Argentina	Estudio M/SG/S/S/S (Spain) with Urgell/Fazio/Penedo/Urgell (Spain)	2000
Munich International Airport (MUC), Terminal 2	Munich, Germany	K+P Architekten und Stadtplaner (Germany)	2003
Munich International Airport (MUC), Airport Center	Munich, Germany	Murphy/Jahn	1999
Munich International Airport (MUC)	Munich, Germany	Von Busse & Partners (Germany)	1992
Orlando International Airport (MCO), Airside 2	Orlando, FL	Hellmuth, Obata & Kassabaum	2000
Ottawa International Airport (YOW), Passenger Terminal	Ottawa, ON, Canada	Brisbin Brook Beynon Architects (Canada); Stantec	2003
Philadelphia International Airport (PHL), International Terminal A-West	Philadelphia, PA	Kohn Pedersen Fox	2003
Pointe à Pitre Le Raizet International Airport (PTP)	Pointe à Pitre, Guadeloupe	Aéroports de Paris (France)	1996

Airport	Location	Architect	Opened
Raleigh-Durham International Airport (RDU), Terminal 2 Phase 1	Raleigh-Durham, NC	Fentress Architects	2008
Raleigh-Durham International Airport (RDU), Terminal 2 Phase 2	Raleigh-Durham, NC	Fentress Architects	2011
Ronald Reagan Washington National Airport (DCA), North Terminal	Washington, DC	Cesar Pelli & Associates; LEO A DALY	1997
Sacramento International Airport (SMF), Central Terminal B and Airside Concourse	Sacramento, CA	Corgan Associates with Fentress Architects	2011
San Francisco International Airport (SFO), International Terminal	San Francisco, CA	Skidmore, Owings & Merrill with Del Campo & Maru and Michael Willis Architects	2000
San Pablo Airport (SVQ)	Seville, Spain	Rafael Moneo (Spain)	1992
Seattle-Tacoma International Airport (SEA), Central Terminal	Seattle, WA	Fentress Bradburn Architects	2005
Seattle-Tacoma International Airport (SEA), Concourse A	Seattle, WA	NBBJ	2004
Sendai International Airport (SDJ)	Natori, Japan	Hellmuth, Obata & Kassabaum; Nikken Sekkei (Japan)	1998
Shanghai Pudong International Airport (PVG), Terminal 2	Shanghai, China	Shanghai Xian Dai Architectural Design Group (China)	2007
Shanghai Pudong International Airport (PVG)	Shanghai, China	Aéroports de Paris (France)	1999
Shenzhen Baoan International Airport (SZX), Domestic Terminal	Shenzhen, China	Llewelyn-Davies Ltd. (UK)	2001
Sheremetyevo International Airport (SVO), Terminal 3	Moscow, Russia	ADPi Designers & Planners (France)	2009
Southampton Airport (SOU)	Southampton, UK	Manser Associates (UK)	1994
Stansted Airport (STN)	London, UK	Foster + Partners (UK)	1991
Suvarnabhumi Airport (BK)	Samut Prakarn (Bangkok), Thailand	MJTA (Murphy/Jahn; TAMS Consultants Inc.; ACT Engineering)	2006
Tianjin Binhai International Airport (TSN), Terminal	Dongli, China	Kohn Pedersen Fox with Netherlands Airport Consultants (Netherlands)	2008
Toulouse-Blagnac International Airport (TLS), Hall D	Toulouse, France	Cardete Huet Architectes (France)	2010
Zurich Airport (ZRH), Airside Centre	Zurich, Switzerland	Nicholas Grimshaw & Partners (UK) with Itten+Brechbühl (Switzerland)	2004

Source: DesignIntelligence

Aquariums

The opening of Boston's New England Aquarium in 1969 ushered in a new age for aquariums, combining the traditional ideas found in the classic aquariums of the early 20th century with new technology and revised educational and research commitments. Aquariums have since proliferated. The following pages highlight the major free-standing aquariums in the United States.

Aquarium	Location	Opened	Cost
Alaska SeaLife Center	Seward, AK	1998	$56 M
Aquarium of the Bay	San Francisco, CA	1996	$38 M
Aquarium of the Pacific	Long Beach, CA	1998	$117 M
Audubon Aquarium of Americas	New Orleans, LA	1990	$42 M
Belle Isle Aquarium	Royal Oak, MI	1904	$175,000
Birch Aquarium at Scripps Institution of Oceanography, UCSD	La Jolla, CA	1992	$14 M
Colorado's Ocean Journey	Denver, CO	1999	$94 M
Flint RiverQuarium	Albany, GA	2004	$30 M
Florida Aquarium	Tampa, FL	1994	$84 M
Georgia Aquarium	Atlanta, GA	2005	$280 M ($110 M addition)
Great Lakes Aquarium	Duluth, MN	2000	$34 M
Greater Cleveland Aquarium	Cleveland, OH	2012	$33 M
John G. Shedd Aquarium	Chicago, IL	1930	$ 3.25 M ($45 M addition)
Maritime Aquarium at Norwalk	Norwalk, CT	1988	$11.5 M ($9 M addition)
Monterey Bay Aquarium	Monterey, CA	1984	$55 M ($57 M addition)
Mystic Aquarium	Mystic, CT	1973	$1.74 M ($52 M expansion)
National Aquarium	Washington, DC	1931	n/a
National Aquarium in Baltimore	Baltimore, MD	1981	$21.3 M ($35 M 1990 addition; $66 M 2005 addition)

Total Square Ft. (original/current)	Tank Capacity (orig./current, in gal.)	Architect
115,000	400,000	Cambridge Seven Associates with Livingston Slone
48,000	707,000	Esherick Homsey Dodge and Davis
156,735	900,000	A joint venture of Hellmuth, Obata & Kassabaum and Esherick Homsey Dodge and Davis
110,000	1.19 M	The Bienville Group: a joint venture of The Mathes Group, Eskew + Architects, Billes/Manning Architects, Hewitt Washington & Associates, Concordia
10,000	32,000	Albert Kahn Associates, Inc.
34,000	150,000	Wheeler Wimer Blackman & Associates
107,000	1 M	Odyssea: a joint venture of RNL and Anderson Mason Dale Architects
30,000	175,000	Antoine Predock Architect with Robbins Bell Kreher Inc.
152,000	1 M	Hellmuth, Obata & Kassabaum and Esherick Homsey Dodge and Davis
500,000/584,000	8 M/9.3 M	Thompson, Ventulett, Stainback & Associates (PGAV Destinations, 2010 expansion)
62,382	170,000	Hammel, Green and Abrahamson
70,000	1 M	Marinescape (New Zealand); (John N. Richardson, original 1892 Powerhouse building)
225,000/395,000	1.5 M/3 M	Graham, Anderson, Probst, & White (Lohan Associates, 1991 addition)
102,000/135,000	150,000	Graham Gund Architects Inc. (original building and 2001 addition)
216,000/307,000	900,000/1.9 M	Esherick Homsey Dodge and Davis (original building and 1996 addition)
76,000/137,000	1.6 M/2.3 M	Flynn, Dalton and van Dijk (Cesar Pelli & Associates, 1999 expansion)
13,500	32,000	York & Sawyer Architects
209,000/324,000/ 389,400	1 M/1.5 M/ 1.578 M	Cambridge Seven Associates (Grieves & Associates, 1990 addition; Chermayeff, Sollogub and Poole, 2005 addition)

Aquariums

Aquarium	Location	Opened	Cost
New England Aquarium	Boston, MA	1969	$8 M ($20.9 M 1998 addition; $19.3 M 2001 expansion)
New Jersey State Aquarium	Camden, NJ	1992	$52 M
New York Aquarium at Coney Island	Brooklyn, NY	1957	n/a
Newport Aquarium	Newport, KY	1999	$40 M ($4.5 M expansion)
North Carolina Aquarium at Fort Fisher	Kure Beach, NC	1976	$1.5 M ($17.5 M expansion)
North Carolina Aquarium at Pine Knoll Shores	Pine Knoll Shores, NC	1976	$4 M ($25 M expansion)
North Carolina Aquarium on Roanoke Island	Manteo, NC	1976	$1.6 M ($16 M expansion)
Oklahoma Aquarium	Tulsa, OK	2003	$15 M
Oregon Coast Aquarium	Newport, OR	1992	$25.5 M
Ripley's Aquarium	Myrtle Beach, SC	1997	$40 M
Ripley's Aquarium of the Smokies	Gatlinburg, TN	2000	$49 M
Seattle Aquarium	Seattle, WA	1977	n/a ($20 M expansion)
South Carolina Aquarium	Charleston, SC	2000	$69 M
Steinhart Aquarium at the California Academy of Science	San Francisco, CA	2008	$438 M*
Tennessee Aquarium	Chattanooga, TN	1992	$45 M ($30 M addition)
Texas State Aquarium	Corpus Christi, TX	1990	$31 M ($14 M addition)
Virginia Aquarium & Science Center	Virginia Beach, VA	1986	$7.5 M ($35 M expansion)
Waikiki Aquarium	Honolulu, HI	1955	$400,000
Wonders of Wildlife at the American National Fish and Wildlife Museum	Springfield, MO	2001	$34 M

* Combines figures for the Steinhart Aquarium, Morrison Planetarium, and Kimball Natural History Museum.

Source: DesignIntelligence

Total Square Ft. (original/current)	Tank Capacity (orig./current, in gal.)	Architect
75,000/1 M	1 M	Cambridge Seven Associates (Schwartz/Silver Architects, 1998 addition; E. Verner Johnson and Associates, 2001 expansion)
120,000	1 M	The Hillier Group
150,000	1.8 M	n/a
100,000/121,200	1 M/1.01 M	GBBN Architects (original and 2005 expansion)
30,000/84,000	77,000/455,000	Cambridge Seven Associates (BMS Architects, 2002 expansion)
29,000/93,000	25,000/433,000	Hayes, Howell & Associates (BMS Architects, 2006 expansion)
34,000/68,000	5,000/400,000	Lyles, Bissett, Carlisle and Wolff Associates of North Carolina Inc. with Cambridge Seven Associates (BMS Architects, 2000 expansion)
71,600	500,000	SPARKS
51,000	1.4 M	SRG Partnership
87,000	1.3 M	Enartec
115,000	1.3 M	Helman Hurley Charvat Peacock/Architects
68,000/86,000	753,000/873,000	Fred Bassetti & Co. (Miller Hull Partnership and Mithun, 2007 expansion)
93,000	1 M	Eskew + Architects with Clark and Menefee Architects
410,000*	500,000	Renzo Piano Building Workshop (Italy) with Stantec Architecture
130,000/190,000	400,000/1.1 M	Cambridge Seven Associates (Chermayeff, Sollogub & Poole, 2005 addition)
43,000/73,800	325,000/725,000	Phelps, Bomberger, and Garza (Corpus Christi Design Associates, 2003 addition)
41,500/120,000	100,000/800,000	E. Verner Johnson and Associates (original building and 1996 expansion)
19,000	152,000	Hart Wood and Edwin A. Weed with Ossipoff, Snyder, and Rowland
92,000	500,000	Cambridge Seven Associates

Art Museums

By some calculations there are more than 16,000 museums in the United States. While the collections they hold are often priceless, the facilities that contain them are frequently significant, especially amidst the recent museum-building boom led by world-class architects. The following chart, while not comprehensive, lists architecturally significant US art museums.

Museum	Location	Architect (original)
Akron Art Museum	Akron, OH	Dalton, van Dijk, Johnson & Partners (conversion of the original 1899 post office)
Albright-Knox Art Gallery	Buffalo, NY	Edward B. Green
Allen Memorial Art Museum	Oberlin, OH	Cass Gilbert
Amon Carter Museum	Fort Worth, TX	Philip Johnson
Anchorage Museum of History and Art	Anchorage, AK	Kirk, Wallace, and McKinley with Schultz/Maynard
Art Institute of Chicago	Chicago, IL	Shepley, Rutan, and Coolidge
Art Museum of South Texas	Corpus Christi, TX	Philip Johnson
Arthur M. Sackler Museum	Cambridge, MA	James Stirling Michael Wilford and Associates (UK)
Asian Art Museum	San Francisco, CA	Gae Aulenti (Italy) with Hellmuth, Obata & Kassabaum, LDa Architects, and Robert Wong Architects (adapted the 1917 main library by George Kelham)
Baltimore Museum of Art	Baltimore, MD	John Russell Pope
Barnes Foundation	Merion, PA	Paul Philippe Cret
Bass Museum of Art	Miami, FL	B. Robert Swartburg (adapted the 1930 Miami Beach Library by Russell Pancoast)
Bechtler Museum of Modern Art	Charlotte, NC	Mario Botta (Switzerland)
Bellevue Art Museum	Bellevue, WA	Steven Holl Architects
Berkeley Art Museum + Pacific Film Archive	Berkeley, CA	Mario J. Ciampi & Associates
Birmingham Museum of Art	Birmingham, AL	Warren, Knight and Davis
Bowdoin College Museum of Art	Brunswick, ME	McKim, Mead and White

Opened	Architect (expansion)
1981	Coop Himmelb(l)au (Austria) with Westlake Reed Leskosky, 2007 John S. and James L. Knight Building
1905	Skidmore, Owings & Merrill, 1961 addition
1917	Venturi, Scott Brown and Associates, 1977 addition
1961	Johnson/Burgee Architects, 1977 expansion; Philip Johnson/Alan Ritchie Architects, 2001 expansion
1968	Kenneth Maynard Associates, 1974 addition; Mitchell	Giurgola Architects with Maynard and Partch, 1986 addition; David Chipperfield Architects with Kumin Associates Inc., 2009 expansion
1893	Skidmore, Owings & Merrill, 1977 Arthur Rubloff Building; Hammond, Beebe and Babka, 1988 Daniel F. and Ada L. Rice Building; Renzo Piano Building Workshop (Italy) , with Interactive Design Inc., 2009 Modern Wing
1972	Legorreta + Legorreta (Mexico) with Dykema Architects, 2006 William B. and Maureen Miller Building
1985	—
2003	—
1929	John Russell Pope, 1937 Jacobs Wing; Wrenn, Lewis & Jancks, 1950 May Wing, 1956 Woodward Wing and 1957 Cone Wing; Bower Lewis & Thrower Architects, 1994 West Wing for Contemporary Art
1925	—
1964	Arata Isozaki & Associates (Japan) with Spillis Candela DMJM	AECOM, 2002 expansion
2010	—
2001	—
1970	—
1959	Warren, Knight and Davis, 1965 west wing, 1967 east wing, 1974 expansion, 1979 addition, and 1980 expansion; Edward Larrabee Barnes Associates, 1993 expansion
1894	Machado and Silvetti Associates, 2007 entry pavilion

Art Museums

Museum	Location	Architect (original)
Brooklyn Museum	Brooklyn, NY	McKim, Mead, and White
Butler Institute of American Art	Youngstown, OH	McKim, Mead and White
Chazen Museum of Art (formerly Elvehjem Museum of Art)	Madison, WI	Harry Weese
Cincinnati Art Museum	Cincinnati, OH	James McLaughlin
Cleveland Museum of Art	Cleveland, OH	Benjamin Hubbell and W. Dominick Benes
Clyfford Still Museum	Denver, CO	Allied Works Architecture
Colorado Springs Fine Arts Center	Colorado Springs, CO	John Gaw Meem
Columbus Museum of Art	Columbus, OH	Richards, McCarty and Bulford
Contemporary Art Museum St. Louis	St. Louis, MO	Allied Works Architecture
Contemporary Arts Museum, Houston	Houston, TX	Gunnar Birkerts and Associates
Corcoran Gallery of Art	Washington, DC	Ernest Flagg
Cranbrook Art Museum	Cranbrook, MI	Eliel Saarinen
Crocker Art Museum	Sacramento, CA	Seth Babson (architect of the original 1872 Crocker family mansion and art gallery)
Crystal Bridges Museum of American Art	Bentonville, AR	Moshe Safdie
Dallas Museum of Art	Dallas, TX	Edward Larrabee Barnes Associates
Dayton Art Institute	Dayton, OH	Edward B. Green
de Young Museum	San Francisco, CA	Herzog & de Meuron (Switzerland) with Fong & Chan Architects
Denver Art Museum	Denver, CO	Gio Ponti (Italy) with James Sudler Associates
Denver Museum of Contemporary Art	Denver, CO	Adjaye Associates (UK)
Des Moines Art Center	Des Moines, IA	Eliel Saarinen
Detroit Institute of Arts	Detroit, MI	James Balfour
Eli and Edythe Broad Art Museum, Michigan State University	East Lansing, MI	Zaha Hadid (UK)
Everson Museum of Art	Syracuse, NY	I.M. Pei & Associates

Opened	Architect (expansion)
1897–1927	Prentice & Chan, Ohlhausen, 1978 addition; Arata Isozaki & Associates (Japan) and James Stewart Polshek & Partners, 1991 Iris and B. Gerald Cantor Auditorium; Polshek Partnership Architects, 2004 front entrance and public plaza addition
1919	Paul Boucherie, 1931 north and south wings; C. Robert Buchanan & Associates, 1967 addition; Buchanan, Ricciuti & Associates, 1986 west wing addition
1970	Machado and Silvetti and Associates with Continuum Architects + Planners, 2011 expansion
1886	Daniel H. Burnham, 1907 Schmidlapp Wing; Garber and Woodward, 1910 Ropes Wing and 1930 Emery, Hanna & French Wings; Rendigs, Panzer and Martin, 1937 Alms Wing; Potter, Tyler, Martin and Roth, 1965 Adams-Emery Wing
1916	J. Byers Hays and Paul C. Ruth, 1958 addition; Marcel Breuer and Hamilton P. Smith, 1971 addition; Dalton, van Dijk, Johnson & Partners, 1984 addition; Rafael Viñoly Architects, 2009 East Wing
2011	
1936	—
1931	Van Buren and Firestone, Architects, Inc., 1974 addition
2003	—
1972	—
1897	Charles Adams Platt, 1927 expansion
1941	Rafael Moneo (Spain), 2002 addition
1978	Gwathmey Siegel & Associates Architects with HMR Architects, Inc., 2010 expansion
2011	—
1984	Edward Larrabee Barnes Associates, 1985 decorative arts wing and 1991 Nancy and Jake L. Hamon Building
1930	Levin Porter Associates, 1997 expansion
2005	—
1971	Studio Daniel Libeskind with Davis Partnership Architects, 2006 Frederic C. Hamilton Building
2006	—
1948	I.M. Pei & Associates, 1968 addition; Richard Meier & Partners Architects, 1985 addition
1888	Cret, Zantzinger, Borie and Medary, 1927 addition; Harley, Ellington, Cowin and Stirton, with Gunnar Birkerts and Associates, 1966 south wings; Harley, Ellington, Cowin and Stirton, 1966 north wing; Michael Graves & Associates with SmithGroup, 2007 expansion
2012	—
1968	—

Art Museums

Museum	Location	Architect (original)
Figge Art Museum	Davenport, IA	David Chipperfield Architects (UK) with Herbert Lewis Kruse Blunck Architecture
Fogg Art Museum	Cambridge, MA	Coolidge, Shepley, Bulfinch, and Abbott
Frances Lehman Loeb Art Center	Poughkeepsie, NY	Cesar Pelli & Associates
Fred Jones Jr. Museum of Art	Norman, OK	Howard and Smais
Frederick R. Weisman Art Museum	Minneapolis, MN	Frank O. Gehry and Associates, Inc.
Freer Gallery Art	Washington, DC	Charles Adams Platt
Frist Center for the Visual Arts	Nashville, TN	Tuck Hinton Architects (adapted the 1934 US Post Office by Marr and Holman Architects)
Frost Art Museum, Florida International University	Miami, FL	Hellmuth, Obata & Kassabaum
Frye Art Museum	Seattle, WA	Paul Albert Thiry
Grand Rapids Art Museum	Grand Rapids, MI	wHY Architecture with Design Plus
Herbert F. Johnson Museum of Art	Ithaca, NY	I.M. Pei & Partners
High Museum of Art	Atlanta, GA	Richard Meier & Partners Architects
Hirshhorn Museum and Sculpture Garden	Washington, DC	Skidmore, Owings & Merrill
Hood Museum of Art	Hanover, NH	Charles Moore and Centerbrook Architects and Planners
Hunter Museum of American Art	Chattanooga, TN	Mead and Garfield (architects of the 1905 mansion adapted to a museum in 1952)
Indiana University Art Museum	Bloomington, IN	I.M. Pei & Partners
Indianapolis Museum of Art	Indianapolis, IN	Richardson, Severns, Scheeler and Associates
Institute for Contemporary Art	Boston, MA	Diller Scofidio + Renfro
Iris & B. Gerald Cantor Center for Visual Arts	Stanford, CA	Percy & Hamilton Architects with Ernest J. Ransome
Isabella Stewart Gardner Museum	Boston, MA	Willard T. Sears
J. Paul Getty Museum	Los Angeles, CA	Richard Meier & Partners Architects
Joslyn Art Museum	Omaha, NE	John and Alan McDonald
Kemper Museum of Contemporary Art and Design	Kansas City, MO	Gunnar Birkerts and Associates
Kimbell Art Museum	Fort Worth, TX	Louis I. Kahn
Kreeger Museum	Washington, DC	Philip Johnson with Richard Foster
Lois & Richard Rosenthal Center for Contemporary Art	Cincinnati, OH	Zaha Hadid Architects (UK) with KZF Design

Opened	Architect (expansion)
2005	—
1927	—
1993	—
1971	Hugh Newell Jacobsen, 2005 Mary and Howard Lester Wing
1993	Gehry Partners, 2011 addition
1923	—
2001	—
2008	—
1952	Olson Sundberg Kundig Allen Architects, 1997 expansion
2007	—
1973	Pei Cobb Freed & Partners, 2011 expansion
1983	Renzo Piano Building Workshop (Italy) with Lord, Aeck and Sargent, 2005 addition
1974	—
1985	—
1952	Derthick, Henley and Wilkerson Architects, 1975 addition; Randall Stout Architects with Derthick, Henley and Wilkerson Architects and Hefferlin + Kronenberg Architects, 2005 addition
1982	—
1970	Edward Larrabee Barnes Associates and John M.Y. Lee, 1990 Mary Fendrich Hulman Pavilion; Browning Day Mullins Dierdorf Architects, 2005 expansion
2006	—
1894	Polshek Partnership Architects, 1999 addition
1903	Renzo Piano Building Workshop (Italy), 2012 expansion
1997	—
1931	Foster + Partners (UK), 1994 Walter and Suzanne Scott Pavilion
1994	—
1972	—
1967	—
2003	—

Art Museums

Museum	Location	Architect (original)
Los Angeles County Museum of Art	Los Angeles, CA	William L. Pereira & Associates
Mead Art Museum	Amherst, MA	McKim, Mead and White
Memphis Brooks Museum of Art	Memphis, TN	James Gamble Rogers with Carl Gutherz
Menil Collection	Houston, TX	Renzo Piano Building Workshop (Italy) with Richard Fitzgerald & Partners
Metropolitan Museum of Art	New York, NY	Calvert Vaux and J. Wrey Mould
Milwaukee Art Museum	Milwaukee, WI	Eero Saarinen with Maynard Meyer
Minneapolis Institute of Arts	Minneapolis, MN	McKim, Mead and White
Modern Art Museum of Fort Worth	Fort Worth, TX	Tadao Ando (Japan)
Munson-Williams-Proctor Arts Institute	Utica, NY	Philip Johnson
Museum of Arts and Design	New York, NY	Allied Works Architecture (renovated the 1965 building by Edward Durrell Stone & Associates)
Museum of Contemporary Art Chicago	Chicago, IL	Josef Paul Kleihues (Germany)
Museum of Contemporary Art Cleveland	Cleveland, OH	Farshid Moussavi (UK) with Westlake Reed Leskosky
Museum of Contemporary Art Denver	Denver, CO	Adjaye Associates (UK)
Museum of Contemporary Art, Los Angeles	Los Angeles, CA	Arata Isozaki & Associates (Japan)
Museum of Contemporary Art San Diego	La Jolla, CA	Irving Gill (originally designed as a residence in 1916)
Museum of Fine Arts, Boston	Boston, MA	Guy Lowell
Museum of Fine Arts, Houston	Houston, TX	William Ward Watkin
Museum of Fine Arts, St. Petersburg	St. Petersburg, FL	John L. Volk

Opened	Architect (expansion)
1965	Hardy Holzman Pfeiffer Associates, 1986 Art of the Americas Building; Bruce Goff, 1988 Pavilion for Japanese Art; Albert C. Martin and Associates, 1998 LACAMA West building (originally the 1946 May Co. building); Renzo Piano Building Workshop (Italy), 2008 Broad Contemporary Art Museum
1949	—
1916	Walk Jones and Francis Mah, 1973 addition; Skidmore, Owings & Merrill with Askew, Nixon, Ferguson & Wolf, 1989 expansion
1987	—
1880	Theodore Weston, 1888 SW wing; Richard Morris Hunt and Richard Howland Hunt, 1902 Central Fifth Avenue facade; McKim, Mead and White, 1906 side wings along Fifth Avenue; Brown, Lawford & Forbes, 1965 Thomas J. Watson Library; Kevin Roche John Dinkeloo & Associates, 1975 Lehman Wing, 1979 Sackler Wing, 1980 American Wing, 1981 Michael C. Rockefeller Wing for Primitive Art, 1988 European Sculpture and Decorative Art Wing; Kevin Roche John Dinkeloo & Associates, 2012 American Wing renovation
1957	Kahler, Fitzhugh and Scott, 1975 addition; Santiago Calatrava (Spain) with Kahler Slater, 2001 Quadracci Pavilion
1915	Kenzo Tange Associates (Japan), 1974 addition; Michael Graves & Associates with RSP Architects, 2006 Target Wing
2002	—
1960	Lund McGee Sharpe Architecture, 1995 Education Wing
2008	—
1996	—
2012	—
2007	—
1986	—
1941	Mosher & Drew, 1950 transition to museum; Mosher & Drew, 1959 Sherwood Auditorium; Venturi, Scott Brown and Associates, 1996 expansion and renovation
1909	Guy Lowell, 1915 Robert Dawson Evans Wing; John Singer Sargent, 1921 Rotunda and 1925 Colonnade; Guy Lowell, 1928 Decorative Arts Wing; Hugh Stubbins & Associates, 1968 Forsyth Wickes Galleries and 1970 George Robert White Wing; I.M. Pei & Partners, 1981 West Wing; Foster + Partners (UK) with Childs Bertman Tseckares, 2010 Art of the Americas Wing and Ruth and Carl J. Shapiro Family Courtyard
1924–26	Kenneth Franzheim, 1953 Robert Lee Blaffer Memorial Wing; Mies van der Rohe, 1958 Cullinan Hall and 1974 Brown Pavilion; Isamu Noguchi (Japan), 1986 Lillie and Hugh Roy Cullen Sculpture Garden; Rafael Moneo (Spain), 2000 Audrey Jones Beck Building
1965	Hellmuth, Obata & Kassabaum, 2008 Hazel Hough Wing

Art Museums

Museum	Location	Architect (original)
Museum of Modern Art	New York, NY	Philip L. Goodwin and Edward Durrell Stone & Associates
Nasher Museum of Art	Durham, NC	Rafael Viñoly Architects
Nasher Sculpture Center	Dallas, TX	Renzo Piano Building Workshop (Italy) with Peter Walker and Partners
National Gallery of Art, East Building	Washington, DC	I.M. Pei & Partners
National Gallery of Art, West Building	Washington, DC	John Russell Pope
National Portrait Gallery and American Art Museum	Washington, DC	Faulkner, Stenhouse, Fryer (adapted the 1836–67 Old Patent Office Building by Robert Mills and Thomas Ustick Walter)
Nelson Fine Arts Center	Tempe, AZ	Antoine Predock Architect
Nelson-Atkins Museum of Art	Kansas City, MO	Wight and Wight
Nevada Museum of Art	Reno, NV	will bruder + PARTNERS
New Museum of Contemporary Art	New York, NY	SANAA with Gensler
New Orleans Museum of Art	New Orleans, LA	Samuel Marx
North Carolina Museum of Art	Raleigh, NC	Edward Durell Stone
Oakland Museum of California	Oakland, CA	Kevin Roche John Dinkeloo & Associates
Ohr-O'Keefe Museum of Art	Biloxi, MS	Gehry Partners; Eley Guild Hardy Architects
Parrish Art Museum	Southampton, NY	Grosvenor Atterbury
Pennsylvania Academy of the Fine Arts	Philadelphia, PA	Frank Furness and George W. Hewitt
Philadelphia Museum of Art	Philadelphia, PA	Horace Trumbauer with Zantzinger, Borie, and Medar
Phoenix Art Museum	Phoenix, AZ	Alden B. Dow
Portland Art Museum	Portland, OR	Pietro Belluschi
Portland Museum of Art	Portland, ME	John Calvin Stevens
Princeton University Art Museum	Princeton, NJ	Ralph Adams Cram
Pulitzer Foundation for the Arts	St. Louis, MO	Tadao Ando (Japan)
Renwick Gallery	Washington, DC	James Renwick Jr.
Rodin Museum	Philadelphia, PA	Paul Philippe Cret and Jacques Gréber
Saint Louis Art Museum	St. Louis, MO	Cass Gilbert
Salvador Dali Museum	St. Petersburg, FL	HOK

Opened	Architect (expansion)
1939	Philip Johnson, 1964 east wing; Cesar Pelli & Associates, 1984 tower; Taniguchi Associates (Japan) with Kohn Pedersen Fox and Cooper, Robertson & Partners, 2004 expansion and 2006 Lewis B. and Dorothy Cullman Education Building
2005	—
2003	—
1978	—
1941	—
1968	Foster + Partners (UK) with SmithGroup, 2007 Robert and Arlene Kogod Courtyard
1989	—
1933	Steven Holl Architects with BNIM Architects, 2007 Bloch Building
2003	—
2007	—
1911	August Perez with Arthur Feitel, 1971 Wisner Education Wing, City Wing, and Stern Auditorium; Eskew Filson Architects with Billes/Manning Architects, 1993 expansion
1984	Thomas Phifer and Partners with Pierce Brinkley Cease + Lee, 2010 expansion
1969	—
2010*	—
1897	Grosvenor Atterbury, 1902 and 1913 wings; Herzog & de Meuron (Switzerland), 2012 expansion
1876	—
1928	Gluckman Mayner Architects, 2008 renovation of the Perelman Building (originally designed by Zantzinger, Borie, and Medary in 1927)
1959	Alden B. Dow, 1965 east wing; Tod Williams Billie Tsien Architects, 1996 and 2006 expansions
1932	Pietro Belluschi, 1939 Hirsch Wing; Pietro Belluschi, with Wolff, Zimmer, Gunsul, Frasca, and Ritter, 1970 Hoffman Wing; Ann Beha Architects, 2000 expansion; Ann Beha Architects with SERA Architects, 2005 expansion
1911	I.M. Pei & Partners, 1983 Charles Shipman Payson Building
1922	Steinman and Cain, 1966 expansion; Mitchell	Giurgola Architects, 1989 Mitchell Wolfson Jr. Wing
2001	—
1859	John Carl Warnecke & Associates and Hugh Newell Jacobsen, 1971 restoration
1929	—
1903	—
2011	—

* The museum opened in 1994, but all of its former buildings were destroyed in Hurricane Katrina.

Art Museums

Museum	Location	Architect (original)
San Diego Museum of Art	San Diego, CA	William Templeton Johnson with Robert W. Snyder
San Francisco Museum of Modern Art	San Francisco, CA	Mario Botta (Italy)
Santa Barbara Museum of Art	Santa Barbara, CA	David Adler (adapted the 1914 Old Post Office designed by Francis Wilson)
Seattle Art Museum	Seattle, WA	Venturi, Scott Brown and Associates
Shaw Center for the Arts	Baton Rouge, LA	Schwartz/Silver Architects with Eskew+Dumez+ Ripple and Jerry M. Campbell Associates
Sheldon Memorial Art Gallery	Lincoln, NE	Philip Johnson
Solomon R. Guggenheim Museum	New York, NY	Frank Lloyd Wright
Speed Art Museum	Louisville, KY	Arthur Loomis
Sterling and Francine Clark Art Institute	Wiliamstown, MA	Daniel Perry
Tacoma Art Museum	Tacoma, WA	Antoine Predock Architect with Olson Sundberg Kundig Allen Architects
Tampa Museum of Art	Tampa, FL	Natoma Architects
Taubman Museum of Art	Roanoke, VA	Randall Stout Architects with Rodriguez Ripley Maddux Motley Architects
Terra Museum of American Art	Chicago, IL	Booth Hansen Associates
Toledo Museum of Art	Toledo, OH	Green & Wicks with Harry W. Wachter
UCLA Hammer Museum of Art	Los Angeles, CA	Edward Larrabee Barnes Associates
University of Michigan Museum of Art	Ann Arbor, MI	Donaldson and Meier Architects
Vincent Price Art Museum	Los Angeles, CA	Arquitectonica
Virginia Museum of Fine Arts	Richmond, VA	Peebles and Ferguson Architects
Wadsworth Atheneum Museum of Art	Hartford, CT	Ithiel Town and Alexander Jackson Davis
Walker Art Center	Minneapolis, MN	Edward Larrabee Barnes Associates
Wexner Center for the Arts	Columbus, OH	Eisenman Architects with Richard Trott & Partners
Whitney Museum of American Art	New York, NY	Marcel Breuer and Associates
Yale Center for British Art	New Haven, CT	Louis I. Kahn
Yale University Art Gallery	New Haven, CT	Louis I. Kahn

Source: DesignIntelligence

Opened	Architect (expansion)
1926	Robert Mosher & Roy Drew, Architects, 1966 west wing; Mosher, Drew, Watson & Associates with William Ferguson, 1974 east wing
1995	—
1941	Chester Carjola, 1942 Katherine Dexter McCormick Wing; Arendt/Mosher/Grants Architects, 1961 Preston Morton Wing and 1962 Sterling Morton Wing; Paul Gray, 1985 Alice Keck Park Wing; Edwards & Pitman, 1998 Peck Wing
1991	Allied Works Architecture with NBBJ, 2007 expansion
2005	—
1963	—
1959	Gwathmey Siegel & Associates Architects, 1992 addition
1927	Nevin and Morgan, 1954 Preston Pope Satterwhite Wing; Brenner, Danforth, and Rockwell, 1973 north wing; Robert Geddes, 1983 south wing
1955	Pietro Belluschi and The Architects Collaborative, 1973 addition; Tadao Ando Architect & Associates (Japan) and Gensler, 2008 Stone Hill Center
2003	—
2010	—
2008	—
1987	—
1912	Edward B. Green and Sons, 1926 wing and 1933 expansion; Frank O. Gehry and Associates, Inc., 1992 Center for the Visual Arts addition; SANAA (Japan), 2006 Glass Pavilion
1990	—
1910	Allied Works Architecture with IDS, 2009 Maxine and Stuart Frankel and Frankel Family Wing
2011	—
1936	Merrill C. Lee, Architects, 1954 addition; Baskervill & Son Architects, 1970 South Wing; Hardwicke Associates, Inc., 1976 North Wing; Hardy Holzman Pfeiffer Associates, 1985 West Wing; Rick Mather Architect (UK) with SMBW, 2010 addition
1844	Benjamin Wistar Morris, 1910 Colt Memorial and 1915 Morgan Memorial; Morris & O'Connor, 1934 Avery Memorial; Huntington, Darbee & Dollard, Architects, 1969 Goodwin Wing
1971	Herzog & de Meuron (Switzerland) with Hammel, Green and Abrahamson, 2005 expansion
1989	—
1966	Gluckman Mayner Architects, 1998 expansion
1977	—
1953	Ennead Architects, 2012 renovation of Swartwout Hall and Street Hall

Convention Centers

In the past decade public spending on convention centers has doubled to $2.4 billion annually, and since 1990 convention space in the US has increased by more than 50 percent. The following is *DesignIntelligence*'s list of the largest US convention centers with their requisite architectural statistics.

Convention Center	Location	Opened	Exhibit Halls (sq. ft.)
America's Center	St. Louis, MO	1977	502,000
AmericasMart Atlanta	Atlanta, GA	1961	800,000
Anaheim Convention Center	Anaheim, CA	1967	815,000
Atlantic City Convention Center	Atlantic City, NJ	1997	518,300
Austin Convention Center	Austin, TX	1992	246,097
Baltimore Convention Center	Baltimore, MD	1979	300,000
Boston Convention and Exhibition Center	Boston, MA	2004	516,000
Charlotte Convention Center	Charlotte, NC	1995	280,000
Cobo Conference/Exhibition Center	Detroit, MI	1960	700,000
Colorado Convention Center	Denver, CO	1990	584,000
Dallas Convention Center	Dallas, TX	1973	726,726
David L. Lawrence Convention Center	Pittsburgh, PA	2003	313,400
Donald E. Stephens Convention Center	Rosemont, IL	1974	840,000
Ernest N. Morial Convention Center	New Orleans, LA	1985	1.1 M
Fort Worth Convention Center	Fort Worth, TX	1968	253,226

Architect (original)	Architect (expansion)
Hellmuth, Obata & Kassabaum	Hellmuth, Obata & Kassabaum, 1993 and 1995 expansions
Edwards and Portman, Architects (Merchandise Mart)	Edwards and Portman, Architects, 1968 Merchandise Mart addition; John Portman & Associates, Architects, 1979 Apparel Mart, 1986 Merchandise Mart addition, 1989 Apparel Mart addition, 1992 Gift Mart; John Portman & Associates, 2009 Building 2 WestWing
Adrian Wilson & Associates	HNTB Architecture, 1974, 1982, 1990, and 1993 expansions; HOK Sport + Venue + Event, 1999–2001 expansion
Wallace Roberts & Todd	—
PageSoutherlandPage	Austin Collaborative Venture (PageSoutherlandPage; Cotera Kolar Negrete & Reed Architects; Limbacher & Godfrey Architects), 2002 expansion
NBBJ with Cochran, Stephenson & Donkervoet expansion	LMN Architects with Cochran, Stephenson & Donkervoet, 1996
HNTB Architecture/Rafael Viñoly Architects, joint venture	—
Thompson, Ventulett, Stainback & Associates with The FWA Group	—
Giffels & Rossetti	Sims-Varner & Associates, 1989 expansion
Fentress Bradburn Architects	Fentress Bradburn Architects, 2004 expansion
Harrell + Hamilton Architects (adapted and expanded the 1957 Dallas Memorial Auditorium by George L. Dahl Architects and Engineers Inc.)	Omniplan, 1984 expansion; JPJ Architects, 1994 expansion; Skidmore, Owings & Merrill and HKS, Inc., 2002 expansion
Rafael Viñoly Architects	—
Anthony M. Rossi Limited	Anthony M. Rossi Limited, subsequent expansions
Perez & Associates and Perkins & James	Perez & Associates and Billes/Manning Architects, 1991 expansion; Convention Center III Architects (Cimini, Meric, Duplantier Architects/Planners, Billes/Manning Architects, and Hewitt Washington & Associates), 1999 expansion
Parker Croston	Carter & Burgess, Inc. and HOK Sport + Venue + Event, 2003 addition

Convention Centers

Convention Center	Location	Opened	Exhibit Halls (sq. ft.)
George R. Brown Convention Center	Houston, TX	1987	893,590
Georgia World Congress Center	Atlanta, GA	1976	1.4 M
Greater Columbus Convention Center	Columbus, OH	1993	426,000
Hawaii Convention Center	Honolulu, HI	1996	204,249
Henry B. Gonzalez Convention Center	San Antonio, TX	1968	440,000
Indianapolis Convention Center & RCA Dome	Indianapolis, IN	1972	567,000
Jacob K. Javits Convention Center	New York, NY	1986	814,000
Kansas City Convention Center	Kansas City, MO	1976	388,800
Las Vegas Convention Center	Las Vegas, NV	1959	2 M
Long Beach Convention & Entertainment Center	Long Beach, CA	1978	224,000
Los Angeles Convention Center	Los Angeles, CA	1972	720,000
Mandalay Bay Convention Center	Las Vegas, NV	2003	934,731
McCormick Place	Chicago, IL	1971	2.6 M

Architect (original)	Architect (expansion)
Goleman & Rolfe Associates, Inc.; John S. Chase; Molina & Associates; Haywood Jordan McCowan, Inc.; Moseley Architects with Bernard Johnson and 3D/International	Golemon & Bolullo Architects, 2003 expansion
Thompson, Ventulett, Stainback & Associates	Thompson, Ventulett, Stainback & Associates, 1985 and 1992 expansions; Thompson, Ventulett, Stainback & Associates with Heery International, 2003 expansion
Eisenman Architects with Richard Trott & Partners	Eisenman Architects, Karlsberger, and Thompson, Ventulett, Stainback & Associates, 2001 expansion
LMN Architects with Wimberly Allison Tong & Goo	—
Noonan and Krocker; Phelps and Simmons and Associates	Cerna Raba & Partners, 1986 expansion; Thompson, Ventulett, Stainback & Associates with Kell Muñoz Architects and Haywood Jordon McCowan, Inc., 2001 expansion
Lennox, James and Loebl (Lennox, Matthews, Simmons and Ford; James Associates; Loebl Schlossman Bennett & Dart)	Blackburn Architects and Browning Day Mullins Dierdorf Architects with Hellmuth, Obata & Kassabaum, 1993 and 2001 expansions; RATIO Architects with BSA LifeStructures, Blackburn Architects, and Domain Architecture Inc., 2011 expansion
I.M. Pei & Partners	—
C.F. Murphy Associates with Seligson Associates, Hormer and Blessing, and Howard Needles Tammen & Bergendoff	Convention Center Associates, Architects; BNIM Architects; HNTB Architecture, 1994 expansion
Adrian Wilson & Associates with Harry Whitney Consulting Architect	Jack Miller & Associates, 1967 South Hall; Adrian Wilson & Associates, 1971 C3 expansion; Jack Miller & Associates, 1975 C4 expansion; JMA, 1980 C5 expansion and 1990 expansion; Domingo Cambeiro Corp. Architects, 1998 North Hall and 2002 South Hall
Killingsworth, Brady, Smith and Associates	Thompson, Ventulett, Stainback & Associates, 1994 expansion
Charles Luckman & Associates	Pei Cobb Freed & Partners with Gruen Associates, 1993 expansion; Gruen Associates, 1997 Kentia Hall addition
Klai Juba Architects	—
C.F. Murphy Associates	Skidmore, Ownings & Merrill, 1986 North Hall; Thompson, Ventulett, Stainback & Associates with Architects Enterprise, 1996 South Hall; Thompson, Ventulett, Stainback & Associates and Mc4West, 2007 West Hall

Convention Centers

Convention Center	Location	Opened	Exhibit Halls (sq. ft.)
Miami Beach Convention Center	Miami Beach, FL	1958	503,000
Minneapolis Convention Center	Minneapolis, MN	1989–91	475,000
Moscone Center	San Francisco, CA	1981	741,308
Orange County Convention Center	Orlando, FL	1983	2.1 M
Oregon Convention Center	Portland, OR	1990	315,000
Pennsylvania Convention Center	Philadelphia, PA	1993	679,000
Phoenix Convention Center	Phoenix, AZ	1985	502,500
Reliant Center	Houston, TX	2004	706,213
Reno-Sparks Convention Center	Reno, NV	1965	381,000
Salt Palace Convention Center	Salt Lake City, UT	1996	515,000
San Diego Convention Center	San Diego, CA	1989	615,701
Tampa Convention Center	Tampa, FL	1990	200,000
Washington Convention Center	Washington, DC	2003	703,000
Washington State Convention and Trade Center	Seattle, WA	1988	205,700

Source: DesignIntelligence

Architect (original)	Architect (expansion)
B. Robert Swartburg	Gilbert M. Fein, 1968 Hall D; Edward Durrell Stone & Associates, Gilbert M. Fein, and Watson, Deutschmann, Kruse & Lyon, 1974 addition; Thompson, Ventulett, Stainback & Associates with Borrelli, Frankel, Biltstein, 1989 and 1991 expansions
Leonard Parker Associates; Setter Leach & Lindstrom; LMN Architects	Convention Center Design Group (Leonard Parker Associates; Setter Leach & Lindstrom; LMN Architects), 2001 expansion
Hellmuth, Obata & Kassabaum	Gensler/DMJM Associate Architects, joint venture, 1992 North Hall; Gensler/Michael Willis Architects/Kwan Henmi, joint venture, 2003 West Hall
Helman Hurley Charvat Peacock/Architects, Inc.	Hellmuth, Obata & Kassabaum and Vickey/Ovresat Assumb Associates, Inc., 1989-90 expansion; Hunton Brady Pryor Maso Architects and Thompson, Ventulett, Stainback & Associates, 1996 expansion; Helman Hurley Charvat Peacock/Architects, Thompson, Ventulett, Stainback & Associates, Inc. and Hunton Brady Pryor Maso Architects, 2003 expansion
Zimmer Gunsul Frasca Partnership	Zimmer Gunsul Frasca Architects, 2003 expansion
Thompson, Ventulett & Stainback Associates with VITETTA and Kelly/Maiello Architects and Planners (including the adaption of the 1893 Reading Terminal Headhouse by Wilson Brothers and F.H. Kimball)	tvsdesign with Vitetta Group and Kelly/Maiello Architects and and Planners, 2011 expansion
GSAS Architects and Planners, Inc. with Howard Needles Tammen & Bergendoff	LEO A DALY/HOK Sport + Venue + Event with van Dijk Westlake Reed Leskosky, 2006 expansion; HOK Sport + Venue + Event and SmithGroup, 2008 North Building
Hermes Reed Architects	—
Richard Neutra with Lockard, Casazza & Parsons	Parsons Design Group, 1981 North Hall; Sheehan, Van Woert Architects, 1991 East Hall; LMN Architects, 2002 expansion
Thompson, Ventulett, Stainback & Associates with GSBS Architects	Leonard Parker Associates with MHTB Architects, 2000 expansion; Edwards & Daniels Architects, Inc., 2006 expansion
Arthur Erickson Architect with Deems Lewis McKinley	HNTB Architecture with Tucker Sadler Architects, 2002 expansion
Hellmuth, Obata & Kassabaum	—
TVS–D&P–Mariani PLLC (Thompson, Ventulett, Stainback & Associates; Devrouax & Purnell Architects; and Mariani Architects Engineers)	—
TRA Architects	LMN Architects, 2001 expansion

Sports Stadiums

From classic ballparks to cutting-edge arenas and stadiums, the following charts provide statistical and architectural highlights for all major-league baseball, basketball, football, and hockey venues in the United States. All cost and architectural information refers to the stadiums as they were originally built and does not include additions, renovations, or expansions.

Baseball

Team	League	Stadium	Location	Opened
Arizona Diamondbacks	National	Chase Field	Phoenix, AZ	1998
Atlanta Braves	National	Turner Field	Atlanta, GA	1997
Baltimore Orioles	American	Oriole Park at Camden Yards	Baltimore, MD	1992
Boston Red Sox	American	Fenway Park	Boston, MA	1912
Chicago Cubs	National	Wrigley Field	Chicago, IL	1914
Chicago White Sox	American	U.S. Cellular Field	Chicago, IL	1991
Cincinnati Reds	National	Great American Ball Park	Cincinnati, OH	2003
Cleveland Indians	American	Progressive Field	Cleveland, OH	1994
Colorado Rockies	National	Coors Field	Denver, CO	1995
Detroit Tigers	American	Comerica Park	Detroit, MI	2000
Houston Astros	National	Minute Maid Park	Houston, TX	2000
Kansas City Royals	American	Kauffman Stadium	Kansas City, MO	1973
Los Angeles Angels of Anaheim	American	Angel Stadium of Anaheim	Anaheim, CA	1966
Los Angeles Dodgers	National	Dodger Stadium	Los Angeles, CA	1962
Miami Marlins	National	Marlins Park	Miami, FL	2012
Milwaukee Brewers	National	Miller Park	Milwaukee, WI	2001
Minnesota Twins	American	Target Field	Minneapolis, MN	2010
New York Mets	National	Citi Field	Flushing, NY	2009
New York Yankees	American	Yankee Stadium	Bronx, NY	2009
Oakland A's	American	O.co Coliseum	Oakland, CA	1966
Philadelphia Phillies	National	Citizens Bank Park	Philadelphia, PA	2004
Pittsburgh Pirates	National	PNC Park	Pittsburgh, PA	2001
San Diego Padres	National	Petco Park	San Diego, CA	2004

Architect	Cost (original)	Capacity (current)	Roof Type	Naming Rights (amt. & expiration)
Ellerbe Becket with Bill Johnson	$355 M	49,033	Convertible	$33.1 M (30 yrs.)
Heery International; Williams-Russell & Johnson, Inc.; Ellerbe Becket	$250 M	49,831	Open-Air	Undisclosed
HOK Sports Facilities Group with RTKL Associates Inc.	$210 M	48,876	Open-Air	—
Osborn Engineering Company	$365,000	33,871	Open-Air	—
Zachary Taylor Davis	$250,000	38,765	Open-Air	—
HOK Sports Facilities Group	$150 M	44,321	Open-Air	$68 M (20 yrs.)
HOK Sport + Venue + Event with GBBN Architects	$290 M	42,053	Open-Air	$75 M (30 yrs.)
HOK Sports Facilities Group	$173 M	43,345	Open-Air	$54 M (15 yrs.)
HOK Sports Facilities Group	$215 M	50,445	Open-Air	$15 M (indefinite)
HOK Sports Facilities Group; SHG Inc.	$300 M	40,637	Open-Air	$66 M (30 yrs.)
HOK Sports Facilities Group	$248.1 M	40,950	Retractable	$170 M (28 yrs.)
HNTB Architecture	$50.45 M	40,625	Open-Air	—
Robert A.M. Stern Architects	$25 M	45,050	Open-Air	—
Emil Praeger	$24.47 M	56,000	Open-Air	—
Populous	$634 M	36,742	Retractable	—
HKS, Inc. with NBBJ and Eppstein Uhen Architects	$399.4 M	42,500	Retractable	$41 M (20 yrs.)
Populous	$545 M	39,504	Open-Air	Undisclosed
Populous	$660 M	41,800	Open-Air	$400 M (20 yrs.)
Populous	$1.5 B	52,325	Open-Air	—
Skidmore, Owings & Merrill	$25.5 M	35,067	Open-Air	$1.2 M (6 yrs.)
EwingCole with HOK Sport + Venue + Event	$346 M	43,000	Open-Air	$57.5 M (25 yrs.)
HOK Sport + Venue + Event; L.D. Astorino Companies	$262 M	38,000	Open-Air	$30 M (20 yrs.)
Antoine Predock Architect with HOK Sport + Venue + Event	$453 M	46,000	Open-Air	$60 M (22 yrs.)

Sports Stadiums

Baseball

Team	League	Stadium	Location	Opened
San Francisco Giants	National	AT&T Park	San Francisco, CA	2000
Seattle Mariners	American	Safeco Field	Seattle, WA	1999
St. Louis Cardinals	National	Busch Stadium	St. Louis, MO	2006
Tampa Bay Rays	American	Tropicana Field	St. Petersburg, FL	1990
Texas Rangers	American	Rangers Ballpark in Arlington	Arlington, TX	1994
Toronto Blue Jays	American	Rogers Centre	Toronto, ON, Canada	1989
Washington Nationals	National	Nationals Park	Washington, DC	2008

Basketball

Team	Conference	Stadium	Location	Opened
Atlanta Hawks	Eastern	Philips Arena	Atlanta, GA	1999
Boston Celtics	Eastern	TD Garden	Boston, MA	1995
Brooklyn Nets	Eastern	Barclays Center	Brooklyn, NY	2012
Charlotte Bobcats	Eastern	Time Warner Cable Arena	Charlotte, NC	2005
Chicago Bulls	Eastern	United Center	Chicago, IL	1994
Cleveland Cavaliers	Eastern	Quicken Loans Arena	Cleveland, OH	1994
Dallas Mavericks	Western	American Airlines Center	Dallas, TX	2001
Denver Nuggets	Western	Pepsi Center	Denver, CO	1999
Detroit Pistons	Eastern	Palace of Auburn Hills	Auburn Hills, MI	1988
Golden State Warriors	Western	Oracle Arena	Oakland, CA	1966
Houston Rockets	Western	Toyota Center	Houston, TX	2003
Indiana Pacers	Eastern	Conseco Fieldhouse	Indianapolis, IN	1999
Los Angeles Clippers	Western	Staples Center	Los Angeles, CA	1999
Los Angeles Lakers	Western	Staples Center	Los Angeles, CA	1999
Memphis Grizzlies	Western	FedEx Forum	Memphis, TN	2004
Miami Heat	Eastern	American Airlines Arena	Miami, FL	1998

Architect	Cost (original)	Capacity (current)	Roof Type	Naming Rights (amt. & expiration)
HOK Sports Facilities Group	$345 M	40,800	Open-Air	$50 M (24 yrs.)
NBBJ	$517.6 M	46,621	Retractable	$40 M (20 yrs.)
HOK Sport + Venue + Event	$344 M	46,816	Open-Air	Undisclosed
HOK Sports Facilities Group; Lescher & Mahoney Sports; Criswell, Blizzard & Blouin Architects	$138 M	45,360	Dome	$30 M (30 yrs.)
David M. Schwarz Architects; HKS, Inc.	$190 M	49,115	Open-Air	—
Rod Robbie and Michael Allen	C$500 M	50,516	Retractable	C$20 M (10 yrs.)
HOK Sport + Venue + Event with Devrouax & Purnell	$611 M	41,888	Open-Air	—

Architect	Cost (original)	Capacity (current)	Naming Rights (amt. & expiration)
HOK Sports Facilities Group; Arquitectonica	$213.5 M	20,300	$180 M (20 yrs.)
Ellerbe Becket	$160 M	18,624	Undisclosed
Ellerbe Becket with SHoP Architects	$950 M	18,103	$200 M (20 yrs.)
Ellerbe Becket with Odell and The Freelon Group	$265 M	18,500	Undisclosed
HOK Sports Facilities Group; Marmon Mok; W.E. Simpson Company	$175 M	21,711	$25 M (20 yrs.)
Ellerbe Becket	$152 M	20,562	Undisclosed
David Schwarz/Architectural Services, Inc. with HKS, Inc.	$420 M	19,200	$40 M (20 yrs.)
HOK Sports Facilities Group	$160 M	19,309	$68 M (20 yrs.)
Rossetti	$70 M	21,454	—
HNTB Architecture	n/a	19,200	$30 M (10 yrs.)
HOK Sports + Venue + Event	$175 M	18,300	Undisclosed
Ellerbe Becket	$183 M	18,345	$40 M (20 yrs.)
NBBJ	$330 M	20,000	$100 M (20 yrs.)
NBBJ	$330 M	20,000	$100 M (20 yrs.)
Ellerbe Becket with Looney Ricks Kiss	$250 M	18,165	$90 M (20 yrs.)
Arquitectonica	$175 M	19,600	$42 M (20 yrs.)

Sports Stadiums

Basketball

Team	Conference	Stadium	Location	Opened
Milwaukee Bucks	Eastern	Bradley Center	Milwaukee, WI	1988
Minnesota Timberwolves	Western	Target Center	Minneapolis, MN	1990
New Orleans Hornets	Western	New Orleans Arena	New Orleans, LA	1999
New York Knicks	Eastern	Madison Square Garden	New York, NY	1968
Oklahoma City Thunder	Western	Ford Center	Oklahoma City, OK	2002
Orlando Magic	Eastern	Amway Center	Orlando, FL	2010
Philadelphia 76ers	Eastern	Wells Fargo Center	Philadelphia, PA	1996
Phoenix Suns	Western	US Airways Center	Phoenix, AZ	1992
Portland Trail Blazers	Western	Rose Garden	Portland, OR	1995
Sacramento Kings	Western	Power Balance Pavilion	Sacramento, CA	1988
San Antonio Spurs	Western	AT&T Center	San Antonio, TX	2002
Toronto Raptors	Eastern	Air Canada Centre	Toronto, ON, Canada	1999
Utah Jazz	Western	EnergySolutions Arena	Salt Lake City, UT	1991
Washington Wizards	Eastern	Verizon Center	Washington, DC	1997

Football

Team	League	Stadium	Location	Opened
Arizona Cardinals	NFC	University of Phoenix Stadium	Glendale, AZ	2006
Atlanta Falcons	NFC	Georgia Dome	Atlanta, GA	1992
Baltimore Ravens	AFC	M&T Bank Stadium	Baltimore, MD	1998
Buffalo Bills	AFC	Ralph Wilson Stadium	Orchard Park, NY	1973
Carolina Panthers	NFC	Bank of America Stadium	Charlotte, NC	1996
Chicago Bears	NFC	Soldier Field	Chicago, IL	2003
Cincinnati Bengals	AFC	Paul Brown Stadium	Cincinnati, OH	2000
Cleveland Browns	AFC	Cleveland Browns Stadium	Cleveland, OH	1999
Dallas Cowboys	NFC	Cowboys Stadium	Arlington, TX	2009

Architect	Cost (original)	Capacity (current)	Naming Rights (amt. & expiration)
HOK Sports Facilities Group	$90 M	18,717	—
KMR Architects	$104 M	19,006	$18.75 M (15 yrs.)
Arthur Q. Davis, FAIA & Partners	$112 M	18,500	—
Charles Luckman	$116 M	19,763	—
The Benham Companies	$89 M	19,599	$8.1 M (15 yrs.)
Populous	$480 M	18,500	$195 M (30 yrs.)
Ellerbe Becket	$206 M	20,444	$40 M (29 yrs.)
Ellerbe Becket	$90 M	19,023	$26 M (30 yrs.)
Ellerbe Becket	$262 M	21,538	—
Rann Haight Architect	$40 M	17,317	Undisclosed (5 yrs.)
Ellerbe Becket with Lake/Flato Architects and Kell Muñoz Architects	$186 M	18,500	$85 M (20 yrs.)
HOK Sports Facilities Group; Brisbin Brook Beynon Architects (Canada)	C$265 M	19,800	C$40 M (20 yrs.)
FFKR Architects	$94 M	19,911	$20 M (10 yrs.)
Ellerbe Becket	$260 M	20,674	$44 M (15 years)

Architect	Cost (original)	Capacity (current)	Roof Type	Naming Rights (amt. & expiration)
Peter Eisenman with HOK Sport + Venue + Event	$370.6 M	65,000	Retractable	$154.5 M (20 yrs.)
Heery International	$214 M	71,149	Dome	—
HOK Sports Facilities Group	$220 M	69,084	Open-Air	$75 M (15 yrs.)
HNTB Architecture	$22 M	73,800	Open-Air	—
HOK Sports Facilities Group	$248 M	73,258	Open-Air	Undisclosed
Wood + Zapata, Inc. with Lohan Caprile Goettsch	$365 M	62,000	Open-Air	—
NBBJ	$400 M	65,535	Open-Air	—
HOK Sports Facilities Group	$283 M	73,200	Open-Air	—
HKS, Inc.	$1.1 B	80,000	Retractable	—

Sports Stadiums

Football

Team	Conference	Stadium	Location	Opened
Denver Broncos	AFC	Sports Authority Field at Mile High Stadium	Denver, CO	2001
Detroit Lions	NFC	Ford Field	Allen Park, MI	2002
Green Bay Packers	NFC	Lambeau Field	Green Bay, WI	1957
Houston Texans	AFC	Reliant Stadium	Houston, TX	2002
Indianapolis Colts	AFC	Lucas Oil Stadium	Indianapolis, IN	2008
Jacksonville Jaguars	AFC	EverBank Field	Jacksonville, FL	1995
Kansas City Chiefs	AFC	Arrowhead Stadium	Kansas City, MO	1972
Miami Dolphins	AFC	Sun Life Stadium	Miami, FL	1987
Minnesota Vikings	NFC	Hubert H. Humphrey Metrodome	Minneapolis, MN	1982
New England Patriots	AFC	Gillette Stadium	Foxboro, MA	2002
New Orleans Saints	NFC	Mercedes-Benz Superdome	New Orleans, LA	1975
New York Giants	NFC	Met Life Stadium	E. Rutherford, NJ	2010
New York Jets	AFC	Met Life Stadium	E. Rutherford, NJ	2010
Oakland Raiders	AFC	Overstock.com Coliseum	Oakland, CA	1966
Philadelphia Eagles	NFC	Lincoln Financial Field	Philadelphia, PA	2003
Pittsburgh Steelers	AFC	Heinz Field	Pittsburgh, PA	2001
San Diego Chargers	AFC	Qualcomm Stadium	San Diego, CA	1967
San Francisco 49ers	NFC	Candlestick Park	San Francisco, CA	1960
Seattle Seahawks	NFC	Century Link Field	Seattle, WA	2002
St. Louis Rams	NFC	Edward Jones Dome	St. Louis, MO	1995
Tampa Bay Buccaneers	NFC	Raymond James Stadium	Tampa, FL	1998
Tennessee Titans	AFC	LP Field	Nashville, TN	1999
Washington Redskins	NFC	FedEx Field	Landover, MD	1996

Architect	Cost (original)	Capacity (current)	Roof Type	Naming Rights (amt. & expiration)
HNTB Architecture with Fentress Bradburn Architects and Bertram A. Burton and Associates	$400.8 M	76,125	Open-Air	$120 M (20 yrs.)
SmithGroup	$500 M	64,355	Dome	$40 M (40 yrs.)
John Somerville	$960,000	60,890	Open-Air	—
HOK Sport + Venue + Event	$325 M	69,500	Retractable	$300 M (30 yrs.)
HKS, Inc.	$625 M	63,000	Retractable	$122 M (20 yrs.)
HOK Sports Facilities Group	$138 M	73,000	Open-Air	$16.6 M (5 yrs.)
Kivett and Meyers	$43 M	79,409	Open-Air	—
HOK Sports Facilities Group	$125 M	74,916	Open-Air	$20 M (5 yrs.)
Skidmore, Owings & Merrill	$55 M	64,121	Dome	—
HOK Sport + Venue + Event	$325 M	68,000	Open-Air	Undisclosed
Curtis & Davis Architects	$134 M	69,065	Dome	Undisclosed $ (10 yrs.)
EwingCole; Skanska; 360 Architecture	$1.6 B	82,566	Open-Air	$425 M–$450 M (25 yrs.)
EwingCole; Skanska; 360 Architecture	$1.6 B	82,566	Open-Air	$425 M–$450 M (25 yrs.)
Skidmore, Owings & Merrill	$25.5 M	62,026	Suspension (fixed)	$1.2 M (6 yrs.)
NBBJ	$320 M	66,000	Open-Air	$139.6 M (20 yrs.)
HOK Sport + Venue + Event with WTW Architects	$281 M	64,440	Open-Air	$58 M (20 yrs.)
Frank L. Hope and Associates	$27 M	71,294	Open-Air	$18 M (20 yrs.)
John & Bolles	$24.6 M	69,843	Open-Air	—
Ellerbe Becket with LMN Architects	$360 M	67,000	Partial Roof	—
HOK Sports Facilities Group	$280 M	66,000	Dome	$31.8 M (12 yrs.)
HOK Sports Facilities Group	$168.5 M	66,000	Open-Air	$32.5 M (13 yrs.)
HOK Sports Facilities Group	$290 M	67,000	Open-Air	$30 M (10 yrs.)
HOK Sports Facilities Group	$250.5 M	80,116	Open-Air	$205 M (27 yrs.)

Sports Stadiums

Hockey

Team	Conference	Stadium	Location	Opened
Anaheim Ducks	Western	Honda Center	Anaheim, CA	1993
Boston Bruins	Eastern	TD Garden	Boston, MA	1995
Buffalo Sabres	Eastern	First Niagara Center	Buffalo, NY	1996
Calgary Flames	Western	Pengrowth Saddledome	Calgary, AB, Canada	1983
Carolina Hurricanes	Eastern	RBC Center	Raleigh, NC	1999
Chicago Blackhawks	Western	United Center	Chicago, IL	1994
Colorado Avalanche	Western	Pepsi Center	Denver, CO	1999
Columbus Blue Jackets	Western	Nationwide Arena	Columbus, OH	2000
Dallas Stars	Western	American Airlines Center	Dallas, TX	2001
Detroit Red Wings	Western	Joe Louis Arena	Detroit, MI	1979
Edmonton Oilers	Western	Rexall Place	Edmonton, AB, Canada	1974
Florida Panthers	Eastern	BankAtlantic Center	Sunrise, FL	1998
Los Angeles Kings	Western	Staples Center	Los Angeles, CA	1999
Minnesota Wild	Western	Xcel Energy Center	St. Paul, MN	2000
Montreal Canadiens	Eastern	Bell Centre	Montreal, QC, Canada	1996
Nashville Predators	Western	Bridgestone Arena	Nashville, TN	1997
New Jersey Devils	Eastern	Prudential Center	Newark, NJ	2007
New York Islanders	Eastern	Nassau Veterans Memorial Coliseum	Uniondale, NY	1972
New York Rangers	Eastern	Madison Square Garden	New York, NY	1968
Ottawa Senators	Eastern	Scotiabank Place	Kanata, ON, Canada	1996
Philadelphia Flyers	Eastern	Wells Fargo Center	Philadelphia, PA	1996
Phoenix Coyotes	Western	Jobing.com Arena	Glendale, AZ	2003
Pittsburgh Penguins	Eastern	Consol Energy Center	Pittsburgh, PA	2010
San Jose Sharks	Western	HP Pavillion	San Jose, CA	1993
St. Louis Blues	Western	Scottrade Center	St. Louis, MO	1994
Tampa Bay Lightning	Eastern	Tampa Bay Times Forum	Tampa, FL	1996
Toronto Maple Leafs	Eastern	Air Canada Centre	Toronto, ON, Canada	1999
Vancouver Canucks	Western	Rogers Arena	Vancouver, BC, Canada	1995
Washington Capitals	Eastern	Verizon Center	Washington, DC	1997
Winnipeg Jets	Eastern	MTS Centre	Winnipeg, MB, Canada	2004

Source: DesignIntelligence

Architect	Cost (original)	Capacity (current)	Naming Rights (amt. & expiration)
HOK Sports Facilities Group	$120 M	17,174	$60 M (15 yrs.)
Ellerbe Becket	$160 M	17,565	Undisclosed
Ellerbe Becket	$127.5 M	18,595	Undisclosed (15 yrs.)
Graham Edmunds Architecture (Canada); Graham McCourt Architects (Canada)	C$176 M	20,140	C$20 M (20 yrs.)
Odell	$158 M	18,176	$80 M (20 yrs.)
HOK Sports Facilities Group; Marmon Mok; W.E. Simpson Co.	$175 M	20,500	$25 M (20 yrs.)
HOK Sports Facilities Group	$160 M	18,129	$68 M (20 yrs.)
Heinlein Schrock Stearns; NBBJ	$150 M	18,500	$135 M (indefinite)
David M. Schwarz Architects with HKS, Inc.	$420 M	18,000	$40 M (20 yrs.)
Smith, Hinchmen and Grylls Associates	$57 M	18,785	—
Phillips, Barrett, Hillier, Jones & Partners with Wynn, Forbes, Lord, Feldberg & Schmidt	C$22.5 M	16,900	Undisclosed
Ellerbe Becket	$212 M	19,452	$27 M (10 yrs.)
NBBJ	$330 M	18,500	Undisclosed
HOK Sports Facilities Group	$130 M	18,064	$75 M (25 yrs.)
Consortium of Quebec Architects (Canada)	C$280 M	21,273	$100 M (20 yrs.)
HOK Sports Facilities Group	$144 M	17,500	Undisclosed
HOK Sport + Venue + Event with Morris Adjmi Architects	$375 M	17,615	$105.3 M (20 yrs.)
Welton Becket	$31 M	16,297	—
Charles Luckman	$116 M	18,200	—
Rossetti	C$200 M	18,500	C$20 M (15 yrs.)
Ellerbe Becket	$206 M	18,168	$40 M (29 yrs.)
HOK Sport + Venue + Event	$220 M	17,653	$25 M (10 yrs.)
Populous	$321 M	18,087	Undisclosed
Sink Combs Dethlefs	$162.5 M	17,483	$55.8 M (18 yrs.)
Ellerbe Becket	$170 M	19,260	Undisclosed
Ellerbe Becket	$139 M	19,500	$25 M (to 2018)
HOK Sports Facilities Group; Brisbin Brook Beynon Architects (Canada)	C$265 M	18,800	C$40 M (20 yrs.)
Brisbin Brook Beynon Architects (Canada)	C$160 M	18,422	Undisclosed (15 yrs.)
Ellerbe Becket	$260 M	19,700	Undisclosed (10 yrs.)
Sink Combs Dethlefs; Number Ten Architectural Group (Canada)	C$133.5 M	15,004	—

AWARDS, STATISTICS & RESOURCES

Top awards to firms and individuals are included in this chapter. Numerous vital statistics for professional reference are also contained herein.

(Note: Bolded text indicates additions to the existing list.)

AIA Gold Medal

The Gold Medal is the **American Institute of Architects' highest award**. Eligibility is open to architects and non-architects, living or dead, whose contribution to the field of architecture has made a lasting impact. The AIA's board of directors grants at least one gold medal each year, occasionally granting none.

www.aia.org

1907	Sir Aston Webb (UK)	1968	Marcel Breuer
1909	Charles F. McKim	1969	William Wurster
1911	George B. Post	1970	R. Buckminster Fuller
1914	Jean Louis Pascal (France)	1971	Louis I. Kahn
1922	Victor Laloux (France)	1972	Pietro Belluschi
1923	Henry Bacon	1977	Richard Neutra* (Germany/US)
1925	Sir Edwin Lutyens (UK)	1978	Philip Johnson
1925	Bertram Grosvenor Goodhue	1979	I.M. Pei
1927	Howard Van Doren Shaw	1981	José Luis Sert (Spain)
1929	Milton B. Medary	1982	Romaldo Giurgola
1933	Ragnar Östberg (Sweden)	1983	Nathaniel Owings
1938	Paul Philippe Cret (France/US)	1985	William Wayne Caudill*
1944	Louis Sullivan	1986	Arthur C. Erickson (Canada)
1947	Eliel Saarinen (Finland/US)	1989	Joseph Esherick
1948	Charles D. Maginnis	1990	E. Fay Jones
1949	Frank Lloyd Wright	1991	Charles Moore
1950	Sir Patrick Abercrombie (UK)	1992	Benjamin Thompson
1951	Bernard Maybeck	1993	Thomas Jefferson*
1952	Auguste Perret (France)	1993	Kevin Roche
1953	William Adams Delano	1994	Sir Norman Foster (UK)
1955	Willem Marinus Dudok (Netherlands)	1995	Cesar Pelli
1956	Clarence S. Stein	1997	Richard Meier
1957	Ralph Thomas Walker	1999	Frank Gehry
1957	Louis Skidmore	2000	Ricardo Legorreta (Mexico)
1958	John Wellborn Root II	2001	Michael Graves
1959	Walter Gropius (Germany/US)	2002	Tadao Ando (Japan)
1960	Ludwig Mies van der Rohe (Germany/US)	2004	Samuel Mockbee*
		2005	Santiago Calatrava (Spain)
1961	Le Corbusier (Charles Édouard Jeanneret) (Switzerland/France)	2006	Antoine Predock
		2007	Edward Larrabee Barnes*
1962	Eero Saarinen*	2008	Renzo Piano (Italy)
1963	Alvar Aalto (Finland)	2009	Glenn Murcutt (Australia)
1964	Pier Luigi Nervi (Italy)	2010	Peter Bohlin
1966	Kenzo Tange (Japan)	2011	Fumihiko Maki (Japan)
1967	Wallace K. Harrison	**2012**	**Steven Holl**

* Honored posthumously

Source: American Institute of Architects

AIA Honor Awards

The American Institute of Architects' Honor Awards celebrate **outstanding design in three areas: architecture, interior architecture, and regional and urban design**. Juries for each category, comprised of designers and executives for the respective disciplines, select the winners.

www.aia.org

2012 Architecture Winners

8 House
Copenhagen, Denmark
BIG (Denmark)

41 Cooper Square
New York, NY
Morphosis Architects

The Gates and Hillman Centers for Computer
  Science, Carnegie Mellon University
  Pittsburgh, PA
Mack Scogin Merrill Elam Architects

Ghost Architectural Laboratory
Upper Kingsburg, NS, Canada
Mackay-Lyons Sweetapple Architects Limited
  (Canada)

LumenHAUS
Virginia Tech Solar Team

Pittman Dowell Residence
La Crescenta, CA
Michael Maltzan Architecture, Inc.

Poetry Foundation
Chicago, IL
John Ronan Architects

Ruth Lilly Visitors Pavilion
Indianapolis, IN
Marlon Blackwell Architect

The Standard
New York, NY
Ennead Architects

2012 Interior Architecture Winners

ARTifacts
Omaha, NE
Randy Brown Architects

Children's Institute, Inc., Otis Booth Campus
Los Angeles, CA
Koning Eizenberg Architecture

David Rubenstein Atrium at Lincoln Center
New York, NY
Tod Williams Billie Tsien Architects

HyundaiCard Air Lounge
Incheon, South Korea
Gensler

Integral House
Toronto, ON, Canada
Shim-Sutcliffe Architects (Canada)

Joukowsky Institute for Archaeology & the
    Ancient World, Brown University
Providence, RI
Anmahian Winton Architects

Memory Temple
Los Angeles, CA
Patrick Tighe Architecture

Prairie Management Group
Northbrook, IL
Goettsch Partners

Record House Revisited
Owings Mill, MD
David Jameson Architect

The Wright at the Guggenheim Museum
New York, NY
Andre Kikoski Architect

2012 Regional & Urban Design Winners

Fayetteville 2030: Transit City Scenario
Fayetteville, AK
University of Arkansas Community Design
    Center

Grangegorman Master Plan
Dublin, Ireland
Moore Ruble Yudell Architects & Planners;
    DMOD Architects (Ireland)

Jordan Dead Sea Development Zone Master
    Plan
Amman, Jordan
Sasaki Associates, Inc.

Master Plan for the Central Delaware
Philadelphia, PA
Cooper, Robertson & Partners;
    KieranTimberlake

Miami Beach City Center Redevelopment
    Project
Miami Beach, FL
Gehry Partners; West 8; Hines Interests
    Limited Partnership

Portland Mall Revitalization
Portland, OR
ZGF Architects

Reinventing the Crescent: Riverfront
    Development Plan
New Orleans, LA
Eskew + Dumez + Ripple

SandRidge Energy Commons
Oklahoma City, OK
Rogers Marvel Architects

Source: American Institute of Architects

Architecture Firm Award

The American Institute of Architects grants its Architecture Firm Award, **the highest honor the AIA can bestow on a firm, annually to an architecture firm for consistently producing distinguished architecture**. Eligible firms must claim collaboration within the practice as a hallmark of their methodology and must have been producing work as an entity for at least 10 years.

www.aia.org

1962	Skidmore, Owings & Merrill
1963	*No award granted*
1964	The Architects Collaborative
1965	Wurster, Bernardi & Emmons
1966	*No award granted*
1967	Hugh Stubbins & Associates
1968	I.M. Pei & Partners
1969	Jones & Emmons
1970	Ernest J. Kump Associates
1971	Albert Kahn Associates
1972	Caudill Rowlett Scott
1973	Shepley Bulfinch Richardson and Abbott
1974	Kevin Roche John Dinkeloo & Associates
1975	Davis, Brody & Associates
1976	Mitchell/Giurgola Architects
1977	Sert Jackson and Associates
1978	Harry Weese & Associates
1979	Geddes Brecher Qualls Cunningham
1980	Edward Larrabee Barnes Associates
1981	Hardy Holzman Pfeiffer Associates
1982	Gwathmey Siegel & Associates, Architects
1983	Holabird & Root
1984	Kallmann, McKinnell & Wood Architects
1985	Venturi, Rauch and Scott Brown
1986	Esherick Homsey Dodge and Davis
1987	Benjamin Thompson & Associates
1988	Hartman-Cox Architects
1989	Cesar Pelli & Associates
1990	Kohn Pedersen Fox Associates
1991	Zimmer Gunsul Frasca Partnership
1992	James Stewart Polshek & Partners
1993	Cambridge Seven Associates
1994	Bohlin Cywinski Jackson
1995	Beyer Blinder Belle
1996	Skidmore, Owings & Merrill
1997	R.M. Kliment & Frances Halsband Architects
1998	Centerbrook Architects and Planners
1999	Perkins+Will
2000	Gensler
2001	Herbert Lewis Kruse Blunck Architecture
2002	Thompson, Ventulett, Stainback & Associates
2003	Miller|Hull Partnership
2004	Lake/Flato Architects
2005	Murphy/Jahn Architects
2006	Moore Ruble Yudell Architects & Planners
2007	Leers Weinzapfel Associates
2008	KieranTimberlake Associates
2009	Olson Sundberg Kundig Allen Architects
2010	Pugh + Scarpa
2011	BNIM Architects
2012	**VJAA**

Source: American Institute of Architects

Arnold W. Brunner Memorial Prize

The American Academy of Arts and Letters annually awards the Arnold W. Brunner Memorial Prize **to architects of any nationality who have contributed to architecture as an art**. The award consists of a $5,000 prize. The prize is named in honor of the notable New York architect and city planner, Arnold William Brunner, who died in 1925.

www.artsandletters.org

1955	Gordon Bunshaft	1984	Peter Eisenman
	Minoru Yamasaki*	1985	William Pedersen and Arthur May
1956	John Yeon	1986	John Hejduk
1957	John Carl Warnecke	1987	James Ingo Freed
1958	Paul Rudolph	1988	Arata Isozaki (Japan)
1959	Edward Larrabee Barnes	1989	Richard Rogers (UK)
1960	Louis I. Kahn	1990	Steven Holl
1961	I.M. Pei	1991	Tadao Ando (Japan)
1962	Ulrich Franzen	1992	Sir Norman Foster (UK)
1963	Edward C. Bassett	1993	Rafael Moneo (Spain)
1964	Harry Weese	1994	Renzo Piano (Italy)
1965	Kevin Roche	1995	Daniel Urban Kiley
1966	Romaldo Giurgola	1996	Tod Williams and Billie Tsien
1967	*No award granted*	1997	Henri Ciriani (France)
1968	John M. Johansen	1998	Alvaro Siza (Portugal)
1969	N. Michael McKinnell	1999	Fumihiko Maki (Japan)
1970	Charles Gwathmey and	2000	Toyo Ito (Japan)
	Richard Henderson	2001	Henry Smith-Miller and
1971	John H. Andrews (Australia)		Laurie Hawkinson
1972	Richard Meier	2002	Kazuyo Sejima + Ryue Nishizawa
1973	Robert Venturi		(Japan)
1974	Hugh Hardy with Norman Pfeiffer	2003	Elizabeth Diller and Ricardo Scofidio
	and Malcolm Holzman	2004	Hans Hollein (Austria)
1975	Lewis Davis and Samuel Brody	2005	Shigeru Ban (Japan)
1976	James Stirling (UK)	2006	Jean Nouvel (France)
1977	Henry N. Cobb	2007	Eric Owen Moss
1978	Cesar Pelli	2008	Peter Zumthor (Switzerland)
1979	Charles Moore	2009	Juhani Pallasmaa (Finland)
1980	Michael Graves	2010	Michael Van Valkenburgh
1981	Gunnar Birkerts	2011	Mack Scogin
1982	Helmut Jahn		Merrill Elam
1983	Frank Gehry	2012	Kathryn Gustafson

* Honorable Mention

Source: American Academy of Arts and Letters

ASLA Firm Award

The American Society of Landscape Architects presents its annual ASLA Firm Award to a **landscape architecture firm that has produced a body of distinguished work for at least 10 years**. Nominees are reviewed for their influence on the profession, their collaborative environment, the consistent quality of their work, and their recognition among fellow practitioners, teachers, allied professionals, and the general public.

www.asla.org

Year	Firm
2003	Jones & Jones Architects and Landscape Architects
2004	Wallace Roberts & Todd
2005	SWA Group
2006	OLIN
2007	Sasaki Associates, Inc.
2008	Design Workshop
2009	EDAW	AECOM
2010	EDSA
2011	JJR
2012	PWP Landscape Architecture

Source: American Society of Landscape Architects

ASLA Medals

The American Society of Landscape Architects awards its highest honor, the ASLA Medal, to individuals who have made a **significant contribution to the field of land-scape architecture** in such areas as landscape design, planning, writing, and public service. The ASLA Design Medal recognizes landscape architects who have produced a body of exceptional design work at a sustained level for at least 10 years.

www.asla.org

ASLA Medal

1971	Hideo Sasaki	1992	Robert S. (Doc) Reich
1972	Conrad L. Wirth	1993	Arthur E. Bye Jr.
1973	John C. Simonds	1994	Edward D. Stone Jr.
1974	Campbell E. Miller	1995	Ervin H. Zube
1975	Garrett Eckbo	1996	John Lyle
1976	Thomas Church	1997	Julius Fabos
1977	Hubert B. Owens	1998	Carol R. Johnson
1978	Lawrence Halprin	1999	Stuart C. Dawson
1979	Norman T. Newton	2000	Carl D. Johnson
1980	William G. Swain	2001	Robert E. Marvin
1981	Sir Geoffrey Jellicoe (UK)	2002	Morgan (Bill) Evans
1982	Charles W. Eliot II	2003	Richard Haag
1983	Theodore Osmundson	2004	Peter Walker
1984	Ian McHarg	2005	Jane Silverstein Ries
1985	Roberto Burle Marx (Brazil)	2006	Cameron R.J. Man
1986	William J. Johnson	2007	William B. Callaway
1987	Philip H. Lewis Jr.	2008	Joseph A. Porter
1988	Dame Sylvia Crowe (UK)	2009	Joseph E. Brown
1989	Robert N. Royston	2010	Edward L. Daugherty
1990	Raymond L. Freeman	2011	Laurie D. Olin
1991	Meade Palmer	2012	Cornelia Hahn Oberlander

ASLA Design Medal

2003	Lawrence Halprin	2008	Kathryn Gustafson
2004	M. Paul Friedberg	2009	Richard W. Shaw
2005	Laurie D. Olin	2010	James van Sweden
2006	Steve Martino	2011	Michael Van Valkenburgh
2007	Richard Haag	2012	Peter Walker

Source: American Society of Landscape Architects

ASLA Professional Awards

With the annual Professional Awards program, the American Society of Landscape Architects honors the **best in landscape architecture from around the globe**. Recipients receive coverage in *Landscape Architecture* magazine; winners in the residential category are also featured in *Garden Design* magazine. The Landmark Award recognizes a distinguished landscape architecture project completed 15 to 50 years ago that retains its original design integrity and contributes significantly to the public realm.

www.asla.org

2012 Award of Excellence Winners

General Design
A Green Sponge for a Water-Resilient City:
    Qunli Stormwater Park
Haerbin City, Heilongjiang Province, China
Turenscape (China)

Residential Design
Drs. Julian and Raye Richardson Apartments
San Francisco, CA
Andrea Cochran Landscape Architecture

Analysis & Planning
The One Ohio State Framework Plan
Columbus, OH
Sasaki Associates

Communications
Digital Drawing for Landscape Architecture:
    Contemporary Techniques and Tools for
    Digital Representation in Site Design
Bradley Cantrell and Wes Michaels

2012 Honor Award Winners

General Design
Canada's Sugar Beach
Toronto, ON, Canada
Claude Cormier + Associés (Canada)

Lafayette Greens: Urban Agriculture, Urban
    Fabric, Urban Sustainability
Detroit, MI
Kenneth Weikal Landscape Architecture

Quarry Garden in Shanghai Botanical Gardens
Songjiant District, Shanghai, China
THUPDI and Tsinghua University (China)

New Academic Complex, Arizona State
    University Polytechnic Campus
Mesa, AZ
Ten Eyck Landscape Architects

200 5th Avenue
New York, NY
Landworks Studio

Powell Street Promenade
San Francisco, CA
Hood Design

Tudela-Culip (Club Med) Restoration Project
Catalonia, Spain
EMF Landscape Architecture (Spain); Ardevols
    Associates Consultants (Spain)

Shangri La Botanical Gardens and Nature
    Center
Orange, TX
Jeffrey Carbo Landscape Architects with
    William T. Arterburn

Winnipeg Skating Shelters
Winnipeg, MB, Canada
Patkau Architects (Canada)

National 9/11 Memorial
New York, NY
PWP Landscape Architecture

Sunnylands Center & Gardens
Rancho Mirage, CA
Office of James Burnett

Residential Design
Quaker Smith Point Residence
Shelburne, VT
H. Keith Wagner Partnership

Quattro by Sansiri
Bangkok, Thailand
TROP Company Limited (Thailand)

New-Century Garden: A Garden of Water
    and Light
Palm Springs, CA
Steve Martino and Associates

Malinalco Private Residence
Malinalco, State of Mexico, Mexico
Mario Schjetnan / Grupo De Diseño Urbano
    (Mexico)

Maple Hill Residence
Westwood, MA
Stephen Stimson Associates Landscape
    Architects

Reordering Old Quarry
Guilford, CT
Reed Hilderbrand

Urban Spring
San Francisco, CA
Bionic

Analysis & Planning
Governors Island Park and Public Space
    Master Plan
New York, NY
West 8 Urban Design & Landscape
    Architecture

Wusong Riverfront: Landscape Infrastructure
    Pilot Project
Kunshan City, Jingsu Province, China
SWA Group

Core Area of Lotus Lake National Wetland
    Park Landscape Planning
Tieling City, Liaoning Province, China
Beijing Tsinghua Urban Planning & Design
    Institute (China)

Coastal Roulette: Planning Resilient
    Communities
Galveston Bay, TX
SWA Group

Nanhu: Farm Town
Big City, Jiaxing, China
SWA Group

A Strategic Master Plan
Dead Sea, Jordan
Sasaki Associates

SW Montgomery Green Street: Connecting
    the West Hills to the Willamette River
Portland, OR
Nevue Ngan Associates

Red Mountain/Green Ribbon: Linking Across
    Birmingham's Great Divide
Birmingham, AL
WRT

ASLA Professional Awards

Communications

"Asphalt to Ecosystems: Design Ideas for
    Schoolyard Transformation"
Sharon Gamson Danks

"Landscape Infrastructure: Case Studies by
    SWA"
SWA Group

Landscape Urbanism Website and Journal
Sarah Peck

What's Out There
Cultural Landscape Foundation

Research

Arizona Department of Transportation
    Ironwood Tree Salvage and Saguaro
    Transplant Survivability Studies
Logan Simpson Designs and Arizona
    Department of Transportation

Productive Neighborhoods: A Case Study
    Based Exploration of Seattle Urban
    Agriculture Projects
Berger Partnership

Source: American Society of Landscape Architects

Best Tall Building Awards

The Best Tall Building Awards recognize projects that have made **extraordinary contributions to the advancement of tall buildings and the urban environment, including sustainability**. The projects must also exhibit processes or innovations that have enhanced the design profession and enriched the cities and lives of their inhabitants. The program is sponsored by the Council on Tall Buildings and Urban Habitats.

www.ctbuh.org

2012 Winners

Americas
Absolute Towers
Mississauga, ON Canada
MAD architects (China) with Burka Architects
    (Canada)

Asia & Australasia
1 Bligh Street
Sydney, Australia
ingenhoven architects (Germany); Architectus
    (Australia)

Europe
Palazzo Lombardia
Milan, Italy
Pei Cobb Freed & Partners with Paolo
    Caputo Partnership (Italy); Sistema Duemila
    Architettura e Ingegneria (Italy)

Middle East & Africa
Doha Tower
Doha, Qatar
Ateliers Jean Nouvel (France)

Source: Council on Tall Buildings and Urban Habitats

Exhibition of School Architecture Awards

The Exhibition of School Architecture Awards, sponsored by the American Association of School Administrators, American Institute of Architects, and Council of Educational Facility Planners International, **showcase how well-designed schools facilitate student achievement**. The Shirley Cooper Award recognizes the project that best meets the educational needs of students. The Walter Taylor Award honors the project that best addresses a difficult design challenge.

www.aasa.org

2011 Winners*

Shirley Cooper Award
Manassas Park Elementary School
Manassas Park, VA
VMDO Architects

Walter Taylor Award
Energy Laboratory, Hawaii Preparatory
    Academy
Waimea, HI
Flansburgh Architects

Honorable Mentions
Park City High School
Park City, UT
VCBO Architecture

Washington-Lee High School
Arlington, VA
Grimm + Parker Architects

Maplewood-Richmond Heights Early
    Childhood Center
St. Louis, MO
Bond Wolfe Architects Inc.

Meldrum Science Center, Westminster College
Salt Lake City, UT
VCBO Architecture

Source: American Association of School Administrators

*The award program is on hiatus for 2012.

Housing Awards

The AIA's Housing Awards recognize the **importance of good housing as a necessity of life, a sanctuary for the human spirit, and a valuable national resource**. Licensed AIA-member architects are eligible to enter US-built projects.

www.aia.org

2012 Winners

One/Two Family Custom Housing
Carmel Residence
Carmel-by-the-Sea, CA
Dirk Denison Architects

Hampden Lane House
Bethesda, MD
Robert M. Gurney, FAIA

Nakahouse
Los Angeles, CA
XTEN Architecture

The Pierre
San Juan Islands, WA
Olson Kundig Architects

Relic Rock
Scottsdale, AZ
DCHGlobal Inc.

One/Two Family Production Housing
Live Work Home
Syracuse, NY
Cook + Fox Architects

Multi-family Living
Drs. Julian and Raye Richardson Apartments
San Francisco, CA
David Baker + Partners, Architects

Optima Camelview Village
Scottsdale, AZ
David Hovey & Associates Architect, Inc.

Specialized Housing
Jesuit Community Center
Fairfield, CT
Gray Organschi Architecture

McMurtry and Duncan Colleges
Houston, TX
Hanbury Evans Wright Vlattas + Company;
  Hopkins Architects

Source: American Institute of Architects

Interior Design Competition

The Interior Design Competition is presented jointly each year by the International Interior Design Association and *Interior Design* magazine. The program was established in 1973 to recognize **outstanding interior design projects and to foster new ideas and techniques**. Winning projects appear in the magazine, and the best-of-competition winner receives a $5,000 cash prize.

www.iida.org

2012 Winners

DOMUSae, Spaces for Culture
Madrid, Spain
APARICIO+DONAIRE (Spain)

Yushe, The Village, Vanke
Shanghai, China
Beijing Newsdays Architectural Design Co.
(China)

Xocolatti
New York, NY
De-Spec

The Pierre
San Juan Islands, WA
Olson Kundig Architects

The Instructional Centre, University of Toronto
Mississauga, ON, Canada
Perkins+Will

Cranbrook Art Museum Collections Building
Addition
Bloomfield Hills, MI
SmithGroupJJR

Source: International Interior Design Association

International Design Excellence Awards

The annual International Design Excellence Awards (IDEA), produced by the Industrial Designers Society of America (IDSA) and sponsored by *Fast Company*, **honor outstanding industrial design projects worldwide**. A jury of business and design executives select winners from categories ranging from commercial and industrial products to interactive product experiences and service design. Gold, silver, and bronze awards are granted.

www.idsa.org

2012 Gold Winners

Commercial & Industrial
37X/38X Clamp Meters with iFlex™
Fluke Corporation

B/E Aerospace Essence Inserts Collection
TEAGUE

Crown RM 6000S MonoLift™ Reach Truck
Crown Equipment Corporation

Communication Tools
Lumia 800
Nokia Design (Finland)

Lumia 900
Nokia Design (Finland)

Design Strategy
GE User Experience Strategy and Capacity
    Building
frog

Digital Design
Teagueduino/teagueduino.org
TEAGUE

Entertainment
Barnes & Noble Nook Simple Touch
Ammunition

Beats by Dr. Dre Beats Mixr
Ammunition

Beats by Dr. Dre Beats Wireless
Ammunition

Propellerhead Balance
Propellerhead Software (Sweden)

Environments
THINK: An Exploration into Making the World
    Work Better
IBM; Ralph Appelbaum Associates Inc.

Kitchens
One-burner Portable Induction Hob
    (CTN431SC01)
Samsung Electronics (South Korea)

OXO Tot Seedling Youth Booster Seat
Smart Design

Leisure & Recreation
Nike+ FuelBand
Nike Digital Sport Design Team; Astro Studios;
    · RGA

Living Room & Bedroom
LED Clear Bulb
Panasonic Corporation (Japan)

Medical & Scientific Products
Cocoon Open MRI Chair
GE Healthcare (France)

DISCOVERY IGS 730
GE Medical Systems (France)

Samsung XGEO GC80
Samsung Electronics (South Korea)

International Design Excellence Awards

Samsung XGEO GU60
Samsung Electronics (South Korea)

Samsung X-ray System User Experience
Samsung Electronics (South Korea)

sleepToo™
Sauder MFG

Office & Productivity
Horizon LED Task Light
Humanscale

TAS Collection
aruliden

Packaging & Graphics
Ecologic Brands Paper Bottle
DW Product Development Inc (Canada)

Social Impact Design
Embrace Infant Warmer
Embrace (India)

UNICEF Project Mwana: Using Mobile
    Technologies to Improve the Lives of
    Underserved Children
frog

Student Designs
Balde a Balde: Safe Agua
Designmatters at Art Center College of Design

C-thru Smoke Diving Helmet
Umeå Institute of Design (Sweden)

DIGIFI: Audionauts
Art Center College of Design

GiraDora: Safe Agua - Washer and Spin Dryer
Designmatters at Art Center College of Design

Medical Toolkit for Surface-Mount Micro
    Dialysis
Umeå Institute of Design (Sweden)

Nursing Kit
National Cheng Kung University (Taiwan)

Smart Squeeze
Emily Carr University of Art & Design (Canada)

The Campus Mini Velo: Redefining Utility
University of Oregon

Source: Industrial Designers Society of America

Library Buildings Awards

The American Institute of Architects and American Library Association present the biennial Library Buildings Awards to encourage **excellence in the design and planning of libraries**. Architects licensed in the United States are eligible to enter any public or private library project from around the world, whether a renovation, addition, conversion, interior project, or new construction. The jury consists of three architects and three librarians with extensive library building experience.

www.ala.org

2011 Winners

Arkansas Studies Institute
Little Rock, AR
Polk Stanley Wilcox

KAUST Library
Thuwal, Jeddah, Saudi Arabia
HOK

Mattapan Branch Library
Boston, MA
William Rawn Associates, Architects, Inc.

Harmon Library
Phoenix, AZ
richard+bauer

William Oxley Thompson Memorial Library,
    Ohio State University
Columbus, OH
GUND Partnership

Source: American Library Association

National Green Building Awards

The National Association of Home Builders presents the annual Green Building Awards to recognize **leaders who have advanced green-home building**. With this program, the NAHB hopes to encourage builders to incorporate green practices into their developments, designs, and construction methodologies and to speed the public's acceptance of sustainable, environmentally friendly building. A jury of industry professionals selects the winners, who are celebrated at the annual NAHB National Green Building Conference.

www.nahb.org

2012 Winners

Project of the Year, Single-Family Custom Builder
Tah.Mah.Lah
MGM Construction

Project of the Year, Single-Family Production Builder
Ploeser Net-Zero
Meritage Homes

Project of the Year, Single-Family Small Volume Builder
Paar Residence
Chandler Design-Build Inc.

Project of the Year, Single-Family Concept and Research-Enterprise
Thomas/Salmon Residence
TC Legend Homes/Zero-Energy Plans

Project of the Year, Single-Family Concept and Research-Academic
INhome
Purdue University

Multifamily Project of the Year
Progresso Point
Reliance Housing Foundation, Inc.; Broward
    County Housing Authority; Trifecta
    Construction Solutions; Sacchina
    Construction

Remodeling Project of the Year, Over $100,000
G HOME
Rocking Horse Redevelopment

Remodeling Project of the Year, Under $100,000
G HOME
Rocking Horse Redevelopment

Builder Advocate of the Year
The Mungo Companies

Remodeler Advocate of the Year
G STREET

Green Outstanding Contribution Award
T.W. Bailey

Source: National Association of Home Builders

National Healthcare Design Awards

The National Healthcare Design Awards showcase the **best of healthcare building design and health design-oriented research**. The program is sponsored by the American Institute of Architects and the Academy of Architecture for Health. Winning projects exhibit conceptual strength and solve aesthetic, civic, urban, and social concerns in addition to the requisite functional and sustainability concerns of a healthcare facility.

www.aia.org/aah

2012 Winners

Built, Less Than $25 Million
Willson Hospice House
Albany, GA
Perkins+Will

Built, More Than $25 Million
Lunder Building at Massachusetts General
   Hospital
Boston, MA
NBBJ

Unbuilt
Kenya Women and Children's Wellness Center
Nairobi, Kenya
Perkins+Will

Innovations in Planning and Design Research, Built and Unbuilt
National Intrepid Center of Excellence
Bethesda, MD
SmithGroupJJR

Source: American Institute of Architects

National Planning Excellence Awards

Through its National Planning Awards program, the American Planning Association recognizes the role cutting-edge planning achievements and outstanding individual contributions play in creating **communities of lasting value**. Excellence Awards are granted to outstanding initiatives by planning agencies, planning teams or firms, community groups, and local authorities.

www.planning.org

2012 Winners

Daniel Burnham Award for a Comprehensive Plan
Vision 2020: New York City Comprehensive Waterfront Plan
New York, NY

HUD Secretary's Opportunity and Empowerment Award
Robert R. Taylor Homes/NorthSide Revitalization
Wilmington, NC

Best Practice
Cool Planning: A Handbook on Local Strategies to Slow Climate Change
Oregon

Grassroots Initiative
Yorktown 2015: A Blueprint for Survival and Sustainability
Philadelphia, PA

Implementation
Contra Costa Centre Transit Village
Contra Costa, CA

Public Outreach
Fast Forward Mobile Outreach Bus
Tulsa, OK

Innovation in Sustaining Places
Re-imagining a More Sustainable Cleveland
Cleveland, OH

Hazard Mitigation and Disaster Planning
Florida Statewide Regional Evacuation Study Program
Florida

Planning Firm
Sasaki Associates
Watertown, MA

Landmark Award
Bennett Plan of the City of Pasadena (1925)
Pasadena, CA

Guiding Principles for Federal Architecture (1962)
US General Services Administration

Pierre L'Efant International Planning Award
Strategic Master Plan I
Petra Region, Jordan

Hard-Won Victory
Candlestick Point-Hunters Point Shipyard Phase II EIR
San Francisco, CA

Advancing Diversity & Social Change in Honor of Paul Davidoff
Leonardo Vazquez
Rutgers, State University of New Jersey

Planning Advocate
Gov. Martin O'Malley: Reinvigorating Smart Growth
Maryland

Source: American Planning Association

National Preservation Awards

The National Trust for Historic Preservation annually recognizes citizens, organizations, and public and private entities for their dedication to and **support of historic preservation**. A jury of preservation professionals selects the winners of the National Preservation Awards using such criteria as the projects' positive effect on the community, pioneering nature, quality, and degree of difficulty. Special interest is also placed on projects that use historic preservation as a method of revitalization.

www.preservationnation.org

2012 Winners

Charles H. Shaw Technology and Learning
    Center
Chicago, IL

Historic Park Inn Hotel
Mason City, IA

Leavenworth Building 19
Leavenworth, KS

New Orleans US Custom House
New Orleans, LA

Accident Fund National Headquarters/Ottawa
    Street Power Station
Lansing, MI

Todd Bolender Center for Dance and
    Creativity
Kansas City, MO

ASM International Headquarters
Materials Park, OH

Oswego Iron Furnace
Lake Oswego, OR

30th Street Main Post Office
Philadelphia, PA

Market Square Place
Pittsburgh, PA

Gullah Museum of Hilton Head Island
    Preservation of Duey's Home
Hilton Head Island, SC

Main Building at Our Lady of the Lake
    University
San Antonio, TX

Washington State Heritage Barn Preservation
    Initiative
Statewide, WA

SIERR Building at McKinstry Station
Spokane, WA

Source: National Trust for Historic Preservation

Praemium Imperiale

The Praemium Imperiale is awarded by the Japan Art Association, Japan's premier cultural institution, for **lifetime achievement in the fields of painting, sculpture, music, architecture, and theater/film**. The following individuals received this honor for architecture, which includes a commemorative medal and a 15,000,000 yen ($130,000) honorarium.

www.praemiumimperiale.org

1989	I.M. Pei	2002	Sir Norman Foster (UK)
1990	James Stirling (UK)	2003	Rem Koolhaas (Netherlands)
1991	Gae Aulenti (Italy)	2004	Oscar Niemeyer (Brazil)
1992	Frank Gehry	2005	Taniguchi Yoshio (Japan)
1993	Kenzo Tange (Japan)	2006	Frei Otto (Germany)
1994	Charles Correa (India)	2007	Jacques Herzog and Pierre de
1995	Renzo Piano (Italy)		Meuron (Switzerland)
1996	Tadao Ando (Japan)	2008	Peter Zumthor (Switzerland)
1997	Richard Meier	2009	Zaha Hadid (UK)
1998	Alvaro Siza (Portugal)	2010	Toyo Ito (Japan)
1999	Fumihiko Maki (Japan)	2011	Ricardo Legorreta (Mexico)
2000	Sir Richard Rogers (UK)	2012	Henning Larsen (Denmark)
2001	Jean Nouvel (France)		

Source: Japan Art Association

Pritzker Architecture Prize

In 1979, Jay and Cindy Pritzker established the Pritzker Architecture Prize to inspire **greater creativity in the profession** and to heighten public awareness about architecture. Today, it is revered as one of the field's highest honors. The prize, which includes a $100,000 grant, is awarded each year to a living architect whose body of work represents a long-standing, significant contribution to the built environment.

www.pritzkerprize.com

1979	Philip Johnson	1997	Sverre Fehn (Norway)
1980	Luis Barragán (Mexico)	1998	Renzo Piano (Italy)
1981	James Stirling (UK)	1999	Sir Norman Foster (UK)
1982	Kevin Roche	2000	Rem Koolhaas (Netherlands)
1983	I.M. Pei	2001	Jacques Herzog and Pierre de
1984	Richard Meier		Meuron (Switzerland)
1985	Hans Hollein (Austria)	2002	Glenn Murcutt (Australia)
1986	Gottfried Boehm (Germany)	2003	Jørn Utzon (Denmark)
1987	Kenzo Tange (Japan)	2004	Zaha Hadid (UK)
1988	Gordon Bunshaft	2005	Thom Mayne
	Oscar Niemeyer (Brazil)	2006	Paulo Mendes da Rocha (Brazil)
1989	Frank Gehry	2007	Sir Richard Rogers (UK)
1990	Aldo Rossi (Italy)	2008	Jean Nouvel (France)
1991	Robert Venturi	2009	Peter Zumthor (Switzerland)
1992	Alvaro Siza (Portugal)	2010	Kazuyo Sejima (Japan)
1993	Fumihiko Maki (Japan)		Ryue Nishizawa (Japan)
1994	Christian de Portzamparc (France)	2011	Eduardo Souto de Moura
1995	Tadao Ando (Japan)		(Portugal)
1996	Rafael Moneo (Spain)	2012	Wang Shu (China)

Source: The Pritzker Architecture Prize

Religious Art & Architecture Design Awards

The annual Religious Art & Architecture Design Awards, co-sponsored by *Faith & Form* magazine and the Interfaith Forum on Religion, Art and Architecture (a professional interest area of the American Institute of Architects), reward the **highest achievements in architecture, liturgical design, and art for religious spaces**. Architects, liturgical consultants, interior designers, artists, and craftpersons worldwide are eligible to enter. Winning projects are featured in *Faith & Form*.

www.faithandform.com

2011 Honor Awards

New Facilities

The Chapel of Our Lady of the Most Holy Trinity
Santa Paula, CA
Duncan G. Stroik Architect

First Unitarian Society Meeting House Addition
Madison, WI
The Kubala Washatko Architects, Inc.

Visual Arts

Internal Glass Window, Basilica of Saint Paul Outside-the-Walls
Rome, Italy
Progetto Arte Poli (Italy)

Rose Window, Eldridge Street Synagogue
New York, NY
Kiki Smith and Deborah Gans

2011 Merit Awards

New Facilities

First Congregational Church, United Church of Christ
Rochester, MI
Constantine George Pappas AIA Architecture/ Planning

Congregation Bet Ha'am
Portland, ME
Shim-Sutcliffe Architects (Canada)

Rio Roca Chapel
Palo Pinto, TX
Maurice Jennings + Walter Jennings Architects

Renovation

St. Paul's Episcopal Church
Indianapolis, IN
Atkin Olshin Schade Architects

St. James Cathedral
Orlando, FL
Kosinski Architecture, Inc.

Restoration

St. Andrew's Episcopal Church
Ann Arbor, MI
Quinn Evans Architects

St. Bernard's Church
Bernardsville, NJ
Historic Building Architects

Liturgical/Interior Design
Catherine McAuley Chapel
Roseburg, OR
Richard Brown Architect, AIA

Church of Jesus the Divine Master
Rome, Italy
Progetto Arte Poli (Italy)

Saint Angela Merici Chapel, Ursuline Academy
of Dallas
Dallas, TX
The Liturgical Design Consultancy

The Shrine of Our Lady of Guadalupe
La Crosse, WI
Duncan G. Stroik Architect

Ceremonial Objects
Peace Lamp, Hyattsville Mennonite Church
Hyattsville, MD
DPConrad, Architect

Visual Arts
"Fourteen Stations of the Cross," Church
of Christ the King
New Vernon, NJ
Leonard Porter Studio

"Gospel of Genesis," Catholic University
of Pusan Theological College
Busan, South Korea
Seunghee.Son (South Korea)

"Andean Christ Breaking Bread"
John Giuliani

Sacred Landscape
Westwood United Methodist Church
Los Angeles, CA
Lehrer Architects

Unbuilt Work
Capilla de Guadalupe & Galeria Capuchina
Santiago, Nuevo Leon, Mexico
Arquipelago

Source: Faith & Form

RIBA Royal Gold Medal

The Royal Institute of British Architects' Royal Gold Medal was inaugurated by Queen Victoria in 1848. It is conferred annually on a **distinguished architect, person, or firm "whose work has promoted, either directly or indirectly, the advancement of architecture."**

www.riba.org

1848	Charles Robert Cockerell (UK)	1886	Charles Garnier (France)
1849	Luigi Canina (Italy)	1887	Ewan Christian (UK)
1850	Sir Charles Barry (UK)	1888	Baron von Hansen (Austria)
1851	Thomas L. Donaldson (UK)	1889	Sir Charles T. Newton (UK)
1852	Leo von Klenze (Germany)	1890	John Gibson (UK)
1853	Sir Robert Smirke (UK)	1891	Sir Arthur Blomfield (UK)
1854	Philip Hardwick (UK)	1892	Cesar Daly (France)
1855	Jacques Ignace Hittorff (France)	1893	Richard Morris Hunt
1856	Sir William Tite (UK)	1894	Lord Frederic Leighton (UK)
1857	Owen Jones (UK)	1895	James Brooks (UK)
1858	Friedrich August Stuler (Germany)	1896	Sir Ernest George (UK)
1859	Sir George Gilbert Scott (UK)	1897	Petrus Josephus Hubertus Cuypers
1860	Sydney Smirke (UK)		(Netherlands)
1861	Jean-Baptiste Cicéron Lesueur	1898	George Aitchison (UK)
	(France)	1899	George Frederick Bodley (UK)
1862	Robert Willis (UK)	1900	Rodolfo Amadeo Lanciani (Italy)
1863	Anthony Salvin (UK)	1901	*No award granted due to the death*
1864	Eugène Emmanuel Violett-le-Duc		*of Queen Victoria*
	(France)	1902	Thomas Edward Collcutt (UK)
1865	Sir James Pennethorne (UK)	1903	Charles F. McKim
1866	Sir Matthew Digby Wyatt (UK)	1904	Auguste Choisy (France)
1867	Charles Texier (France)	1905	Sir Aston Webb (UK)
1868	Sir Henry Layard (UK)	1906	Sir Lawrence Alma-Tadema (UK)
1869	C.R. Lepsius (Germany)	1907	John Belcher (UK)
1870	Benjamin Ferrey (UK)	1908	Honore Daumet (France)
1871	James Fergusson (UK)	1909	Sir Arthur John Evans (UK)
1872	Baron von Schmidt (Austria)	1910	Sir Thomas Graham Jackson (UK)
1873	Thomas Henry Wyatt (UK)	1911	Wilhelm Dorpfeld (Germany)
1874	George Edmund Street (UK)	1912	Basil Champneys (UK)
1875	Edmund Sharpe (UK)	1913	Sir Reginald Blomfield (UK)
1876	Joseph Louis Duc (France)	1914	Jean Louis Pascal (France)
1877	Charles Barry Jr. (UK)	1915	Frank Darling (Canada)
1878	Alfred Waterhouse (UK)	1916	Sir Robert Rowand Anderson (UK)
1879	Marquis de Vogue (France)	1917	Henri Paul Nenot (France)
1880	John L. Pearson (UK)	1918	Ernest Newton (UK)
1881	George Godwin (UK)	1919	Leonard Stokes (UK)
1882	Baron von Ferstel (Austria)	1920	Charles Louis Girault (France)
1883	Francis C. Penrose (UK)	1921	Sir Edwin Lutyens (UK)
1884	William Butterfield (UK)	1922	Thomas Hastings
1885	H. Schliemann (Germany)	1923	Sir John James Burnet (UK)

1924	*No award granted*	1969	Jack Antonio Coia (UK)
1925	Sir Giles Gilbert Scott (UK)	1970	Sir Robert Matthew (UK)
1926	Ragnar Östberg (Sweden)	1971	Hubert de Cronin Hastings (UK)
1927	Sir Herbert Baker (UK)	1972	Louis I. Kahn
1928	Sir Guy Dawber (UK)	1973	Sir Leslie Martin (UK)
1929	Victor Laloux (France)	1974	Powell & Moya (UK)
1930	Sir Percy Scott Worthington (UK)	1975	Michael Scott (Ireland)
1931	Sir Edwin Cooper (UK)	1976	Sir John Summerson (UK)
1932	Hendrik Petrus Berlage (Netherlands)	1977	Sir Denys Lasdun (UK)
1933	Sir Charles Reed Peers (UK)	1978	Jørn Utzon (Denmark)
1934	Henry Vaughan Lanchester (UK)	1979	The Office of Charles and Ray Eames
1935	Willem Marinus Dudok (Netherlands)	1980	James Stirling (UK)
1936	Charles Henry Holden (UK)	1981	Sir Philip Dowson (UK)
1937	Sir Raymond Unwin (UK)	1982	Berthold Lubetkin (Georgia)
1938	Ivar Tengbom (Sweden)	1983	Sir Norman Foster (UK)
1939	Sir Percy Thomas (UK)	1984	Charles Correa (India)
1940	Charles Francis Annesley Voysey (UK)	1985	Sir Richard Rogers (UK)
1941	Frank Lloyd Wright	1986	Arata Isozaki (Japan)
1942	William Curtis Green (UK)	1987	Ralph Erskine (Sweden)
1943	Sir Charles Herbert Reilly (UK)	1988	Richard Meier
1944	Sir Edward Maufe (UK)	1989	Renzo Piano (Italy)
1945	Victor Vesnin (USSR)	1990	Aldo van Eyck (Netherlands)
1946	Sir Patrick Abercrombie (UK)	1991	Sir Colin Stansfield Smith (UK)
1947	Sir Albert Edward Richardson (UK)	1992	Peter Rice (UK)
1948	Auguste Perret (France)	1993	Giancarlo de Carlo (Italy)
1949	Sir Howard Robertson (UK)	1994	Sir Michael and Lady Patricia
1950	Eleil Saarinen (Finland/US)		Hopkins (UK)
1951	Emanuel Vincent Harris (UK)	1995	Colin Rowe (UK/US)
1952	George Grey Wornum (UK)	1996	Harry Seidler (Australia)
1953	Le Corbusier (Charles-Édouard	1997	Tadao Ando (Japan)
	Jeanneret) (Switzerland/France)	1998	Oscar Niemeyer (Brazil)
1954	Sir Arthur Stephenson (Australia)	1999	Barcelona, Spain
1955	John Murray Easton (UK)	2000	Frank Gehry
1956	Walter Gropius (Germany/US)	2001	Jean Nouvel (France)
1957	Alvar Aalto (Finland)	2002	Archigram (UK)
1958	Robert Schofield Morris (Canada)	2003	Rafael Moneo (Spain)
1959	Ludwig Mies van der Rohe	2004	Rem Koolhaas (Netherlands)
	(Germany/US)	2005	Frei Otto (Germany)
1960	Pier Luigi Nervi (Italy)	2006	Toyo Ito (Japan)
1961	Lewis Mumford	2007	Jacques Herzog and Pierre
1962	Sven Gottfrid Markelius (Sweden)		de Meuron (Switzerland)
1963	Lord William Graham Holford (UK)	2008	Edward Cullinan (UK)
1964	E. Maxwell Fry (UK)	2009	Álvaro Siza (Portugal)
1965	Kenzo Tange (Japan)	2010	I.M. Pei
1966	Ove Arup (UK)	2011	David Chipperfield
1967	Sir Nikolaus Pevsner (UK)	2012	Herman Hertzberger (Netherlands)
1968	R. Buckminster Fuller		

Source: Royal Institute of British Architects

SCUP/AIA-CAE Excellence in Planning, Landscape Architecture, and Architecture Awards

The Society for College and University Planning and the American Institute of Architects' Committee on Architecture for Education jointly present the annual Excellence in Planning, Landscape Architecture, and Architecture Awards to **outstanding projects developed for higher education institutions**. The jury considerations include the quality of the physical environment as well as the comprehensiveness of the planning process. The award is presented to all members of the project team.

www.scup.org

2012 Honor Awards

Planning for a New Campus
Grangegorman Urban Quarter Master Plan, Dublin Institute of Technology and Health Executive Services
Dublin, Ireland
Moore Ruble Yudell Architects & Planners

Planning for an Existing Campus
Drexel University Campus Master Plan
Philadelphia, PA
Goody Clancy

Landscape Architecture – General Design
Midway Crossings, University of Chicago
Chicago, IL
BauerLatoza Studio; James Carpenter Design Associates

Buchanan Courtyards, University of British Columbia
Vancouver, BC, Canada
Phillips Farevaag Smallenberg (Canada)

Architecture for a New Building
Energy. Environment. Experiential Learning, University of Calgary
Calgary, AB, Canada
DIALOG; Perkins+Will

Brockman Hall for Physics, Rice University
Houston, TX
Kieran Timberlake

Algonquin Centre for Construction Excellence, Algonquin College of Applied Arts and Technology
Ottawa, ON, Canada
Diamond Schmitt Architects (Canada); Edward J. Cuhaci and Associates Architects Inc., Architects (Canada)

Architecture for Building Additions or Adaptive Reuse
Chevron Chemistry Annex, University of Pittsburgh
Pittsburgh, PA
Wilson Architects, Inc.

University of California, Berkeley School of Law, Renovation and South Addition
Berkeley, CA
Ratcliff; Hargreaves Associates

Architecture for Restoration or Preservation
Gasson Hall, Boston College
Boston, MA
Shawmut Design and Construction

2012 Merit Awards

Planning for a New Campus
Universidad del Istmo Master Plan
Guatemala City, Guatemala
Sasaki Associates, Inc.

Planning for a District or Campus Component
Indiana University Bloomington Campus
    Master Plan
Bloomington, IN
SmithGroupJJR

Landscape Architecture – General Design
Walkways and Gardens in the Main
    Quadrangle Landscape, University of
    Chicago
Chicago, Illinois
Hoerr Schaudt Landscape Architects

Landscape Architecture – Open Space Planning and Design
Duke University for Building Connections
    Through Landscape: Duke University
    Campus Drive Planning Study
Durham, NC
Reed Hilderbrand; Pelli Clarke Pelli Architects;
    William Rawn Associates, Architects, Inc.

Architecture for a New Building
Emery Community Arts Center, University of
    Maine at Farmington
Farmington, ME
designLAB architects

Arbol de la Vida Residence Hall, University of
    Arizona
Tucson, AZ
NAC Architecture

Frick Chemistry Laboratory, Princeton
    University
Princeton, NJ
Payette; Hopkins Architects

Architecture for Building Additions or Adaptive Reuse
The Paramount Center, Emerson College
Boston, MA
Elkus Manfredi Architects; Silverman
    Associates

Architecture for Restoration or Preservation
Fariborz Maseeh Residence Hall,
    Massachusetts Institute of Technology
Cambridge, MA
Miller Dyer Spears Inc.

Source: Society for College and University Planning

Star Award

The International Interior Design Association's Star Award celebrates **individuals and organizations that have made extraordinary contributions to the interior design profession**. As the Star Award is merit-based, it is not necessarily granted each year. Although non-members are eligible, the IIDA board of directors (the selection body) only accepts nominations from IIDA fellows, chapter presidents, and directors.

www.iida.org

1985	Lester Dundes	2000	Eva L. Maddox
1986	William Sullivan	2001	Andrée Putman (France)
1987	Orlando Diaz-Azcuy	2002	Karim Rashid
1988	Paul Brayton	2003	Ray Anderson
1989	Florence Knoll Bassett	2004	Kevin Kampschroer
1990	Beverly Russell	2005	Target Corporation
1991	Stanley Abercrombie	2006	*Fast Company*
1992	M. Arthur Gensler Jr.	2007	Karen Stephenson
1993	Sivon C. Reznikoff	2008	Gordon Segal
1994	Michael Kroelinger	2009	Hilda Longinotti
1995	Douglas R. Parker	2010	Majora Carter
1997	Michael Wirtz	2011	The Center for Health Design
1998	Charles and Ray Eames	2012	Four Seasons Hotel Corporation
1999	Michael Brill		

Source: International Interior Designers Association

Top Green Projects

The American Institute of Architects' Committee on the Environment annually selects the Top Green Projects to highlight **viable architectural design solutions that protect and enhance the environment**. Winning projects address significant environmental challenges, such as energy and water conservation, use of recycled materials, and improved indoor air quality. Responsible use of building materials, daylighting, efficient heating and cooling, and sensitivity to local environmental issues are some of the jury's considerations.

www.aiatopten.org

2012 Winners

1315 Peachtree Street/Perkins+Will
Atlanta, GA
Perkins+Will

ASU Polytechnic Academic District
Mesa, AZ
RSP Architects; Lake Flato Architects

Chandler City Hall
Chandler, AZ
SmithGroupJJR

Iowa Utilities Board Office of Consumer
    Advocate Office Building
Des Moines, IA
BNIM

Mercy Corps Global Headquarters
Portland, OR
THA Architecture

Kensington High School for the Creative and
    Performing Arts
Philadelphia, PA
SMP Architects with SRK Architects

Music and Science Building, Hood River
    Middle School
Hood River, OR
Opsis Architecture

Newberg Center, Portland Community College
Newberg, OR
Hennebery Eddy Architects

Bagley Classroom Building, University of
    Minnesota, Duluth
Duluth, MN
Salmela Architect

2009 Long Range Development Plan,
    University of California, Merced
Merced, CA
University of California, Merced

Source: American Institute of Architects

Twenty-five Year Award

The American Institute of Architects' Twenty-five Year Award celebrates **buildings that excel under the test of time**. Eligible projects must have been completed within the past 25 to 35 years by a licensed US architect, though the buildings may be located worldwide. Winning designs are still operating under the tenets of the original program, demonstrating continued viability in function and form, and contributing meaningfully to American life and architecture.

www.aia.org

1969	Rockefeller Center
	New York, NY, 1931–40
	Reinhard & Hofmeister with
	Corbett, Harrison & MacMurray
	and Hood & Fouilhoux
1971	Crow Island School
	Winnetka, IL, 1939
	Perkins, Wheeler & Will and Eliel
	and Eero Saarinen
1972	Baldwin Hills Village
	Los Angeles, CA, 1941
	Reginald D. Johnson with Wilson,
	Merrill & Alexander and
	Clarence S. Stein
1973	Taliesin West
	Paradise Valley, AZ, 1938
	Frank Lloyd Wright
1974	S.C. Johnson & Son Administration
	Building
	Racine, WI, 1939
	Frank Lloyd Wright
1975	Philip Johnson Residence
	(The Glass House)
	New Canaan, CT, 1949
	Philip Johnson
1976	860-880 North Lakeshore Drive
	Apartments
	Chicago, IL, 1948–51
	Ludwig Mies van der Rohe
1977	Christ Lutheran Church
	Minneapolis, MN, 1948–51
	Saarinen, Saarinen & Associates
	with Hills, Gilbertson & Hays
1978	Eames House
	Pacific Palisades, CA, 1949
	Charles and Ray Eames

1979	Yale University Art Gallery
	New Haven, CT, 1954
	Louis I. Kahn with Douglas W. Orr
1980	Lever House
	New York, NY, 1952
	Skidmore, Owings & Merrill
1981	Farnsworth House
	Plano, IL, 1950
	Ludwig Mies van der Rohe
1982	Equitable Savings and Loan
	Association Building
	Portland, OR, 1948
	Pietro Belluschi
1983	Price Tower
	Bartlesville, OK, 1956
	Frank Lloyd Wright
1984	Seagram Building
	New York, NY, 1957
	Ludwig Mies van der Rohe
1985	General Motors Technical Center
	Warren, MI, 1951
	Saarinen, Saarinen & Associates
	with Smith, Hinchman and
	Grylls Associates
1986	Solomon R. Guggenheim
	Museum
	New York, NY, 1959
	Frank Lloyd Wright
1987	Bavinger House
	Norman, OK, 1953
	Bruce Goff
1988	Dulles International Airport
	Terminal Building
	Chantilly, VA, 1962
	Eero Saarinen & Associates

1989	Vanna Venturi House Chestnut Hill, PA, 1964 Robert Venturi	2001	Weyerhaeuser Headquarters Tacoma, WA, 1971 Skidmore, Owings & Merrill
1990	Gateway Arch St. Louis, MO, 1965 Eero Saarinen & Associates	2002	Fundació Joan Miró Barcelona, Spain, 1975 Sert Jackson and Associates
1991	Sea Ranch Condominium I The Sea Ranch, CA, 1965 Moore Lyndon Turnbull Whitaker	2003	Design Research Headquarters Building Cambridge, MA, 1969 BTA Architects Inc.
1992	Salk Institute for Biological Studies La Jolla, CA, 1966 Louis I. Kahn	2004	East Building, National Gallery of Art Washington, DC, 1978 I.M. Pei & Partners
1993	Deere & Company Administrative Center Moline, IL, 1963 Eero Saarinen & Associates	2005	Yale Center for British Art New Haven, CT, 1977 Louis I. Kahn
1994	Haystack Mountain School of Crafts Deer Isle, ME, 1962 Edward Larrabee Barnes Associates	2006	Thorncrown Chapel Eureka Springs, AR, 1980 E. Fay Jones
1995	Ford Foundation Headquarters New York, NY, 1968 Kevin Roche John Dinkeloo & Associates	2007	Vietnam Veterans Memorial Washington, DC, 1982 Maya Lin
1996	Air Force Academy Cadet Chapel Colorado Springs, CO, 1962 Skidmore, Owings & Merrill	2008	Atheneum New Harmony, IN, 1979 Richard Meier & Partners Architects
1997	Phillips Exeter Academy Library Exeter, NH, 1972 Louis I. Kahn	2009	Faneuil Hall Marketplace Boston, MA various renovations Benjamin Thompson & Associates
1998	Kimbell Art Museum Fort Worth, TX, 1972 Louis I. Kahn	2010	Hajj Terminal, King Abdul Aziz International Airport Jeddah, Saudi Arabia, 1981 Skidmore, Owings & Merrill
1999	John Hancock Center Chicago, IL, 1969 Skidmore, Owings & Merrill	2011	John Hancock Tower Boston, MA I.M. Pei & Partners
2000	Smith House Darien, CT, 1967 Richard Meier & Partners Architects	2012	Gehry Residence Santa Monica, CA, 1978 Gehry Partners

Source: American Institute of Architects

UIA Gold Medal

Every three years at its World Congress, the International Union of Architects awards its Gold Medal to a **living architect who has made outstanding achievements in the field of architecture**. This honor recognizes the recipient's lifetime of distinguished practice, contribution to the enrichment of mankind, and the promotion of the art of architecture.

www.uia-architectes.org

1984	Hassan Fathy (Egypt)	2002	Renzo Piano (Italy)
1987	Reima Pietila (Finland)	2005	Tadao Ando (Japan)
1990	Charles Correa (India)	2008	Teodoro González de León (Mexico)
1993	Fumihiko Maki (Japan)		
1996	Rafael Moneo (Spain)	2011	Alvaro Siza (Portugal)
1999	Ricardo Legorreta (Mexico)		

Source: International Union of Architects

Fellows of the Design Futures Council

Fellowship in the Design Futures Council is granted annually to an outstanding individual(s) who has provided noteworthy leadership to the advancement of design, design solutions, and/or the design professions. Senior fellows of the DFC are recognized for **significant contributions toward the understanding of changing trends, new research, and applied knowledge that improve the built environment and the human condition**. Any person worldwide may nominate candidates. The final selection of the senior fellows is made by the Senior Fellows Selection Committee.

Ava Abramowitz, Professor of Negotiations, George Washington University Law School

Harold Adams, Chairman Emeritus, RTKL

David M. Adamson, Visiting Professor, UCL and UWE

David Adjaye, Principal, Adjaye Associates

Ray Anderson*, Founder and Chairman, Interface Inc.

Rodrigo Arboleda, Chairman & CEO, One Laptop Per Child Association

James F. Barker, President, Clemson University

Peter Beck, Managing Partner and CEO, The Beck Group

Janine M. Benyus, Biomimicry & Sustainability Expert

Robert J. Berkebile, Founding Principal, BNIM Architects

Phil Bernstein, Technology and Professional Practice Authority, Yale University; Vice President for Industry Strategy & Relations, AEC Solutions, Autodesk

Peter Bohlin, Founder, Bohlin Cywinski Jackson

Friedl Bohm, Owner, White Oaks Partners

Penny Bonda, Eco Editor, *Interior Design* magazine

John Seely Brown, Co-Chairman, Deloitte Center for Edge Innovation

Barbara White Bryson, Associate Vice President of Facilities, Engineering & Planning, Rice University

Carrie Byles, Managing Director and Partner, Skidmore, Owings & Merrill

Santiago Calatrava, Pioneering Forms and Spaces, Santiago Calatrava Architects

Robert Campbell, Architecture Critic, *Boston Globe*

John Cary, President and CEO, *Next American City*

Wing T. Chao, Former Vice Chairman of Development, Walt Disney World

David Childs, Consulting Design Partner, Skidmore, Owings & Merrill

William Chilton, Founding Principal, Pickard Chilton

Clayton Christensen, Robert and Jane Cizik Professor of Business Administration, Harvard Business School

Steve Chu, Nobel Laureate and Secretary of Energy, U.S. Dept. of Energy

Daniel P. Coffey, Founder and President, Daniel P. Coffey & Associates Ltd.

Cindy Coleman, Partner, Frankel + Coleman; Associate Professor, School of the Art Institute of Chicago

Carol Coletta, President and CEO, CEOs for Cities

James P. Cramer, Resident Fellow and Foresight Advisor, Design Futures Council; Co-Founder, Design Futures Council; Chairman and CEO, Greenway Group

Michael Crichton*, Design Advocate, Author, Film Director

Sylvester Damianos, Architect, Sculptor, Damianosgroup

Nigel Dancey, Senior Partner, Foster and Partners

Fellows of the Design Futures Council

Clark Davis, Vice Chairman, HOK
Betsy del Monte, Principal, The Beck Group
Lauren Della Bella, President, SHP Leading Design
Frank Duffy, Co-Founder, DEGW
Williston (Bill) Dye, Principal, TSA Inc.
Phil Enquist, Partner, Skidmore, Owings & Merrill
Del Eulberg, Booz Allen Hamilton; USAF (ret.)
Richard Farson, Ph.D., President, Western Behavioral Sciences Institute
Rick Fedrizzi, President and CEO, U.S. Green Building Council
Edward Feiner, Principal, Perkins + Will
Curtis Fentress, President, Fentress Architects
Martin Fischer, Director, Center for Integrated Facility Engineering, Stanford University
Tom Fisher, Dean, College of Design, University of Minnesota
Steve Fiskum, COO and Partner, Hammel, Green and Abrahamson
Richard Florida, Author
Jim Follett, Organizational Growth Pioneer, Gensler
Sir Norman Foster, Founder and Chairman, Foster and Partners
Harrison Fraker, Professor, University of California, Berkeley
Neil Frankel, Principal, Frankel + Coleman
Roger Frechette, President, PositivEnergy Practice
Ed Friedrichs, Entrepreneur and Author, Friedrichs Group
R. Buckminster (Bucky) Fuller*, Engineer, Inventor, Educator, and Architectural Innovator
Thomas Galloway*, Georgia Institute of Technology
Jan Gehl, Principal, Gehl Architects
Frank Gehry, Architect, Gehry Partners
Arthur Gensler, Founder and Chairman, Gensler
Milton Glaser, Founder, Milton Glaser Inc.
Roger Godwin, Partner, DAG Architects

Paul Goldberger, Architecture Critic, *The New Yorker*
Al Gore, Former Vice President of the United States
David Gottfried, Managing Partner, Regenerative Ventures; Founder, U.S. Green Building Council
Michael Graves, Architect, Michael Graves & Associates
Robert Greenstreet, Dean, University of Wisconsin-Milwaukee; Director of Planning and Design, City of Milwaukee, Wisc.
Robert C. Grupe, Director, Architecture & Technology, USG Building Systems
Zaha Hadid, Architect, Zaha Hadid Architects
Gerry Hammond*, President and CEO, SHP Leading Design
Jeremy Harris, Former Mayor, Honolulu, Hawaii
Phil Harrison, President and CEO, Perkins+Will
Scott Harrison, President and Founder, charity: water
Craig W. Hartman, Design Partner, Skidmore, Owings & Merrill
Paul Hawken, Founder, Natural Capital Institute
H. Ralph Hawkins, Chairman and CEO, HKS Inc.
Barbara Heller, CEO, Design + Construction Strategies
Jerry Hobbs, Former Chairman, VNU North America
Carl Hodges, Founder and Chairman, Seawater Foundation
Steven Holl, Principal, Steven Holl Architects
Bjarke Ingels, Principal, BIG, Copenagen
Robert Ivy, Executive Vice President and CEO, American Institute of Architects
Richard Jackson, Professor & Chair, Environmental Health Sciences, UCLA
Jane Jacobs*, Urban Theorist, Author, Educator & Community Activist
Mary Margaret Jones, President and Senior Principal, Hargreaves Associates
Chris Jordan, Photographer

Louis I. Kahn*, Architect and Educator, University of Pennsylvania

Blair Kamin, Architecture Critic, *Chicago Tribune*

Don Kasian, President and CEO, Kasian Architecture Interior Design and Planning

Bruce Katz, Vice President, Brookings Institution

Larry Keeley, Thought Leader, Doblin, Inc.

Tom Kelley, General Manager, IDEO

Stephen Kieran, Founding Partner, KieranTimberlake

A. Eugene Kohn, Founding Partner and Chairman, Kohn Pedersen Fox Associates

Norman Koonce, Former CEO, American Institute of Architects

Ray Kurzweil, Inventor, Author, and Futurist

Theodore C. Landsmark, President, Boston Architectural College

Gary Lawrence, Vice President and Chief Sustainability Officer, AECOM

Mary Ann Lazarus, Firmwide Director of Sustainable Design, HOK

Laura Lee, Professor, Carnegie Mellon University; Thinker in Residence, South Australia

Debra Lehman-Smith, Principal, Lehman Smith McLeish

Maya Lin, Artist and Designer, Maya Lin Studio

Amory Lovins, Chief Scientist and Founder, Rocky Mountain Institute

Lucinda Ludwig*, Design Forum Architect, Engineer, Design Integration and Value Innovator, Leo A Daly

Chris Luebkeman, Director for Global Foresight & Innovation, Arup

John Maeda, President, Rhode Island School of Design

Marvin Malecha, Dean and Professor, College of Design, North Carolina State University

Janet Martin, President, Communication Arts Inc / Stantec

Bruce Mau, Chief Creative Officer, Bruce Mau Design Inc.

Thom Mayne, Founder and Design Director, Morphosis

Ed Mazria, Environmental Advocate and Founder, Architecture 2030

Steve McKay, Senior Principal, DLR Group

William McDonough, Architect, William McDonough + Partners

Alisdair McGregor, Global Sustainability Fellow, Arup

Richard Meier, Managing Partner, Richard Meier & Partners Architects

Sandra Mendler, Sustainability Leader and Principal, Mithun

Raymond F. Messer, Chairman and CEO, Walter P Moore

Gordon Mills, Former President, Durrant Group; Former President, National Council of Architectural Registration Boards

Glen Morrison, President, Alcoa Building and Construction Systems

Glenn Murcutt, Professor and Architect

John Ochsendorf, Associate Professor, Massachusetts Institute of Technology

Liz Ogbu, Fellow in Residence, IDEO.org

Ruy Ohtake, Architect, Brazil

Doug Parker, Managing Principal, Greenway Group

Alexander (Sandy) Pentland, Ph.D., Educator and Researcher, MIT Media Lab

Renzo Piano, Architect, Renzo Piano Building Workshop

B. Joseph Pine II, Branding Strategist and Author, Strategic Horizons LLP

Dan Pink, Author and Economics Lecturer

William Bradley (Brad) Pitt, Actor and environmental advocate

Jane Poynter, Chairwoman and President, Paragon Space Development Corp.

Antoine Predock, Principal, Antoine Predock Architect PC

Richard Rogers, Founder & Pritzker Prize Laureate, Rogers Stirk Harbour + Partners

Witold Rybczynski, Myerson Professor, Wharton School of Business, University of Pennsylvania

Fellows of the Design Futures Council

Moshe Safdie, Architect, Moshe Safdie and Associates

Jonas Salk*, M.D., Co-Founder, Design Futures Council; Founder, Salk Institute

Adele Santos, Dean, School of Architecture & Planning, Massachusetts Institute of Technology

Michael Schrage, Research Fellow, MIT Sloan School's Center for Digital Business

Peter Schwartz, Co-Founder, Global Business Network

Kate Schwennsen, Chair, School of Architecture, Clemson University

Terrence J. Sejnowski, Ph.D., Brain Scientist, Salk Institute

Stephen J. Senkowski, CEO, Xella Aircrete North America

William Sharples, Founding Principal, SHoP Architects and SHoP Construction

Scott Simpson, Principal/Senior Director- Cambridge, KlingStubbins

Cameron Sinclair, Co-Founder, Architecture for Humanity

Adrian Smith, Principal, Adrian Smith + Gordon Gill Architecture

Alex Steffen, Co-founder, Worldchanging

Karen Stephenson, Professor, Rotterdam School of Management, Erasmus University; Founder, NetForm International

Cecil Steward, President, Joslyn Institute for Sustainable Communities

RK Stewart, Associate Principal, Perkins + Will

Sarah Susanka, Architect, Susanka Studios

David Suzuki, Co-Founder, David Suzuki Foundation

Richard N. Swett, President, Swett Associates

Susan Szenasy, Chief Editor, *Metropolis* magazine

Jack Tanis, Strategic Planning and Workplace Design Thought Leader

Marilyn Taylor, Dean, School of Design, University of Pennsylvania

April Thornton, Leading Voice for Integrated Design Services

James Timberlake, Founding Partner, KieranTimberlake

Lene Tranberg, Head Architect and Co-Founder, Lundgaard & Tranberg

Alan Traugott, Principal, CJL Engineering

Robert Tucker, President, The Innovation Resource

John Carl Warnecke*, Architect and Contextual Design Advocate

Alice Waters, Founder, Chez Panisse Foundation

Alan Webber, Founding Editor, *FastCompany*

Jon Westling, Professor, Boston University

Gary Wheeler, Architect and Workspace Design Leader, WheelerKänik LLP

Allison Williams, Principal, Perkins + Will

Arol Wolford, President, SmartBIM

Richard Saul Wurman, Founder, Access Guide and TED

Jocelyn Wyatt, Co-Leader & Executive Director, IDEO.org

Scott Wyatt, Managing Partner, NBBJ

Nicholas You, Planner & Director, UN-Habitat

* Deceased
† Resident fellow and foresight advisor

Source: Design Futures Council

Benjamin Russell Hospital for Children, Birmingham, AL | HKS

Blake Marvin/HKS, Inc.

© James Wong

Kaiser Permanente, Ontario Vineyard Medical Center, Ontario, CA I HDR

Central Washington Hospital, Wenatchee, WA I HDR

City of Alexandria, Public Safety Headquarters, Alexandria, VA I HDR

Diné College Library, Shiprock, NM | DLR Group

Casper College, University of Wyoming Student Center, Casper, WY | DLR Group

RTKL Associates Inc.

Shanghai Zhabei Suzhou Creek, Shanghai, China | RTKL Associates Inc.

St. John's on the Lake, Milwaukee, WI I Perkins Eastman

Sasaki Associates, Inc.

Ohio State University South High Rises, Columbus, OH | Sasaki Associates, Inc.

Durstan Saylor

Sustainable Design in Connecticut, Norwalk, CT I DuJardin Design Associates

John McKinnon

Savannah College of Art and Design (SCAD), School of Building Art in Eichberg Hall, Savannah, GA | SCAD

SCAD

SCAD's Flagship Building, Poetter Hall, Savannah, GA | SCAD

SCAD, Student Center, Savannah, GA | SCAD

Courtesy of Conrad Koh Samui

Conrad Koh Samui, Koh Samui, Thailand | Wilson

Firm Anniversaries

The following currently practicing US architecture firms were founded in 1913, 1938, 1963, and 1988 respectively.

Founded 1913 (Firms Celebrating their 100th Anniversaries)
Potter Lawson, Madison, WI
Saxelbye Architects, Jacksonville, FL

1938 (75th Anniversaries)
Corgan, Dallas, TX
CTA Architects Engineers, Billings, MT
Harvard Jolly, St. Petersburg, FL
Heyward Boyd Architects, Charlottesville, VA
JBA Architects, Neward, OH
Mahlum Architects, Seattle, WA
McCleary German Architects, Houston, TX

1963 (50th Anniversaries)
AAIC, Collinsville, IL
Anderson Wade & Witty, Minot, ND
Beacon Architectural Associates, Boston, MA
BRR Architecture, Merriam, KS
Buttrick White & Burtis, New York, NY
Christner, St. Louis, MO
DeWolff Partnership Architects, Rochester, NY
Ennead Architects (formerly Polshek
    Partnership), New York, NY
Flansburgh Architects, Boston, MA
Fugleberg Koch, Winter Park, FL
Fusco, Shaffer & Pappas, Farmington Hills, MI
H + L Architecture, Denver, CO
Hanhfeld Hoffer Stanford, Fort Worth, TX
Holt Architects, Ithaca, NY
Kaestle Boos, New Britain, CT
KMD Architects, San Francisco, CA
Larson & Darby Group, Rockford, IL
Lindsay Shives Associates, Still River, MA
Melichar Architects, Lake Forest, IL
Morton M. Gruber, Atlanta, GA
MS Consultants, Columbus, OH
RCM Architects, Findlay, OH
Richard Meier & Partners Architects,
    New York, NY

RKT&B Architecture & Urban Design,
    New York, NY
Ron Yeo Architect, Corona Del Mar, CA
Wallace Roberts & Todd, Philadelphia, PA

1988 (25th Anniversaries)
AHAdams&Company, Willow Grove, PA
ALB Designs, San Rafael, CA
Alfonso Architects, Tampa, FL
Anderson Architecture, Boca Raton, FL
Andreozzi Architects, Barrington, RI
Archimages, St. Louis, MO
Architectura, Rochester, NY
Architecture Design Group, South Bend, IN
Arkinetics, Cleveland, OH
Artekna, Indianapolis, IN
Barry Davis Architects, Birmingham, AL
Bell/Knott & Associates, Leawood, KS
Blackney Hayes Architects, Philadelphia, PA
Bondurant Associates, Portsmouth, VA
Bouril Design Studio, Madison, WI
Brasher Design, Columbia, MD
Buckman Architectural Group, Kenilworth, NJ
Busch Architects, Minneapolis, MN
BWA Architecture + Planning, Philadelphia, PA
Catalyst Architects, Lexington, SC
D.W. Arthur Associates Architecture,
    Boston, MA
Destefano Partners, Chicago, IL
DTJ Design, Boulder, CO
Elena Kalman Architect, Stamford, CT
Elkus Manfredi Architects, Boston, MA
Escher Design, Dorset, VT
Ferraro Choi, Honolulu, HI
Gardner Architects, Delaware, OH
Gignac Associates, Corpus Christi, TX
Hagemeister and Mack Architects,
    St. Cloud, MN
Harold Massop Associates Architects,
    Aurora, CO

Firm Anniversaries

Highland Associates, Clarks Summit, PA
Hilliard Architects, San Francisco, CA
Integrated Architecture, Grand Rapids, MI
Jeffrey Berman Architect, New York, NY
Jochum Architects, San Anselmo, CA
John Lape Architect, Portland, OR
John Schlesinger Architect, San Francisco, CA
JRC Design, Phoenix, AZ
KAA Design, Los Angeles, CA
Kenneth Boroson Architects, New Haven, CT
Kluber, Batavia, IL
Koch Architects, Berkeley, CA
LineSync Architecture, Wilmington, VT
Lockwood Architects, Fort Collins, CO
Lyman Davidson Dooley, Atlanta, GA
Margulies Perruzzi Architects, Boston, MA
McElrath and Oliver Associates,
    St. Gadsden, AL
MHAWorks, Durham, NC
Morgan Gick McBeath & Associates,
    Falls Church, VA
MWA Architects, San Francisco, CA
Nashawtuc Architects, Concord, MA
Neil Hauck Architects, Darien, CT

Oakley Collier Architects, Rocky Mount, NC
Peacock Architects, Atlanta, GA
PF&A Design, Norfolk, VA
RicciGreene Associates, New York, NY
Richard Brown Architect, Lexington, MA
Robert V. Sierzega and Associates,
    Chicago, IL
Setzer Architects, Red Wing, MN
Shiffler Associates Architects, Des Moines, IA
Smith Consulting Architects, San Diego, CA
Song + Associates, West Palm Beach, FL
Stemper Architects & Engineers, Seattle, WA
Stephen J. Kramer Architecture + Design,
    San Antonio, TX
Steven Heller Architect, Haiku, HI
Strobel & Hunter, Pensacola, FL
Theodore + Theodore Architects,
    Arrowsic, ME
TRK Architecture & Facilities Management,
    Phoenix, AZ
Vetter Design Group, Toledo, OH
Voith & Mactavish, Philadelphia, PA
WGM Design, Charlotte, NC

Source: DesignIntelligence

Firm Statistics: Architecture

	Number of Establishments[1]	Annual Payroll ($1,000s)	Paid Employees[2]
Alabama	214	82,948	1,328
Alaska	48	25,291	360
Arizona	504	146,685	2,677
Arkansas	138	65,060	1,111
California	3,148	1,673,732	22,372
Colorado	758	206,671	3,393
Connecticut	278	131,806	1,887
Delaware	31	7,801	166
District of Columbia	158	227,944	2,659
Florida	1,530	383,922	6,945
Georgia	543	267,629	4,423
Hawaii	178	74,017	1,092
Idaho	140	31,170	697
Illinois	1,033	440,156	6,780
Indiana	245	125,108	2,111
Iowa	116	55,886	906
Kansas	159	90,494	1,480
Kentucky	147	54,943	983
Louisiana	285	127,653	2,098
Maine	120	38,593	658
Maryland	395	190,486	2,834
Massachusetts	716	372,439	5,289
Michigan	422	173,217	3,113
Minnesota	381	208,520	3,229
Mississippi	109	44,649	754
Missouri	389	248,152	3,770
Montana	135	35,116	685
Nebraska	91	79,995	1,233
Nevada	143	68,066	1,140
New Hampshire	70	20,410	335
New Jersey	656	210,191	3,442
New Mexico	165	53,472	1,057
New York	2,147	1,097,226	15,814

Firm Statistics: Architecture

	Number of Establishments[1]	Annual Payroll ($1,000s)	Paid Employees[2]
North Carolina	574	196,094	3,332
North Dakota	44	12,979	264
Ohio	593	295,925	4,968
Oklahoma	181	80,684	1,448
Oregon	307	136,705	2,392
Pennsylvania	748	418,787	6,555
Rhode Island	79	17,640	360
South Carolina	248	69,196	1,305
South Dakota	40	13,012	255
Tennessee	270	136,384	2,234
Texas	1,348	774,278	11,308
Utah	222	70,689	1,392
Vermont	90	19,001	413
Virginia	519	297,459	4,339
Washington	669	306,175	5,040
West Virginia	39	20,666	318
Wisconsin	251	124,161	2,116
Wyoming	48	11,532	216
US Total	21,862	10,060,815	155,076

[1] All numbers are 2010.
[2] Paid employees for the pay period including March 12.

Source: US Census Bureau

Architecture

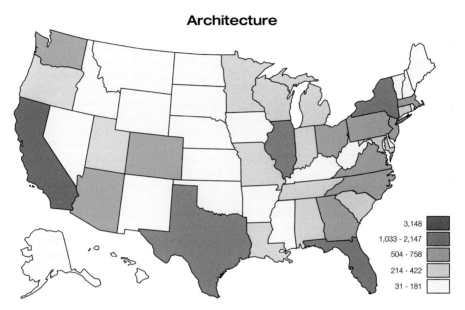

3,148	
1,033 - 2,147	
504 - 758	
214 - 422	
31 - 181	

The District of Columbia contains 158 establishments. US Total of Establishments: 21,862.

Firm Statistics: Interior Design

	Number of Establishments[1]	Annual Payroll ($1,000s)	Paid Employees[2]
Alabama	102	5,633	207
Alaska	11	1,757	44
Arizona	244	21,804	633
Arkansas	57	2,907	n/a
California	1,531	315,597	4,974
Colorado	397	38,406	1,021
Connecticut	136	12,805	299
Delaware	29	3,557	89
District of Columbia	61	38,858	522
Florida	1,442	117,799	3,456
Georgia	432	51,047	1,177
Hawaii	32	4,819	n/a
Idaho	28	2,137	71
Illinois	607	62,815	1,513
Indiana	147	14,566	468
Iowa	59	3,175	n/a
Kansas	80	4,485	182
Kentucky	83	6,295	198
Louisiana	88	7,984	287
Maine	25	1,022	n/a
Maryland	214	28,489	690
Massachusetts	268	41,674	707
Michigan	215	15,623	485
Minnesota	204	19,273	532
Mississippi	39	3,827	129
Missouri	137	10,606	337
Montana	37	1,860	80
Nebraska	57	6,008	165
Nevada	84	10,036	244
New Hampshire	23	1,416	45
New Jersey	334	31,755	779
New Mexico	42	2,255	131
New York	1,232	230,473	3,863

	Number of Establishments[1]	Annual Payroll ($1,000s)	Paid Employees[2]
North Carolina	312	22,982	745
North Dakota	13	430	n/a
Ohio	220	29,002	719
Oklahoma	93	7,701	256
Oregon	123	18,081	481
Pennsylvania	265	53,517	1,072
Rhode Island	43	6,600	158
South Carolina	158	12,241	454
South Dakota	12	532	n/a
Tennessee	135	15,599	405
Texas	724	101,621	2,551
Utah	96	7,226	254
Vermont	17	1,718	41
Virginia	329	32,902	875
Washington	228	18,872	659
West Virginia	19	1,414	n/a
Wisconsin	107	11,079	329
Wyoming	17	1,539	n/a
US Total	11,388	1,463,819	32,327

[1] All numbers are 2010.
[2] Paid employees for the pay period including March 12.

Source: US Census Bureau

Firm Statistics: Number of Establishments

Interior Design

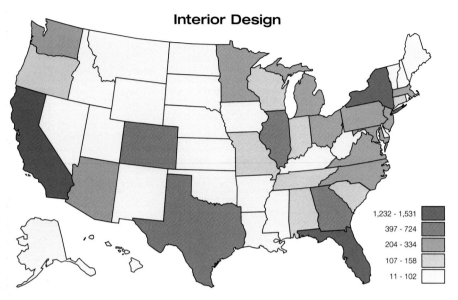

1,232 - 1,531	
397 - 724	
204 - 334	
107 - 158	
11 - 102	

The District of Columbia contains 61 establishments. US Total of Establishments: 11,388.

Landscape Architecture

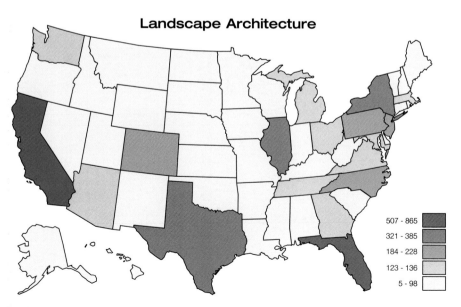

507 - 865	
321 - 385	
184 - 228	
123 - 136	
5 - 98	

The District of Columbia contains 25 establishments. US Total of Establishments: 5,604.

Source: DesignIntelligence

Firm Statistics: Landscape Architecture

	Number of Establishments[1]	Annual Payroll ($1,000s)	Paid Employees[2]
Alabama	35	6,851	n/a
Alaska	7	n/a	n/a
Arizona	133	25,891	538
Arkansas	13	835	n/a
California	865	283,527	5,105
Colorado	228	45,921	844
Connecticut	81	13,347	235
Delaware	11	2,186	61
District of Columbia	25	4,445	119
Florida	507	92,603	2,026
Georgia	136	22,502	538
Hawaii	36	13,158	206
Idaho	38	3,655	108
Illinois	345	53,593	947
Indiana	73	7,599	214
Iowa	17	1,343	41
Kansas	26	3,702	116
Kentucky	38	6,334	171
Louisiana	63	13,751	405
Maine	27	3,409	69
Maryland	131	23,880	579
Massachusetts	184	72,111	1,034
Michigan	130	18,946	407
Minnesota	80	8,965	166
Mississippi	21	1,712	61
Missouri	57	7,895	212
Montana	22	1,266	35
Nebraska	11	n/a	n/a
Nevada	23	4,977	n/a
New Hampshire	22	2,819	54
New Jersey	228	35,813	625
New Mexico	24	4,792	128
New York	385	85,653	1,425

Firm Statistics: Landscape Architecture

	Number of Establishments[1]	Annual Payroll ($1,000s)	Paid Employees[2]
North Carolina	208	33,778	814
North Dakota	5	n/a	n/a
Ohio	93	17,430	431
Oklahoma	44	5,811	178
Oregon	95	13,620	317
Pennsylvania	199	53,110	1,011
Rhode Island	19	3,128	56
South Carolina	81	7,004	272
South Dakota	11	1,346	n/a
Tennessee	98	13,096	391
Texas	321	75,055	1,816
Utah	55	6,937	205
Vermont	23	3,010	74
Virginia	123	34,473	758
Washington	136	26,762	565
West Virginia	6	n/a	n/a
Wisconsin	58	9,616	162
Wyoming	7	1,501	n/a
US Total	**5,604**	**1,179,158**	**23,519**

[1] All numbers are 2010.
[2] Paid employees for the pay period including March 12.

Source: US Census Bureau

Number of Licensed Architects

Licensed architects in each state are divided into two categories: resident and recipro-cal, or non-resident, registrants. Based on current population levels, the chart below also calculates the per capita number of resident architects in each state. The following information is from the National Council of Architectural Registration Boards' 2011 survey.

State	Resident Architects	Reciprocal Registrations	Total	Population	Per capita # of Resident Arch. (per 100,000)
Alabama	823	1,789	2,612	4,802,740	17
Alaska	249	343	592	722,718	34
Arizona	2,412	5,238	7,650	6,482,505	37
Arkansas	507	930	1,437	2,937,979	17
California	15,575	3,907	19,482	37,691,912	41
Colorado	3,193	3,937	7,130	5,116,796	62
Connecticut	1,438	2,656	4,094	3,580,709	40
Delaware	123	1,526	1,649	907,135	14
D.C.	780	2,438	3,218	617,996	126
Florida	4,904	4,272	9,176	19,057,542	26
Georgia	2,404	2,952	5,356	9,815,210	24
Hawaii	972	1,192	2,164	1,374,810	71
Idaho	497	1,140	1,637	1,584,985	31
Illinois	5,499	3,646	9,145	12,869,257	43
Indiana	957	2,224	3,181	6,516,922	15
Iowa	501	1,181	1,682	3,062,309	16
Kansas	930	1,756	2,686	2,871,238	32
Kentucky	718	1,641	2,359	4,369,356	16
Louisiana	1,176	2,017	3,193	4,574,836	26
Maine	415	1,028	1,443	1,328,188	31
Maryland	1,934	3,667	5,601	5,828,289	33
Massachusetts	3,666	2,965	6,631	6,587,536	56
Michigan	2,588	3,125	5,713	9,876,187	26
Minnesota	1,896	1,538	4,434	5,344,861	35
Mississippi	350	1,564	1,914	2,978,512	12
Missouri	2,062	2,932	4,994	6,010,688	34
Montana	432	903	1,326	998,199	43

Number of Licensed Architects

State	Resident Architects	Reciprocal Registrations	Total	Population	Per capita # of Resident Arch. (per 100,000)
Nebraska	598	1,233	1,831	1,842,641	32
Nevada	766	2,377	3,143	2,723,322	28
New Hampshire	323	1,436	1,759	1,318,194	25
New Jersey	3,066	4,762	7,828	8,821,155	35
New Mexico	728	1,479	2,207	2,082,224	35
New York	9,467	6,592	16,059	19,465,197	49
North Carolina	2,306	3,005	5,311	9,656,401	24
North Dakota	141	653	794	683,932	21
Ohio	3,279	3,343	6,622	11,544,951	28
Oklahoma	732	1,479	1,927	3,791,508	19
Oregon	1,631	1,308	2,939	3,871,859	42
Pennsylvania	3,742	4,326	8,068	12,742,886	29
Rhode Island	314	1,367	1,681	1,051,302	30
South Carolina	1,015	2,465	3,480	4,679,230	22
South Dakota	101	674	775	824,082	12
Tennessee	1,299	1,716	3,015	6,403,353	20
Texas	7,333	3,882	11,215	25,674,681	29
Utah	771	1,455	2,226	2,817,222	27
Vermont	485	568	1,053	626,431	77
Virginia	2,774	4,185	6,959	8,096,604	34
Washington	3,956	2,285	6,241	6,830,038	58
West Virginia	92	891	983	1,855,364	5
Wisconsin	1,617	3,031	4,648	5,711,767	28
Wyoming	120	978	1,098	568,158	21
Totals	**103,657**	**117,997**	**222,361**	**311,591,917**	

Source: National Council of Architectural Registration Boards and DesignIntelligence

Oldest Architecture Firms

The following North American architecture firms were founded prior to 1914 (their specific founding dates indicated below) and are still operational today.

1853	Luckett & Farley, Louisville, KY SmithGroup, Detroit, MI
1868	Jensen and Halstead, Chicago, IL King & King Architects, Syracuse, NY
1870	Harriman, Auburn, ME

1871	Scholtz Gowey Gere Marolf
	    Architects & Interior Designers
	    (SGGM), Davenport, IA

1873	Graham, Anderson, Probst, & White, Chicago, IL
1874	Shepley Bulfinch Richardson and Abbott, Boston, MA
1876	Keffer/Overton Architects, Des Moines, IA
1878	The Austin Company, Kansas City, MO Ballinger, Philadelphia, PA

1880	Beatty, Harvey, Coco Architects,
	    New York, NY
	Holabird & Root, Chicago, IL
	Zeidler Partnership Architects,
	    Toronto, Canada

1884	SMRT, Portland, ME
1885	Cromwell Architects Engineers, Little Rock, AR HLW International, New York, NY
1887	Bradley & Bradley, Rockford, IL

1889	CSHQA, Boise, ID
	MacLachlan, Corneliu & Filoni,
	    Pittsburgh, PA
	Wank Adams Slavin Associates,
	    New York, NY

1891	Mathes Brierre Architects,
	    New Orleans, LA
	SSP Architectural Group,
	    Somerville, NJ

1892	FreemanWhite, Raleigh, NC
1893	Foor & Associates, Elmira, NY
1894	Colgan Perry Lawler Aurell Architects, Nyack, NY Freese and Nichols, Fort Worth, TX
1895	Brooks Borg Skiles Architecture Engineering, Des Moines, IA Albert Kahn Associates, Detroit, MI
1896	Hummel Architects, Boise, ID
1897	Baskervill, Richmond, VA Ittner Architects, St. Louis, MO

1898	Beardsley Design Associates,
	    Auburn, NY
	Berners-Schober Associates
	    (BSA, Inc.), Green Bay, WI
	Burns & McDonnell,
	    Kansas City, MO
	Eckles Architecture,
	    New Castle, PA
	FEH Associates Inc.,
	    Des Moines, IA
	Foss Architecture & Interiors,
	    Fargo, ND & Moorhead, MN
	PageSoutherlandPage, Austin, TX

1901	SHP Leading Design, Cincinnati, OH Wiley & Wilson, Lynchburg, VA
1902	WBRC Architects, Engineer, Bangor, ME

Oldest Architecture Firms

1906	AC Martin Partners, Los Angeles, CA
	CJMW, Winston Salem, NC
	Ratcliff, Emeryville, CA
	Swanke Hayden Connell Architects, New York, NY
	Zimmerman Architectural Studios, Milwaukee, WI

1907 Eppstein Uhen Architects, Milwaukee, WI
Fletcher Thompson, Shelton, CT
H2L2, Philadelphia, PA
Richter Cornbrooks Gribble, Baltimore, MD

1908 Harley Ellis Devereaux, Southfield, MI
Kahler Slater Architects, Milwaukee, WI
Somdal Associates, Shreveport, LA

1909 Howell Rusk Dodson Architects, Atlanta, GA
Lionakis, Sacramento, CA
Moeckel Carbonell Associates, Wilmington, DE
TRO/Jung Brannen, Boston, MA

1910 HFR Design, Nashville, TN

1911 IKM Incorporated, Pittsburgh, PA

1912 Graham, Anderson, Probst, & White, Chicago, IL

1913 Potter Lawson, Madison, WI
Saxelbye Architects, Jacksonville, FL

Source: DesignIntelligence

Tallest Buildings in the World

The following list ranks the world's 100 tallest buildings as determined by the Council on Tall Buildings and Urban Habitat. Buildings that have reached their full height but are still under construction are deemed eligible and are indicated with a UC in the year category along with the anticipated completion date, if known.

	Building	Yr.	Location	Height (ft./m.)	(# stories)	Architect
1	Burj Khalifa	2010	Dubai, UAE	2,717/828	163	Skidmore, Owings & Merrill
2	Makkah Royal Clock Tower Hotel	UC12	Mecca, Saudia Arabia	1,972/601	120	Dar Al-Handasah Architects (Lebanon)
3	Taipei 101	2004	Taipei, Taiwan	1,667/508	101	C.Y. Lee & Partners (Taiwan)
4	Shanghai World Financial Center	2008	Shanghai, China	1,614/492	101	Kohn Pedersen Fox Associates; East China Architectural Design & Research Institute Co. Ltd. (China)
5	International Commerce Centre	2010	Hong Kong, China	1,588/484	108	Wong & Ouyang Ltd. (Hong Kong); Kohn Pedersen Fox Associates
6	Petronas Tower 1	1998	Kuala Lumpur, Malaysia	1,483/452	88	Cesar Pelli & Associates
7	Petronas Tower 2	1998	Kuala Lumpur, Malaysia	1,483/452	88	Cesar Pelli & Associates
8	Zifeng Tower	2010	Nanjing, China	1,476/450	66	Skidmore, Owings & Merrill
9	Willis Tower	1974	Chicago, IL	1,451/442	108	Skidmore, Owings & Merrill
10	Guangzhou International Finance Center	2010	Guangzhou, China	1,451/442	108	Wilkerson Eyre Architects (UK)
11	KK100 Development	2011	Shenzhen, China	1,449/442	100	TFP Farrells (UK)
12	Trump International Hotel & Tower	2009	Chicago, IL	1,398/423	98	Skidmore, Owings & Merrill
13	Jin Mao Building	1999	Shanghai, China	1,380/421	88	Skidmore, Owings & Merrill
14	Princess Tower	2012	Dubai, UAE	1,356/413	101	Adnan Saffarini (UAE)
15	Al Hamra Firdous Tower	2011	Kuwait City, Kuwait	1,354/413	80	Skidmore, Owings & Merrill; Al Jazera Consultants (Kuwait); Callison
16	Two International Finance Centre	2003	Hong Kong, China	1,352/412	88	Cesar Pelli & Associates
17	23 Marina	2012	Dubai, UAE	1,289/393	90	Hafeez Contractor (India)
18	CITIC Plaza	1996	Guangzhou, China	1,280/390	80	Dennis Lau & Ng Chun Man Architects & Engineers (China)
19	Shun Hing Square	1996	Shenzhen, China	1,260/384	69	K.Y. Cheung Design Associates (China)
20	The Domain	UC13	Abu Dhabi, UAE	1,251/381	88	Foster + Partners (UK)
21	Empire State Building	1931	New York, NY	1,250/381	102	Shreve, Lamb & Harmon
22	Elite Residence	2012	Dubai, UAE	1,248/380	87	Adnan Saffarini (UAE)

Tallest Buildings in the World

	Building	Yr.	Location	Height (ft./m.)	(# stories)	Architect
23	Central Plaza	1992	Hong Kong, China	1,227/374	78	Ng Chun Man & Associates (China)
24	Bank of China Tower	1989	Hong Kong, China	1,205/367	72	Pei Cobb Freed & Partners
25	Bank of America Tower	2009	New York, NY	1,200/366	55	Cook+Fox Architects; Adamson Associates Architects
26	The Pinnacle	2012	Guangzhou, China	1,181/360	60	Make Architects (China)
27	Almas Tower	2008	Dubai, UAE	1,181/360	68	WS Atkins & Partners (UK)
28	Emirates Tower One	2000	Dubai, UAE	1,163/355	54	Norr Group Consultants (Canada)
29	J.W. Marriott Marquis Hotel Dubai Tower 1	UC12	Dubai, UAE	1,166/355	82	Archgroup Consultants (UAE)
30	J.W. Marriott Marquis Hotel Dubai Tower 2	UC13	Dubai, UAE	1,166/355	82	Archgroup Consultants (UAE)
31	Tuntex Sky Tower	1997	Kaohsiung, Taiwan	1,140/348	85	C.Y. Lee & Partners (Taiwan); Hellmuth, Obata & Kassabaum
32	Aon Centre	1973	Chicago, IL	1,136/346	83	Edward Durrell Stone & Associates
33	The Center	1998	Hong Kong, China	1,135/346	73	Dennis Lau & Ng Chun Man Architects & Engineers (China)
34	John Hancock Center	1969	Chicago, IL	1,128/344	100	Skidmore, Owings & Merrill
35	Tianjin World Financial Center	2011	Tianjin, China	1,105/337	76	Skidmore, Owings & Merrill
36	The Torch	2011	Dubai, UAE	1,105/337	79	Khatib & Alami (UAE)
37	Keangnam Hanoi Landmark Tower	2012	Hanoi, Vietnam	1,102/336	70	Heerim Architects & Planners (South Korea); Samoo Architects & Engineers (South Korea); HOK
38	Shimao International Plaza	2006	Shanghai, China	1,094/333	60	Ingenhoven Architekten (Germany); East China Architectural Design & Research Institute Co. Ltd. (China)
39	Rose Rayhaan by Rotana	2007	Dubai, UAE	1,093/333	72	Khatib & Alami (Lebanon)
40	Minsheng Bank Building	2008	Wuhan, China	1,086/331	68	Wuhan Architectural Design Institute (China)
41	Ryugyong Hotel	UC12	Pyongyang, North Korea	1,083/330	105	Baikdoosan Architects & Engineers (North Korea)
42	China World Trade Center Tower III	2009	Beijing, China	1,083/330	74	Skidmore, Owings & Merrill
43	Longxi International Hotel	2011	Jiangyin, China	1,076/328	74	A+E Design Co. (China)
44	Al Yaqoub Tower	UC12	Dubai, UAE	1,076/328	69	Adnan Saffarini (UAE)

Building	Yr.	Location	Height (ft./m.)	(# stories)	Architect
45 The Index	2010	Dubai, UAE	1,070/326	80	Foster + Partners (UK); Woods Bagot (UAE); Khatib & Alami (UAE)
46 The Landmark	UC12	Dubai, UAE	1,063/324	72	Cesar Pelli & Associates
47 Q1	2005	Gold Coast, Australia	1,058/323	78	The Buchan Group (Australia)
48 Wenzhou Trade Center	2010	Wenzhou, China	1,056,322	68	RTKL Associates Inc.; Shanghai Institute of Architectural Design & Research Co. (China)
49 Burj Al Arab Hotel	1999	Dubai, UAE	1,053/321	60	WS Atkins & Partners (UK)
50 Nina Tower I	2007	Hong Kong, China	1,046/319	80	Arthur CS Kwok Architects & Associates (China); Casa Design International (China); Dennis Lau & Ng Chun Man Architects & Engineers (China)
51 Chrysler Building	1930	New York, NY	1,046/319	77	William Van Alen
52 New York Times Tower	2007	New York, NY	1,046/319	52	Renzo Piano Building Workshop (Italy); FXFOWLE Architects
53 HHHR Tower	2010	Dubai, UAE	1,042/318	72	Al Hashemi (UAE)
54 Bank of America Plaza	1993	Atlanta, GA	1,040/317	55	Kevin Roche John Dinkeloo & Associates
55 Moi Center Tower A	UC13	Shenyang, China	1,020/311	62	Shenzhen Tongli Architects (China)
56 U.S. Bank Tower	1990	Los Angeles, CA	1,018/310	73	Pei Cobb Freed & Partners
57 Ocean Heights	2010	Dubai, UAE	1,017/310	83	Aedas (UAE) with ECG Engineering Consultants Group (Egypt)
58 Menara Telekom	2000	Kuala Lumpur, Malaysia	1,017/310	55	Hijjas Kasturi Associates (Malaysia)
59 Pearl River Tower	2012	Guangzhou, China	1,016/310	71	Skidmore, Owings & Merrill
60 Emirates Tower Two	2000	Dubai, UAE	1,014/309	56	Norr Group Consultants (Canada)
61 Franklin Center North Tower	1989	Chicago, IL	1,007/307	60	Skidmore, Owings & Merrill
62 Infinity Tower	UC13	Dubai, UAE	1,005/306	76	Skidmore, Owings & Merrill
63 One57	UC13	New York, NY	1,004/306	79	Atelier Christian de Portzamparc (France)
64 East Pacific Center Tower A	UC13	Shenzhen, China	1,004/306	85	Wong & Ouyang (Hong Kong)
65 The Shard	UC13	London, UK	1,004/306	73	Renzo Piano Building Workshop (Italy)
66 Etihad Towers T2	2011	Abu Dhabi, UAE	1,002/305	80	DBI Design (Australia)
67 JP Morgan Chase Tower	1982	Houston, TX	1,002/305	75	I.M. Pei & Partners
68 NE Asia Trade Tower	2010	Incheon, South Korea	1,001/305	68	Kohn Pedersen Fox Associates
69 Baiyoke Tower II	1997	Bangkok, Thailand	997/304	85	Plan Architects Co. (Thailand)

Tallest Buildings in the World

	Building	Yr.	Location	Height (ft./m.)	(# stories)	Architect
70	Two Prudential Plaza	1990	Chicago, IL	995/303	64	Loebl Schlossman Dart & Hackl
71	Leatop Plaza	2012	Guangzhou, China	993/303	64	Murphy/Jahn
72	Wells Fargo Plaza	1983	Houston, TX	992/302	71	Skidmore, Owings & Merrill
73	Kingdom Centre	2002	Riyadh, Saudi Arabia	991/302	41	Ellerbe Becket; Omrania & Associates (Saudi Arabia)
74	The Address Downtown Dubai	2008	Dubai, UAE	991/302	63	WS Atkins & Partners (UK)
75	Gate of the Orient	UC13	Suzhou, China	990/302	68	RMJM
76	Capital City Moscow Tower	2010	Moscow, Russia	990/302	76	NBBJ
77	Arraya Tower	2009	Kuwait City, Kuwait	984/300	60	Fentress Architects
78	Doosan Haeundae We've the Zenith Tower A	2011	Busan, South Korea	984/300	80	DeStefano + Partners
79	Aspire Tower	2007	Doha, Qatar	984/300	36	AREP Group (France) with Hadi Simaan Partners (Qatar)
80	Gran Torre Costanera	UC13	Santiago, Chile	984/300	64	Cesar Pelli & Associates
81	Abeno Harukas	UC14	Osaka, Japan	984/300	62	Pelli Clarke Pelli Architects
82	One Island East	2008	Hong Kong, China	979/298	69	Wong & Ouyang Ltd. (Hong Kong)
83	First Bank Tower	1975	Toronto, ON, Canada	979/298	72	Bregman + Hamann Architects (Canada)
84	Eureka Tower	2006	Melbourne, Australia	975/297	91	Fender Katsalidis Architects (Australia)
85	Comcast Center	2008	Philadelphia, PA	974/297	57	Robert A.M. Stern Architects with Kendall/Heaton Associates Inc.
86	Landmark Tower	1993	Yokohama, Japan	972/296	73	The Stubbins Associates
87	Emirates Crown	2008	Dubai, UAE	971/296	63	DAR Consult (Sudan)
88	Khalid Al Attar Tower 2	2011	Dubai, UAE	965/294	66	Eng. Adnan Saffarini (UAE)
89	Trump Ocean Club International Hotel & Tower	2011	Panama City, Panama	961/293	68	Arias Serna Saravia (Colombia)
90	311 South Wacker Drive	1990	Chicago, IL	961/293	65	Kohn Pedersen Fox Associates
91	Sky Tower	2011	Abu Dhabi, UAE	958/292	74	Arquitectonica
92	Haeundae I'Park Marina Tower 2	2011	Busan, South Korea	958/292	72	Studio Daniel Libeskind
93	SEG Plaza	2000	Shenzhen, China	957/292	71	Hua Yi Designing Consultants Ltd (China)
94	American International Building/ 70 Pine Street	1932	New York, NY	952/290	67	Clinton & Russell

	Building	Yr.	Location	Height (ft./m.)	(# stories)	Architect
95	Key Tower	1991	Cleveland, OH	947/289	57	Cesar Pelli & Associates
96	Yingli International Finance Centre	2012	Chongqing, China	945/288	58	Cesar Pelli & Associates; Rocco Design Architects Limited (Hong Kong)
97	Plaza 66	2001	Shanghai, China	945/288	66	Kohn Pedersen Fox Associates with East China Architectural Design & Research Institute Co. Ltd. (China) and Frank C.Y. Feng Architects & Associates (China)
98	One Liberty Place	1987	Philadelphia, PA	945/288	61	Murphy/Jahn
99	Millennium Tower	2006	Dubai, UAE	935/285	59	-WS Atkins & Partners (UK)
100	Sulafa Tower	2010	Dubai, UAE	935/285	75	National Engineering Bureau (UAE)

Source: ©Council on Tall Buildings and Urban Habitat

AIGA, the professional association for design

One of the oldest and largest membership associations for professionals engaged in visual communication and graphic design, AIGA, the professional association for design was founded in 1914 as the American Institute of Graphic Arts. Its more than 20,000 members include professional designers, educators, and students in traditional communication design fields, such as type and book design, as well as such newer disciplines as interaction design, experience design, and motion graphics. In addition, AIGA supports the interests of those involved in design in other disciplines, professions, and businesses who are committed to advancing the understanding of the value of design. AIGA serves as a hub of information and activity within the design community through conferences, competitions, exhibitions, publications, educational activities, and its website.

the professional association for design

Address

164 Fifth Avenue
New York, NY 10010
(212) 807-1990
www.aiga.org

Mission

AIGA's mission is to advance designing as a professional craft, strategic tool, and vital cultural force.

American Architectural Foundation

The American Architectural Foundation is a national nonprofit 501(c)(3) organization that educates individuals and communities about the power of architecture to transform lives and improve the places where we live, learn, work, and play. The AAF's programs include the Mayors' Institute on City Design and Great Schools by Design—highly regarded initiatives that help improve the built environment through the collaboration of thought leaders, designers, and local communities. Through its outreach programs, grants, exhibitions, and educational resources, the AAF helps people become thoughtful and engaged stewards of the world around them. The AAF is headquartered in The Octagon, an 1801 Federal-style home designed by William Thornton.

Address

1020 19th Street NW, Suite 525
Washington, DC 20036
(202) 787-1001
www.archfoundation.org

Mission

The American Architectural Foundation's mission is to educate the public on the power of architecture to improve lives and transform communities. The AAF is a national resource that helps provide information and best practices to communities and leaders, promotes collaboration, and encourages design excellence.

American Institute of Architects

Representing the professional interests of America's architects since 1857, the American Institute of Architects provides education, government advocacy, community redevelopment, and public outreach activities with and for its 83,000 members. With more than 300 local and state AIA organizations, the institute closely monitors legislative and regulatory actions at all levels of government. It provides professional development opportunities, industry-standard contract documents, information services, and a comprehensive awards program.

Address

1735 New York Avenue NW
Washington, DC 20006
(202) 626-7300
www.aia.org

Mission

The American Institute of Architects is the voice of the architecture profession dedicated to serving its members, advancing their value, and improving the quality of the built environment.

American Planning Association

The American Planning Association promotes good planning practices to build better communities while protecting the environment so residents have choices in housing, transportation, and employment. The group's 43,000 members include engaged citizens, planning professionals, and elected and appointed officials. The APA strives to engage all citizens in the planning process so it is open, transparent, and reflects the needs and desires of all community members. The association has offices in Washington, DC, and Chicago. It operates local chapters across the country as well as interest-specific divisions, and provides extensive research, publications, and training opportunities. The APA's professional institute, the American Institute of Certified Planners, certifies planners and promotes high ethical standards of professional practice.

Address

205 North Michigan Avenue
Suite 1200
Chicago, IL 60601
(312) 431-9100
www. planning.org

1030 15th Street NW
Suite 750 West
Washington, DC 20005
(202) 872-0611
www.planning.org

Mission

The American Planning Association is a nonprofit public interest and research organization committed to urban, suburban, regional, and rural planning. The APA and its professional institute, the American Institute of Certified Planners, advance the art and science of planning to meet the needs of people and society.

American Society of Interior Designers

The American Society of Interior Designers was formed in 1975 with the consolidation of the American Institute of Designers and the National Society of Interior Designers. It serves more than 36,000 members with continuing education and government affairs departments, conferences, publications, online services, and more. Members include residential and commercial designers; 2,700 manufacturers of design-related products and services, also known as industry partners; and 10,500 interior design students. ASID operates 48 local chapters throughout the United States.

Address

608 Massachusetts Avenue NE
Washington, DC 20002
(202) 546-3480
www.asid.org

Mission

The mission of the American Society of Interior Designers is to advance the interior design profession through knowledge genera- tion and sharing, advocacy of interior designers' right to practice, professional and public education, and expansion of interior design markets.

American Society of Landscape Architects

Representing the landscape architecture profession in the United States since 1899, the American Society of Landscape Architects currently serves more than 16,000 members through 48 chapters across the country. The ASLA's goal is to advance knowledge, education, and skill in the art and science of landscape architecture. The benefits of membership include a national annual meeting, *Landscape Architecture* magazine, continuing education credits, seminars and workshops, profes- sional interest groups, government advocacy, and award programs. In addition, the US Department of Education has certified the Landscape Architectural Accreditation Board of the ASLA as the accrediting agency for landscape architecture programs at US colleges and universities.

AMERICAN
SOCIETY OF
LANDSCAPE
ARCHITECTS

Address

636 Eye Street NW
Washington, DC 20001
(202) 898-2444
www.asla.org

Mission

The mission of the American Society of Landscape Architects is to lead, to educate, and to participate in the careful steward- ship, wise planning, and artful design of our cultural and natural environments.

Construction History Society of America

Founded in 2007 as an independent branch of the British-based Construction History Society, the CHSA provides a forum for everyone interested in the history of the American construction industry in all its aspects. The society attracts members from all sectors of the industry. It publishes newsletters and a well-regarded journal called *Construction History*. Biennial national meetings are held and local interest groups are forming. The next national meeting will be in Chicago in 2013 and the society will be hosting the 5th International Construction History Congress in Chicago in 2015.

Address

PO Box 93461
Atlanta, GA 30377
www.constructionhistorysociety.org

Mission

The Construction History Society of America's mission is to encourage the study and research of the history of the American construction industry.

Design Futures Council

The Design Futures Council is a global think tank of design and building industry leaders who collaborate through a series of regular meetings, summits, and *DesignIntelligence*, the bi-monthly journal. The group shares information among its fellows and members on best practices and new trends in order to help member organizations anticipate change and increase competitive fitness. Recent summit topics have included sustainability and innovation. Members include leading architecture and design firms, preferred manufacturers, service providers, and forward-thinking AEC companies taking an active interest in their future.

Address

25 Technology Parkway South, Suite 101
Atlanta, GA 30092
(800) 726-8603
www.di.net

Mission

The Design Futures Council is a think tank with the mission to explore trends, changes, and new opportunities in design, architecture, engineering, and building technology for the purpose of fostering innovation and improving the performance of member organizations.

Industrial Designers Society of America

Founded in 1965, the Industrial Designers Society of America is a professional association of industrial designers, educators, and students dedicated to the promotion of the profession. By fostering innovation and high standards of design, the IDSA communicates the value of design to the public and mentors young designers in their professional career development. The organization serves its constituency through the professional journal *Innovation*, award programs, an annual conference, research sponsorship, networking opportunities, and the promotion of the practice at all levels of government.

Address

555 Grove Street, Suite 200
Herndon, VA 20170
(703) 707-6000
www.idsa.org

Mission

The mission of the Industrial Designers Society of America is to lead the profession by expanding our horizons, connectivity and influence, and our service to members; inspire design quality and responsibility through professional development and education; and elevate the business of design and improve our industry's value.

International Interior Design Association

The International Interior Design Association provides a variety of services and benefits to its more than 11,000 members through 10 specialty forums, and more than 32 chapters around the world. This professional networking and educational association promotes the interior design practice to the public and serves its members as a clearinghouse for industry information. The IIDA was founded in 1994 as the result of a merger of the Institute of Business Designers, the International Society of Interior Designers, and the Council of Federal Interior Designers. The goal of the merger was to create an international association with a united mission that would represent interior designers worldwide.

Address

222 Merchandise Mart Plaza, Suite 567
Chicago, IL 60654
(312) 467-1950
www.iida.org

Mission

The International Interior Design Association is committed to enhancing the quality of life through excellence in interior design and advancing interior design through knowledge. The IIDA advocates for interior design excellence, provides superior industry information, nurtures a global interior design community, maintains educational standards, and responds to trends in business and design.

National Trust for Historic Preservation

The National Trust for Historic Preservation is a private nonprofit membership organization dedicated to saving historic places and revitalizing America's communities. Since NTHP's founding in 1949, it has worked to preserve historic buildings and neighborhoods through leadership, educational programs, publications (such as its award-winning *Preservation* magazine), financial assistance, and government advocacy. Staff at the Washington, DC, headquarters, six regional offices, and 27 historic sites work with its 200,000 members and thousands of preservation groups nationwide to protect the irreplaceable places that tell America's story.

Address
1785 Massachusetts Avenue NW
Washington, DC 20036
(202) 588-6000
www.preservationnation.org

Mission
The National Trust for Historic Preservation is a privately funded, nonprofit organization that provides leadership, education, advocacy, and resources to save America's diverse historic places and revitalize our communities.

Society for Environmental Graphic Design

The Society for Environmental Graphic Design is a nonprofit organization formed in 1973 to promote public awareness of and professional development in environmental graphic design. This interdisciplinary field encompasses the talents of many design professionals, including graphic designers, architects, landscape architects, product designers, planners, interior designers, and exhibition designers who create graphic elements to help identify, direct, inform, interpret, and visually enhance our surroundings through such means as wayfinding or maps. Resources available to SEGD members include a quarterly color magazine, a bi-monthly newsletter, an annual conference, a design award program, technical bulletins, job bank listings, and many other formal and informal materials.

Address
1000 Vermont Avenue NW, Suite 400
Washington, DC 20005
(202) 638-5555
www.segd.org

Mission
The Society for Environmental Graphic Design is an international nonprofit educational organization providing resources for design specialists in the field of environmental graphic design; architecture; and landscape, interior, and industrial design.

Society for Marketing Professional Services

Established in 1973, the Society for Marketing Professional Services is a network of over 6,000 marketing and business development professionals representing architectural, engineering, planning, interior design, construction, and specialty consulting firms throughout the United States and Canada. The society's benefits include a certification program (Certified Professional Services Marketer), an annual marketing and management conference (www.buildbusiness.org), an annual marketing communications competition, educational programs, resources, and publications highlighting the latest trends and best practices in professional services marketing in the AEC industry. SMPS is supported by 55 chapters in the United States.

Address

123 North Pitt Street, Suite 400
Alexandria, VA 22314
(703) 549-6117
www.smps.org

Mission

The mission of the Society for Marketing Professional Services is to advocate for, educate, and connect leaders in the building industry.

Society of Architectural Historians

Since its founding in 1940, the Society of Architectural Historians has sought to promote the history of architecture. The membership of the SAH ranges from professionals, such as architects, planners, preservationists, and academics, to those simply interested in architecture. The society produces a quarterly journal and monthly newsletter and organizes study tours and an annual conference. There are also a number of associated, although independent, local chapters. The SAH's national headquarters is located in Chicago's architecturally significant Charnley-Persky House, designed in 1891 by the firm of Dankmar Adler and Louis Sullivan. Guided tours of the house are offered.

Address

1365 North Astor Street
Chicago, IL 60610
(312) 573-1365
www.sah.org

Mission

The mission of the Society of Architectural Historians is to advance knowledge and understanding of the history of architecture, design, landscape, and urbanism worldwide.

Urban Land Institute

Formed in 1936 as a research arm of the National Association of Real Estate Boards (now the National Association of Realtors), the Urban Land Institute is an independent organization for those engaged in the entrepreneurial and collaborative process of real estate development and land-use policymaking. The ULI has more than 34,000 members worldwide and a $53-million operating budget. ULI members include the people that plan, develop, and redevelop neighborhoods, business districts, and communities across the United States and around the world, working in private enterprise and public service. The institute's activities include research, forums and task forces, awards, education, and publishing.

Address
1025 Thomas Jefferson Street NW
Suite 500 West
Washington, DC 20007
(202) 624-7000
www.uli.org

Mission
The mission of the Urban Land Institute is to provide responsible leadership in the use of land to enhance the total environment.

US Green Building Council

The US Green Building Council was formed in 1993 to integrate, educate, and provide leadership for building industry leaders, environmental groups, designers, retailers, and building owners as they strive to develop and market products and services that are environmentally progressive and responsible. The council includes nearly 13,000 member organizations, 181,000 LEED professionals, and 79 regional chapters with a common interest in green building practices, technologies, policies, and standards. Its most visible program, the LEED™ Green Building Rating System, is a voluntary consensus-based rating system that provides a national standard on what constitutes a green building. It also offers professional accreditation to certify individuals who have demonstrated the ability to serve on a LEED project team and provide detailed knowledge of LEED project certification requirements and processes.

Address
2101 L Street NW, Suite 500
Washington, DC 20037
(202) 742-3792
www.new.usgbc.org

Mission
The US Green Building Council's core purpose is to transform the way buildings and communities are designed, built, and operated, enabling an environmentally and socially responsible, healthy, and prosperous environment that improves the quality of life.

Architectural Outreach

Countless volunteer opportunities abound for architects, designers, and others interested in the built environment, ranging from disaster relief and recovery to community empowerment, restoration, and historic preservation. The following is a partial list of organizations, coalitions, and resources aimed at the coordination and operation of national and international volunteer programs that are focused on architecture, planning, design, and community development initiatives.

**Adventures in Preservation
(formerly Heritage Conservation
Network)**
1557 North Street
Boulder, CO 80304
(303) 444-0128
www.adventuresinpreservation.org

Heritage Conservation Networks' hands-on building conservation workshops bring people to historic sites around the world to provide much-needed labor and technical assistance to preservation projects. Participants work with and learn from experts in the field of heritage conservation; all levels of experience are welcome.

Architecture for Humanity
848 Folsom, Suite 201
San Francisco, CA 94107
(415) 963-3511
www.architectureforhumanity.org

Architecture for Humanity promotes architectural and design solutions to global, social, and humanitarian crises. Through competitions, workshops, educational forums, partnerships with aid organizations, and other activities, Architecture for Humanity creates opportunities for architects and designers from around the world to help communities in need.

Builders Without Borders
119 Kingston Main Street
Hillsboro, NM 88042
(510) 525-0525
www.builderswithoutborders.org

With volunteers, including architects, engineers, contractors, and others in the AEC field, Builders Without Borders specializes in affordable housing, both domestically and abroad, emphasizing sustainable structures built with locally available materials. Generally, BWB provides technical assistance to improve designs.

buildOn
PO Box 16741
Stamford, CT 06905
(203) 585-5390
www.buildon.org

buildOn enhances education and empowers youth in the United States to make a positive difference in their communities while helping people of developing countries increase their self-reliance through education and the development of educational resources.

Caribbean Volunteer Expeditions

PO Box 388
Corning, NY 14830
(607) 962-7846
www.cvexp.org

Caribbean Volunteer Expeditions is a non-profit agency dedicated to the preservation and documentation of the historical heritage of the Caribbean. Members and volunteers measure and document historical plantations, windmills, and other structures to help local Caribbean agencies keep a record of their architectural heritage. Professional assistance is appreciated.

Habitat for Humanity International

121 Habitat Street
Americus, GA 31709-3498
(800) 422-4828
www.habitat.org

Habitat for Humanity International seeks to eliminate poverty housing and homelessness from the world and to make decent shelter a matter of conscience and action. Through volunteer labor and donations of money and materials, Habitat builds and rehabilitates simple, decent houses with the help of the homeowner (partner) families.

La Sabranenque

rue de la Tour de l'Oume
30290 Saint Victor la Coste
France
www.sabranenque.com

La Sabranenque works toward the preservation of the traditional Mediterranean habitat and architecture. Working with volunteers, it preserves, restores, and rebuilds sites that can range from a simple village path to a complex of buildings using traditional construction techniques while introducing volunteers to the values of vernacular architecture and traditional construction.

National Park Service

Volunteers-In-Parks Program
1849 C Street NW
Washington, DC 20240
(202) 208-3818
www.nps.gov

The Volunteers-In-Parks Program provides a vehicle through which the National Park Service can accept and utilize voluntary help and services from the public.

Open Architecture Network

Architecture for Humanity
848 Folsom, Suite 201
San Francisco, CA 94107-1173
(415) 963-3511
www.openarchitecturenetwork.org

The Open Architecture Network is an online, open-source community dedicated to improving living conditions through innovative and sustainable design. Here designers of all persuasions can share their ideas, designs and plans; view and review designs posted by others; collaborate to address specific design challenges; manage design projects from concept to implementation; protect their intellectual property rights using the Creative Commons licensing system; and build a more sustainable future.

Peace Corps

1111 20th Street NW
Washington, DC 20526
(800) 424-8580
www.peacecorps.gov

Peace Corps Volunteers serve in countries across the globe: Africa, Asia, the Caribbean, Central and South America, Europe, and the Middle East. Collaborating with local community members, volunteers work in such areas as education, youth outreach and community development, the environment, and information technology.

Architectural Outreach

Public Architecture 1% Solution
1211 Folsom Street, 4th Floor
San Francisco, CA 94103
(415) 861-8200
www.theonepercent.org
www.publicarchitecture.org

The 1% Solution program grew out of a real-ization that there are no formal mechanisms supporting or recognizing pro bono architectural work within the profession. The goal of the 1% Solution is to direct one percent of all architects' working hours to matters of public interest, pro bono.

Rebuilding Together
1899 L Street NW, Suite 1000
Washington, DC 20036
(800) 473-4229
www.rebuildingtogether.org

Rebuilding Together preserves and revitalizes houses and communities, assuring that low-income homeowners, from the elderly and disabled to families with children, live in warmth, safety, and independence. Its goal is to make a sustainable impact in partnership with the community.

Red Feather Development Group
PO Box 907
Bozeman, MT 59771
(406) 585-7188
www.redfeather.org

Red Feather educates and empowers American Indian nations to create sustain- able solutions to the severe housing crisis within reservation communities. Red Feather teaches affordable, replicable, and sustainable approaches to home construction, working with volunteers alongside tribal members to build desperately needed homes.

Shelter For Life International
10201 Wayzata Boulevard, Suite 230
Minnetonka, MN 55305
(763) 253-4082
www.shelter.org

Shelter for Life International is a faith-based humanitarian organization that enables people affected by conflict and disaster to rebuild their communities and restore their lives through appropriate shelter and community develop-ment programs. Shelter for Life has occasional volunteer opportunities in project manage-ment, construction, community development, engineering, architecture, and cross-cultural relations.

slowLab
c/o New York Foundation for the Arts
20 Jay Street, 7th Floor
Brooklyn, NY 11201
(212) 366-6900
www.slowlab.net

The goal of slowLab is to promote slowness as a positive catalyst of individual, socio-cultural, and environmental well-being. Current and future programs include public lectures, discussions and exhibitions, a dynamic online project observatory and communication portal, academic programs, and publishing projects.

Southface Energy Institute
241 Pine Street NE
Atlanta, GA 30308
(404) 872-3549
www.southface.org

Southface promotes sustainable homes, work-places, and communities through education, research, advocacy, and technical assistance.

United Nations Volunteers

United Nations Campus
Langer Eugen
Hermann-Ehlers-Str.10
53113 Bonn, Germany
+49 228 815 2000
www.unvolunteers.org

The United Nations Volunteers supports sustainable human development globally through the promotion of volunteerism, including the mobilization of volunteers. It serves the causes of peace and development through enhancing opportunities for participation by all people.

World Hands Project

1406 Bishops Lodge Road
Santa Fe, NM 87506
(505) 989-7000
www.worldhandsproject.org

The World Hands Project is a group of concerned citizen-activists from diverse backgrounds that works worldwide creating solutions that address the basic needs for clean water, food production, sanitation, and shelter. Through workshops and studios, participants work with communities to establish a better quality of life by combining technical knowledge and skills with the traditional wisdom of indigenous peoples.

World Shelters for Humanitarian Needs

550 South G Street, Suite 3
Arcata, CA 95521
(707) 822-6600
www.worldshelters.org

World Shelters designs, produces, and delivers temporary and permanent structures for both emergency response and long-term humanitarian needs.

Source: DesignIntelligence

Architecture Critics

Below is a listing of major US publications that regularly feature architectural writing and criticism. Some publications have a staff architecture critic while others an art critic or critic-at-large who routinely covers architecture stories.

Arizona Republic
200 East Van Buren Street
Phoenix, AZ 85004
(602) 444-8000
www.azcentral.com

Atlanta Journal-Constitution
Chris Quinn
Features Assignment Editor
cquinn@ajc.com
223 Perimeter Center
    Parkway
Atlanta, GA 30346
(404) 526-2160
www.ajc.com

Austin American-Statesman
Jeanne Claire van Ryzin
Arts Critic
jvanryzin@statesman.com
PO Box 670
Austin, Texas 78767
(512) 445-3500
www.statesman.com
www.austin360.com

Baltimore Sun
Mary Carole McCauley
Arts Reporter
mary.mccauley@baltsun.com
501 North Calvert Street
Baltimore, MD 21278
(410) 332-6704
www.baltimoresun.com

Boston Globe
Robert Campbell
Architecture Critic
Rebecca Ostriker
Arts Editor
ostriker@globe.com
135 Morrissey Boulevard
Boston, MA 02125
(617) 929-2800
www.boston.com

Boston Herald
Sandra Kent
Arts and Lifestyle Editor
Sandra.kent@bostonherald.com
One Herald Square
Boston, MA 02118
(617) 426-3000
www.bostonherald.com

Charleston Post and Courier
Robert Behre
rbehre@postandcourier.com
Architecture Critic
134 Columbus Street
Charleston, SC 29403
(843) 577-7111
www.postandcourier.com

Charlotte Observer
Allen Norwood
Home Columnist
homeinfo@embarqmail.com
600 South Tryon Street
Charlotte, NC 28202
(704) 358-5000
www.charlotteobserver.com

Chicago Sun-Times
350 North Orleans Street
Chicago, IL 60654
(312) 321-3000
www.suntimes.com

Chicago Tribune
Blair Kamin
Architecture Critic
bkamin@tribune.com
435 North Michigan Avenue
Chicago, IL 60611
(312) 222-3232
www.chicagotribune.com

Cleveland Plain Dealer
Steven Litt
Art & Architecture Critic
Plain Dealer Plaza
1801 Superior Avenue
Cleveland, OH 44114
(216) 999-5000
www.plaindealer.com

Dallas Morning News
508 Young Street
Dallas, TX 75202
(214) 977-8222
www.dallasnews.com

Dayton Daily News
Michelle Fong
News Editor
1611 South Main Street
Dayton, OH 45409
(937) 225-2271
www.daytondailynews.com

Denver Post
Ray Ranaldi
Fine Arts Critic
rranaldi@denverpost.com
101 West Colfax Avenue
Denver, CO 80202
(303) 954-1540
www.denverpost.com

Detroit Free Press
Mark Stryker
Fine Arts Critic
mstryker@freepress.com
615 West Lafayette
 Boulevard
Detroit, MI 48226
(313) 222-6459
www.freep.com

Los Angeles Times
Christopher Hawthorne
Architecture Critic
christopher.hawthorne@lat-
 imes.com
202 West First Street
Los Angeles, CA 90012
(213) 237-5000
www.latimes.com

Louisville Courier-Journal
Veda Morgan
Features Editor
vmorgan@courier-journal.
 com.
PO Box 740031
Louisville, KY 40201
(502) 582-4215
www.courier-journal.com

Milwaukee Journal Sentinel
Mary Louise Schumacher
Art and Architecture Critic
mschumacher@journalsenti-
 nel.com
PO Box 371
Milwaukee, WI 53201
(414) 224-2000
www.jsonline.com

New York Times
Michael Kimmelman
Architecture Critic
229 West 43rd Street
New York, NY 10036
(212) 556-1234
www.nytimes.com

Newark Star-Ledger
Dan Bischoff
Art Critic
dbischoff@starledger.com
1 Star-Ledger Plaza
Newark, NJ 07102
(973) 392-4040
www.nj.com/starledger

Newport News Daily Press
Mark St. John Erickson
Arts/Museum/History
 Reporter
merickson@dailypress.com
7505 Warwick Boulevard
Newport News, VA 23607
(757) 247-4600
www.dailypress.com

Philadelphia Inquirer
Inga Saffron
Architecture Critic
isaffron@phillynews.com
PO Box 8263
Philadelphia, PA 19101
(215) 854-2000
www.philly.com

Pittsburgh Post-Gazette
34 Boulevard of the Allies
Pittsburgh, PA 15222
(412) 263-1100
www.post-gazette.com

Providence Journal
Bill Van Siclen
Art Critic
bvansicl@projo.com
75 Fountain Street
Providence, RI 02902
(401) 277-7000
www.providencejournal.com

Raleigh News & Observer
Carole Miller
Features Editor
cmiller@newsobserver.com
215 South McDowell Street
Raleigh, NC 27602
(919) 829-4500
www.newsobserver.com

The Record
John Zeaman
Art Critic
features@northjersey.com
North Jersey Media Group
1 Garret Mountain Plaza
Woodland Park, NJ 07424
(201) 646-4000
www.northjersey.com

San Antonio Express-News
Jennifer Hiller
Arts Critic
jhiller@express-news.net
301 Avenue E
San Antonio, TX 78205
(210) 250-3000
www.mysanantonio.com

Architecture Critics

San Diego Union-Tribune
350 Camino de la Reina
San Diego, CA 92108
(619) 299-3131
www.utsandiego.com

San Francisco Chronicle
John King
Urban Design Writer
jking@sfchronicle.com
901 Mission Street
San Francisco, CA 94103
(415) 777-1111
www.sfgate.com

Seattle Times
Rebecca Teagarden
Reporter, Pacific NW
    Magazine
bteagarden@seattletimes.
    com
PO Box 70
Seattle, WA 98111
(206) 748-5808
seattletimes.com

South Florida Sun-Sentinel
500 East Broward Boulevard
Fort Lauderdale, FL 33394
(954) 356-4000
www.sun-sentinel.com

Wall Street Journal
Ada Louise Huxtable
Architecture Critic
1211 Avenue of the
    Americas
New York, NY, 10036
(212) 416-2000
www.wsj.com

Washington Post
Philip Kennicott
Art and Architecture Critic
1150 15th Street NW
Washington, DC 20071
(202) 334-6000
www.washingtonpost.com

Source: DesignIntelligence

Bookstores

The following is a list of US architecture and design bookstores, including rare and out-of-print dealers that specialize in design titles.

ARIZONA

Builder's Book Depot
1001 East Jefferson, Suite 5
Phoenix, AZ 85034
(800) 284-3434
www.buildersbookdepot.com

CALIFORNIA

Arcana: Books on the Arts
@ The Historic Helms Bakery
8675 Washington Boulevard
Culver City, CA 90232
(310) 458-1499
www.arcanabooks.com

Builder's Book
8001 Canoga Avenue
Canoga Park, CA 91304
(800) 273-7375
www.buildersbook.com

Builders Booksource
1817 Fourth Street
Berkeley, CA 94710
(800) 843-2028
www.buildersbooksource.com

Hennessey + Ingalls
214 Wilshire Boulevard
Santa Monica, CA 90401
(310) 458-9074
www.hennesseyingalls.com

J.B. Muns Fine Arts Books
1162 Shattuck Avenue
Berkeley, CA 94707
(510) 525-2420

MAK Center for Art and Architecture Bookstore
835 North Kings Road
West Hollywood, CA 90069
(323) 651-1510
www.makcenter.org

Moe's Books
2476 Telegraph Avenue
Berkeley, CA 94704
(510) 849-2087
www.moesbooks.com

Potterton Books
Pacific Design Building, G154
8687 Melrose Avenue
West Hollywood, CA 90069
(310) 289-1247
www.pottertonbooksusa.com

Sullivan Goss
7 East Anapamu Street
Santa Barbara, CA 93101
(805) 730-1460
www.sullivangoss.com

William Stout Architectural Books
804 Montgomery Street
San Francisco, CA 94133
(415) 391-6757

1605 Solano at Tacoma
Berkeley, CA 94707
(510) 356-4740
www.stoutbooks.com

COLORADO

Tattered Cover Bookstore
2526 East Colfax Avenue
Denver, CO 80206
(303) 322-7727

1628 16th Street
Denver, CO 80202
(303) 436-1070

9315 Dorchester Street
Highlands Ranch, CO 80129
(303) 470-7050
www.tatteredcover.com

DISTRICT OF COLUMBIA

AIA Bookstore
1735 New York Avenue NW
Washington, DC 20006
(202) 626-7475
www.aia.org/store

National Building Museum Shop
401 F Street NW
Washington, DC 20001
(202) 272-2448
www.nbm.org

ILLINOIS

Chicago Architecture Foundation
Bookstore
224 South Michigan Avenue
Chicago, IL 60604
(312) 922-3432
www.architecture.org/shop

INDIANA

AIA Indiana Bookstore
1200 South Madison
Suite LL20
Indianapolis, IN 46225
(317) 634-6993
www.aiaindiana.org

MARYLAND

Baltimore AIA Bookstore
11 1/2 West Chase Street
Baltimore, MD 21201
(410) 625-2585
www.aiabalt.com

Bookstores

MASSACHUSETTS

Ars Libri
500 Harrison Avenue
Boston, MA 02118
(617) 357-5212
www.arslibri.com

**Charles B. Wood III
Antiquarian Booksellers**
PO Box 382369
Cambridge, MA 02238
(617) 868-1711
www.cbwoodbooks.com

F.A. Bernett
144 Lincoln Street
Boston, MA 02111
(617) 350-7778
www.fabernett.com

MISSOURI

St. Louis AIA Bookstore
911 Washington Avenue
Suite 100
St. Louis, MO 63101
(314) 621-3484
www.aia-stlouis.org

NEW YORK

Argosy Bookstore
116 East 59th Street
New York, NY 10022
(212) 753-4455
www.argosybooks.com

**Cooper-Hewitt Museum
Bookstore**
2 East 91st Street
New York, NY 10128
(212) 849-8355
www.cooperhewittshop.org

Hacker Art Books
45 West 57th Street
New York, NY 10019
(212) 688-7600

Neue Galeria Bookstore
1048 Fifth Avenue
New York, NY 10028
(212) 628-6200
www.neuegalerie.org

**New York School of
Interior Design Bookstore**
170 East 70th Street
New York, NY 10021
(212) 472-1500
www.nysid.edu

Potterton Books
D & D Building
Lobby Level
979 Third Avenue
New York, NY 10022
(212) 644-2292
www.pottertonbooksusa.com

Rizzoli Bookstore
31 West 57th Street
New York, NY 10019
(212) 759-2424
www.rizzoliusa.com

Royoung Bookseller
564 Ashford Avenue
Ardsley, NY 10502
(914) 693-6116
www.royoung.com

Strand Book Store
828 Broadway
New York, NY 10003
(212) 473-1452
www.strandbooks.com

Ursus Books
699 Madison Avenue, 3rd
   Floor
New York, NY 10065
(212) 772-8787
www.ursusbooks.com

OREGON

Powell's City of Books
1005 West Burnside
Portland, OR 97209

Powell's Books Building 2
40 Northwest 10th Avenue
Portland, OR 97209

**Powell's Books at Cedar
Hills Crossing**
3415 Southwest Cedar Hills
Boulevard
Beaverton, OR 97005

**Powell's Books on
Hawthorne**
3723 Southeast Hawthorne
Boulevard
Portland, OR 97214

Powell's Books at PDX
7000 Northeast Airport Way,
Suite 2250
Portland, OR 97218
(503) 228-4651
www.powells.com

PENNSYLVANIA

**AIA Bookstore & Design
Center**
1218 Arch Street
Philadelphia, PA 19107
(215) 569-3186
www.aiaphila.org

Joseph Fox Bookshop
1724 Sansom Street
Philadelphia, PA 19103
(215) 563-4184
www.foxbookshop.com

TEXAS

Brazos Bookstore
2421 Bissonnet Street
Houston, TX 77005
(713) 523-0701
www.brazosbookstore.com

WASHINGTON

AIA Spokane Bookstore
335 West Sprague Avenue
Spokane, WA 99201
(509) 747-5498
www.aiaspokane.org

Hinck & Wall
760 Hemlock Street
Edmonds, WA 98020
(800) 561-1203
www.gardenhistory.com

**Peter Miller Architecture
and Design Books**
1930 First Avenue
Seattle, WA 98101
(206) 441-4114
www.petermiller.com

Source: DesignIntelligence

Museums

There are many museums around the world devoted solely to architecture and design. In addition, many major museums maintain strong design collections and regularly host architecture and design-related exhibits. The following contains the contact information for these organizations.

US Museums

A+D Architecture and Design Museum
6032 Wilshire Boulevard
Los Angeles, CA 90036
(323) 932-9393
www.aplusd.org

Art Institute of Chicago
111 South Michigan Avenue
Chicago, IL 60603
(312) 443-3600
www.artic.edu

Athenaeum of Philadelphia
219 South Sixth Street
Philadelphia, PA 19106
(215) 925-2688
www.philaathenaeum.org

Center for Architecture
536 LaGuardia Place
New York, NY 10012
(212) 683-0023
www.cfa.aiany.org

Chicago Architecture Foundation
224 South Michigan Avenue
Chicago, IL 60604
(312) 922-3432
www.architecture.org

Cooper-Hewitt, National Design Museum, Smithsonian Institution
2 East 91st Street
New York, NY 10128
(212) 849-8400
www.cooperhewitt.org

Heinz Architectural Center
Carnegie Museum of Art
4400 Forbes Avenue
Pittsburgh, PA 15213
(412) 622-3131
www.cmoa.org

MAK Center for Art & Architecture Los Angeles
The Schindler House
835 North Kings Road
West Hollywood, CA 90069
(323) 651-1510
www.makcenter.org

Museum of Arts & Design
2 Columbus Circle
New York, NY 10019
(212) 299-7777
www.madmuseum.org

Museum of Contemporary Art, Los Angeles
MOCA at California Plaza
250 South Grand Avenue
Los Angeles, CA 90012
(213) 626-6222
www.moca.org

Museum of Design Atlanta
1315 Peachtree Street NE
Atlanta, GA 30309
(404) 979-6455
www.museumofdesign.org

Museum of Modern Art
11 West 53rd Street
New York, NY 10019
(212) 708-9400
www.moma.org

National Building Museum
401 F Street Northwest
Washington, DC 20001
(202) 272-2448
www.nbm.org

Octagon Museum
1799 New York Avenue Northwest
Washington, DC 20006
(202) 638-3221
www.artcom.com/Museums/vs/mr/20006.htm

Price Tower Arts Center
510 Dewey Avenue
Bartlesville, OK 74003
(918) 336-4949
www.pricetower.org

San Francisco Museum of Craft + Design
2569 Third Street
San Francisco, CA 94107
(415) 773-0303
www.sfmcd.org

San Francisco Museum of Modern Art
151 Third Street
San Francisco, CA 94103
(415) 357-4000
www.sfmoma.org

Skyscraper Museum
39 Battery Place
New York, NY 10280
(212) 968-1961
www.skyscraper.org

Storefront for Art and Architecture
97 Kenmare Street
New York, NY 10012
(212) 431-5795
www.storefrontnews.org

Van Alen Institute
30 West 22 Street, 6th Floor
New York, NY 10010
(212) 924-7000
www.vanalen.org

Virginia Center for Architecture
2501 Monument Avenue
Richmond, VA 23220
(804) 644-3041
www.virginiaarchitecture.org

International Museums

Alvar Aalto Museum
(Alvar Aalto Museo)
Alvar Aallon katu 7
Jyväskylä, Finland
+358 14 266 7113
www.alvaraalto.fi

Architecture Center of Vienna
(Architekturzentrum Wien)
Museumsplatz 1, im MQ
A-1070 Vienna, Austria
+43 522 3115
www.azw.at

Bauhaus Archive/Museum of Design
(Bauhaus-Archiv/Museum für Gestaltung)
Klingelhöferstraße 14
10785 Berlin, Germany
+49 30 254 00 20
www.bauhaus.de

Canadian Centre for Architecture
1920, rue Baile
Montreal, QC, Canada H3H 2S6
(514) 939-7026
www.cca.qc.ca

Museums

Danish Architecture Center
(Dansk Arkitektur Center)
Strandgade 27B
1401 Copenhagen K, Denmark
+45 32 57 19 30
www.dac.dk

Danish Design Center
(Dansk Design Center)
27 H C Andersens Boulevard
1553 Copenhagen V, Denmark
+45 33 69 33 69
www.ddc.dk

Design Museum, Finland
(Designmuseo)
Korkeavuorenkatu 23
00130 Helsinki, Finland
+35 89 622 0540
www.designmuseum.fi

Design Museum, London
Shad Thames
London SE1 2YD, UK
+44 20 7403 6933
www.designmuseum.org

Design Museum at the Cultural Center of Belém
(Museu do Design, Centro Cultural de Belém)
Praça do Império
1499-003 Lisbon, Portugal
+351 213 612 400
www.ccb.pt

German Centre for Architecture
(Deutsches Architektur Zentrum)
Direktorin Kristien Ring
Köpenicker Straße 48/49
10179 Berlin, Germany
+49 30 278799-29
www.daz.de

German Architecture Museum
(Deutsches Architektur Museum)
Schaumainkai 43
60596 Frankfurt am Main
Germany
+49 69-212 38844
www.dam-online.de

International Center for Urbanism
(Centre International pour la Ville, l'Architecture et le Paysage)
Rue de l'Ermitage 55 Kluisstraat
Brussels 1050, Belgium
+32 (0)2 642 24 50
www.civa.be

The Lighthouse: Scotland's Centre for Architecture, Design & the City
11 Mitchell Lane
Glasgow, G1 3NU, Scotland
United Kingdom
+44 141 276 5360
www.thelighthouse.co.uk

Museum of Architecture in Wroclaw
(Muzeum Architektury we Wroclawiu)
ul. Bernardynska 5
PL 50-156 Wroclaw, Poland
+48 (71) 344 82 79
www.ma.wroc.pl

Museum of Estonian Architecture
(Eesti Arhitektuurimuuseum)
Arts centre
Rotermann's Salt Storage
Ahtri 2, Tallinn 10151
tel. +372 625 7000
www.arhitektuurimuuseum.ee

Museum of Finnish Architecture
(Suomen Rakennustaiteen Museo)
Kasarmikatu 24, 00130
Helsinki, Finland
+358 9 8567 5100
www.mfa.fi

Netherlands Architecture Institute
(Nederlands Architectuurinstituut)
Museumpark 25
3015 CB Rotterdam, Netherlands
+3110-4401200
www.nai.nl

National Museum of Art, Architecture and Design
(Nasjonalmuseet for Kunst, Arkitektur og Design)
Kristian Augusts gate 23
Oslo, Norway
+47 21 98 20 00
www.nationalmuseum.no

Palladio Centre and Museum
(Centro Internazionale di Studi di Architettura Andrea Palladio)
Contra' Porti 11
I-36100 Vicenza, Italy
+39 (04) 44 32 30 14
www.cisapalladio.org

RIBA Architecture Gallery
66 Portland Place
London W1B 1AD, UK
+44 20 7580 5533
www.architecture.com

Röhsska Museum of Design and Applied Art
(Röhsska Museet för Konsthantverk och Design)
Vasagatan 37-39
SE-400 15 Göteborg, Sweden
+46 31-36 83 150
www.designmuseum.se

Schusev State Museum of Architecture
Vozdvizhenka str., 5
119019 Moscow, Russia
+7 495 691 21 09
www.muar.ru

Swedish Museum of Architecture
(Arkitekturmuseet)
Skeppsholmen
SE-111 49 Stockholm, Sweden
+46 8 587 270 00
www.arkitekturmuseet.se

Swiss Architecture Museum
(Schweizerisches Architekturmuseum)
Steinenberg 7
Postfach 911
CH-4001 Basel, Switzerland
+41 61 261 1413
www.sam-basel.org

Victoria and Albert Museum
Cromwell Road
London SW7 2RL, UK
+44 20 7942 2000
www.vam.ac.uk

Vitra Design Museum
Charles-Eames-Str. 2
D-79576 Weil am Rhein
Germany
+49 7621 702 32 00
www.design-museum.de

Zurich Museum of Design
(Museum für Gestaltung Zürich)
Ausstellungsstrasse 60
8005 Zürich, Switzerland
+41 43 446 67 67
www.museum-gestaltung.ch

Source: DesignIntelligence

NOTES

NOTES

NOTES

NOTES

NOTES

About the Editors

James P. Cramer is the founding editor and publisher of the *Almanac of Architecture & Design* as well as *DesignIntelligence*, a journal on trends and strategies published by Greenway Communications on behalf of the Design Futures Council. Cramer is one of the country's foremost management consultants to the design industry and is the founder and CEO of the Greenway Group, a leading strategy consulting and business networking firm. He is the author or co-author of several hundred articles and several books, including the critically acclaimed *Design Plus Enterprise: Seeking a New Reality in Architecture* and the bestselling *How Firms Succeed: A Field Guide to Design Management Solutions*. Cramer is the former chief executive of the American Institute of Architects, a Richard Upjohn Fellow of the AIA, and a Fellow of the International Leadership Forum. He is president of the Washington, DC-based think tank the Design Futures Council and has more than 80 honors to his credit for service to the architecture and design community.

Jane Paradise Wolford, Ph.D., is an architectural historian and the editor of the *Almanac of Architecture & Design*. She is also a senior consultant with Greenway Communications and an editor for the Ostberg Library of Design Management. Wolford has a doctorate in architectural history, theory, and criticism from the Georgia Institute of Technology as well as a Master of Science degree in architectural history from there. Her doctoral thesis established the theoretical and practical framework for architectural contextualism in its definitions and aspects of construction that enable buildings to relate better to each other and encourage a more sustainable, cohesively built environment. She is a LEED accredited professional. She also studied at Westmont College in Santa Barbara, CA, where she earned her bachelor's degree in English, and the University of California Berkeley, where she received her teaching credential. She and her husband, Arol Wolford, founded Construction Market Data in 1981, a leading international construction information service. Enlightening the public about the transformational potential of architecture is her quest.

Jennifer Evans Yankopolus is an architectural historian and the editorial advisor to the *Almanac of Architecture & Design*. She works with numerous architecture and design publications as an editor. In addition to a master's degree in architecture history from the Georgia Institute of Technology, she holds a master's degree in heritage preservation from Georgia State University and a BS in business from Drake University.

östberg

Library of Design Management

Every relationship of value requires constant care and commitment. At Östberg, we are relentless in our desire to create
and bring forward only the best ideas in design, architecture,
interiors, and design management. Using diverse mediums of
communications, including books and the Internet, we are constantly searching for thoughtful ideas that are erudite, witty, and
of lasting importance to the quality of life. Inspired by the architecture of Ragnar Östberg and the best of Scandinavian design
and civility, the Östberg Library of Design Management seeks
to restore the passion for creativity that makes better products,
spaces, and communities. The essence of Östberg can be
summed up in our quality charter to you: "Communicating con-
cepts of leadership and design excellence."

NOTES

NOTES

DATE DUE

Demco, Inc. 38-293